Turning Woode

Turning Wooden Toys

Terry Lawrence

Guild of Master Craftsman Publications Ltd

First published 1994 by
Guild of Master Craftsman Publications Ltd
166 High Street, Lewes
East Sussex BN7 1XU

ISBN 0 946819 61 0

Designed by Gellatly Norman Associates

Printed and bound in Great Britain by Hillman Printers (Frome) Ltd

Contents

Introduction

If you are a woodturner, I expect that you have been through a similar learning curve to mine. You may have been attracted to the hobby by persuasive advertisements for equipment and numerous magazine articles, which frequently put forward the view that bowls or 'hollow vessels' are the epitome of the craft.

I've got a boxful of bowls in the loft, my friends all have a bowl which I've made for them, and I couldn't sell the surplus at the local craft fair as there are already several turners there with their wares. Platters, boxes and goblets all followed the same route.

given for design. I don't agree with this approach. If the club judges were arbiters of fine art, they would give so few marks to Picasso, because they could see his brush marks and because the lines were not straight, that the poor chap would have sold nothing.

For me, design is the most important thing, although of course I cannot and have not ignored finish. Because design is so important, and satisfying, I started to create my own one-off projects. I was interested in creating something using similar techniques to those used to create bowls and platters, but which had a little extra to make it different, and also fun to make. My ideas soon turned naturally to toys; as a low-paid civil servant with two sets of twins, I started making toys a long time ago, because I couldn't afford to buy them. I didn't have the tools then which I have now, but even so, the things I made

were fun to design and build, were different from the shop-bought equivalent, and were strong enough to outlast the child's interest.

Nowadays, a toy catalogue is a display of hi-tech chemistry, with all the types of plastic in use. I once designed a modern dolls' house which had sliding perspex patio doors all round, an open tread teak staircase, fitted carpets and so on. It was beaten on the marketplace not because of its design, but because of the materials, which priced it beyond the competition. The company who wanted a dolls' house eventually produced a plastic one, very flimsy and rather garish, and they admitted that it was not meant to last; it was built, nay extruded and pressed, down to a low price and not up to a quality.

Something different was needed to sustain my interest, other than seeking perfection of shape or surface. This business of surface finish is a vexed one indeed. I know one professional who spends as much as 20 hours polishing one of his turned pieces, and in the monthly competition in the woodturning club to which I belong, a perfect finish is paramount. Marks are knocked off for any surface blemish, but absolutely no marks are

Now that I have a lathe, and a couple of other bits of equipment, the same reasons for building toys still apply. In making your own

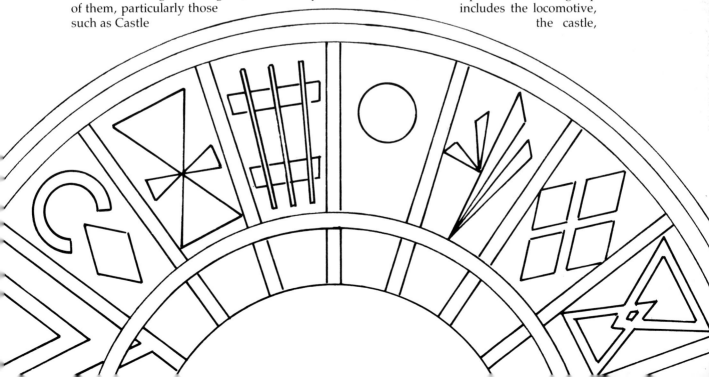

toys on the lathe you can use natural materials, and add something to make the piece different from that made by anyone else. It is not difficult; after all, if you look at the picture of Noah's Ark, for example, you will note at once that it is only a bowl with a little house on top. The Starship *Moth*, a flying saucer, is only a couple of platters put together.

There are a few materials which I use that may be unfamiliar to your own hobby experiences, such as marquetry veneers, leather, etc. I use whatever accessories are to hand: brass eyelets, glass rod, car decor strip, cocktail sticks, and so on – all easily obtained items. However, I do stress that the techniques, such as the marquetry inlay, and the leather work, are quite rudimentary, and well within the capacity of anyone who can turn wood on a lathe.

As far as equipment is concerned, I am sure that most woodturners have more equipment than just their lathe. Most have a band saw, or access to one, and a bench drill. Many have a scroll saw, and, if not, a hand fret saw can be used instead. That's about all you need, really. I don't have (or have room in my workshop for) a circular saw or a planer/ thicknesser, but only twice have I needed to have timber machined for me (so far!) because of this.

I think you will find this book different because the designs are original, and in many of them, particularly those such as Castle

Crécy (the fort), *Nautilus*, Starship *Moth*, and the Ark, there is ample scope for you to personalize it by adding detail of your own, or to add bits which your son or daughter particularly ask for. That is, if they are ever allowed to get their hands on it!

None of the designs is simplified to the point where it loses reality, though as a consequence, very few of the items can be made in a day. As far as the turning element of each project is concerned, there are really three grades of difficulty. There are four projects which I consider easy: the Ninepins (or skittles), the Radiolaria, the Colourmix Tops, and the Extraterrestrial Calculator. Anyone who can turn a piece on a faceplate, or between centres, can make these with no trouble.

The bulk of the projects I would class as intermediate; that is to say, comfortable to anyone who has a little experience, and this group includes the locomotive, the castle, the fort, the ark, the bridge, and the flying saucer. Only one is what I think of as difficult, namely *Nautilus*, but the difficulty consists in taking extra care, and not rushing things, rather than a high risk of failure.

Even the simplest designs have something to offer. The Ninepins are a good exercise in repetition turning, and a good excuse, if you need it, to experience working on ten different timbers. You can judge for yourself the ease or difficulty of turning particular woods, and perhaps add one or two new

gives you a chance to do some miniature turning, and perhaps a little thatching. The Gamesphere offers some simple marquetry – mostly straight-sided geometric inlays. King Billy, the locomotive, has proper loco wheels cut on the scroll saw after turning, and features some exotic timbers. The Extraterrestrial Calculator is a conversation piece adorned with a variety of inlaid cabbalistic signs, which need patience rather than skill to achieve. Castle Quint exercises your ability to cut longitudinal quadrants from the turned towers, and also a little bolection. Crécy, the fort, whose battlements are ideal for toy soldiers, has a wealth of corbelled machicolation (yes, I had to look it up too; it means crenels and voids, or crenellations, supported by little triangular bits underneath). These will keep your scroll saw or fret saw warm. The flying saucer, *Moth,* gives you a chance to do some large-diameter turning, and also to make a wooden chuck plate.

favourites to your list of friendly timbers. The Radiolaria need a bit of precision (or at least accurate) drilling, particularly the Urchin, which I found the most rewarding of the set. That of course may be because I recently learned to become a scuba diver under the Red Sea, and met many real urchins, some with spines a foot long. The Colourmix Tops, meanwhile, give you a chance to use your paint set.

You will probably find the intermediate group of the greatest interest, because they all use different turning techniques and all utilize 'extra bits' beyond the basic turned shape. The Fantasy Bridge offers a wide variety of shapes to turn between centres, and the use of thin plywood and sheet veneer for covering. Noah's Ark

Nautilus is not the one to start with, I suggest, if you are a beginner. Its hull is oval in cross section and is a compound turning made from two shells cut from a hollow cigar, itself made from 10 sections. It is still quite a bit quicker than carving from the solid!

What I hope you will discover is that some at least of the projects have an heirloom quality. Just like grandmother's dolls' house, some of these pieces are worth making well, to hand down to your next generation.

There is also the sense of personal satisfaction which you get from crafting something quite complex, using your own hands and using basic materials, rather than going to a shop and buying a kit whose parts are mainly prefabricated. There is the matter of cost, too. For example, if you buy kiln-dried timber for *Nautilus*, the whole vessel, made of hardwood and lined with suede leather and with as much detail as you care to cram in, will cost about £12–15 (US$19–24; A$24–30).

Contrast that with a kit I saw recently for a model boat made from pre-printed cardboard which cost £32 (US$51; A$64)!

Short of a survey, there is no telling what other craft experiences the average woodturner has acquired. Even if he or she now has a preference for the lathe, few I suspect have no experience in other forms of woodwork, even if it has been of the do-it-yourself variety, like fitting shelves in your library. Whatever your experience, I am sure that few of you will baulk at the simple extras which, in this book, transform a turning into a characterful construction or vehicle. There is nothing difficult in gluing four strips of wood together to make a deckhouse for the Ark, for example. Covering the Fantasy Bridge with thin plywood is a simple task, compared to turning the towers which will rise above it.

I have been lucky enough to have been making things from wood for fifty years (and it don't seem a day too much). I started with a solid, scale model aircraft at the age of nine which was not very good, although it could just

than just those whose advertisements I have seen (*see* page 170). I've had good stuff from them.

I have tried to include a wide variety of subjects from which you may choose projects to build. In time, we travel from 4000 BC (a guess as to when old Noah was busy with his saw), to 2068 AD when *Moth* was built. In space, we travel from a planet in a distant galaxy where the Fantasy Bridge crosses a far river, to under the sea with *Nautilus*. In size, we range from a great castle, to a microscopic organism.

Finally, you will note that many of the chapters start with a paragraph introducing the project, and you may find these a little fanci-

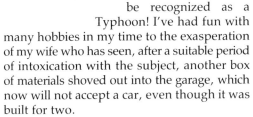

ful. Well, in the words of the immortal Frankie Howerd, 'mock not'. They helped me, at least, to set the scene, and I don't mind if you think me childish; I am!

Publisher's Note
Many of the drawings in this book have, for reasons of space, been reproduced at less than full size. It is suggested that, where necessary, these drawings are photocopied using a photocopier with a facility for enlargement. For this purpose, a symbol ( ) followed by a percentage (e.g. 143%) has been printed by each of these drawings to indicate the percentage increase required to bring them up to full size.

be recognized as a Typhoon! I've had fun with many hobbies in my time to the exasperation of my wife who has seen, after a suitable period of intoxication with the subject, another box of materials shoved out into the garage, which now will not accept a car, even though it was built for two.

The net result is that I have more junk materials lying around than most people, which helps me enormously when I am designing. However, I do mention in the text the sources of items which are outside the normal woodturner's box of useful bits. At the end of the book I also provide a short list of UK suppliers whom I have used, rather

CHAPTER I

Ninepins

This is a nice straightforward project which will give you an opportunity to do some repetition turning – a short run of nine identical shapes. There is also a sphere to turn and, if you wish, some laminated work or inlays. For son or daughter, there is a set of indoor skittles to play with on the carpet when it is raining outside.

One good thing about this project, I found, is that it is cheap in materials. I was able to find all the timber on my small stock trolley, so the only cost was the time involved.

I decided that it would be interesting to make the skittles all from different timbers; the shape alone would be the unifying factor. I used ash, brown oak, opepe, afrormosia, olive ash, mahogany, beech, taun and spalted hackberry. The base of the stand is walnut, and the stand centre and pegs are of bodo. Quite a variety, and you may feel that it would look better in only one timber. Well, it's your set, so choose what pleases you.

There is one other point to make. For the skittles themselves you need nine pieces of timber 6in × 2in × 2in (152mm × 51mm × 51mm), preferably with the grain running along the 6in (152mm) length. If you have only thin planks of timber, or you choose to be different, then you can create your own patterns with laminations or inlay. I have made three examples just to suggest simple variations; the first is three lengths of oak, with Macassar ebony veneer sandwiched between them. The second is made of discs of oak, again with veneer between them, to give horizontal rings around the skittle. The third is a plain skittle, inlaid at its waist after turning with a band of Rio rosewood. The variations on these simple themes are numerous; you can also – or as an alternative – insert plugs of a contrasting timber, or even just paint the pieces.

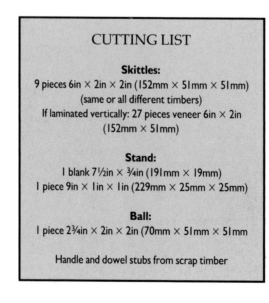

CUTTING LIST

Skittles:
9 pieces 6in × 2in × 2in (152mm × 51mm × 51mm)
(same or all different timbers)
If laminated vertically: 27 pieces veneer 6in × 2in
(152mm × 51mm)

Stand:
1 blank 7½in × ¾in (191mm × 19mm)
1 piece 9in × 1in × 1in (229mm × 25mm × 25mm)

Ball:
1 piece 2¾in × 2in × 2in (70mm × 51mm × 51mm

Handle and dowel stubs from scrap timber

CONSTRUCTION

Turning the Pins

There is no need to write detailed instructions for shaping the pieces as they are all the same as the pattern shown in Fig 1.1. They are turned between centres at about 900rpm for turning the blank to a

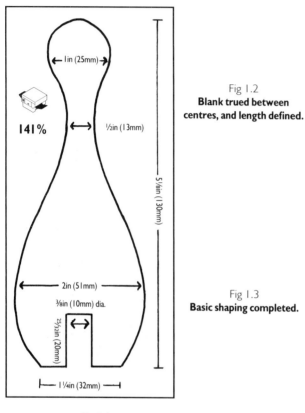

Fig 1.1
Skittle shape and dimensions.

the skittle so that the rim of the hole made a ring on the head. You can avoid this by placing a thin piece of leather or cloth over the hole first.

Turn the blank to a cylinder then, with a narrow parting tool, define the length of the skittle (*see* Fig 1.2). The blank, at 6in (152mm), gives plenty of

Fig 1.2
Blank trued between centres, and length defined.

Fig 1.3
Basic shaping completed.

cylinder, and at about 1500rpm for the shaping. The maximum diameter is 2in (51mm), which occurs 1in (25mm) above the base. The height is 5⅛in (130mm), and there is a ½in (13mm) hole drilled centrally in the base so it can sit on a peg on the stand. You can drill this hole first in the blank, if you wish, and the drive can then be a slightly tapered stub ½in (13mm) in diameter, held in a Jacobs chuck in the headstock (or in ½in (13mm) mini jaws of a Multistar chuck in compression mode). I chose to drill after turning and finishing, setting a block of waste timber in the vice on my bench drill table. The block had a ⅞in (22mm) hole drilled into it to locate the head of the skittle when placed into position upside down ready for the drilling. There is a danger at this point of marking the head of the skittle. I managed to do this on the softer timbers when the drill pressed

room at either end to avoid marks of drive and tailstock centres. Reduce the diameter of the waste at the headstock end to just greater than the drive dog. This will give plenty of room to shape the base of the piece. The tools used are up to you: spindle gouge, scraper, skew chisel, whichever you prefer. The whole job can be done with a round-nosed scraper if you wish.

You may find that it helps to make a card template for the shape to ensure accuracy. I sometimes do this but for a change I used the first piece as the model for the following ones, holding it above the spinning workpiece to check the curvatures, after establishing the 2in (51mm) waist and 1in (25mm) diameters. If you move your head along above the pieces, comparison is quite easy. There will be some variation of course but I found, after I had finished, that the variation was about ¹⁄₁₆in (2mm) between the fattest and the thinnest pieces (which was acceptable to me, though perhaps not to you).

and left them for 24 hours. It is not really necessary to leave them so long, certainly not if you use veneer with a more open grain. In the

Fig 1.4
Oak planks and macassar ebony inserts for variant no. 1.

Fig 1.5
Variant No. 1 glued and clamped.

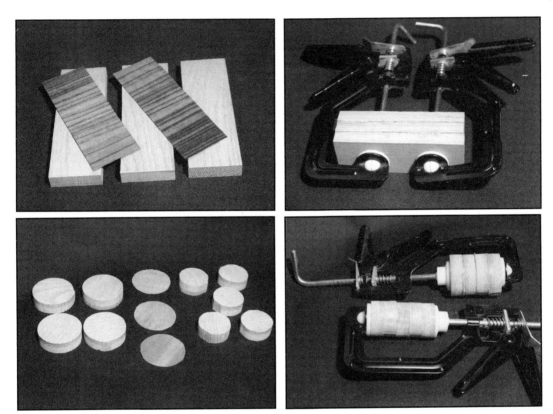

Fig 1.6
Oak discs and mahogany inserts for variant no. 2.

Fig 1.7
Variant no. 2 glued and clamped (base and neck).

Sand with your usual progression of grits (I used 2in (51mm) velcro discs of 120, 180, 240 and 400 grits) followed by a coat of sanding sealer or melamine, and then a wax finish.

Variations
The first of these was made up of three pieces of oak, with a smooth planed surface on both sides, each piece 6in × 2in × ⅝in (152mm × 51mm × 16mm) thick. For contrast, I chose Macassar ebony veneer to go between these pieces (*see* Fig 1.4), and cut the two pieces of ebony so that their grain was at right angles to that of the oak. Ebony is a very dense timber, and I was concerned about glue penetration, so after applying white PVA glue to the pieces, I clamped them (*see* Fig 1.5),

event there was no problem. The five-part block turned safely and there was no separation, whichever tool was used.

The next variation is one using the same oak, but in horizontal layers. The piece is made up of discs of oak ⅝in (16mm) thick, cut on the scroll saw and sanded lightly so that any edge fibres are flattened. I used three discs of veneer, this time of mahogany ¹⁄₁₆in (2mm) thick (the type used for antique furniture restoration). For the oak, you need four discs 2in (51mm) in diameter, and five discs 1½in (38mm) in diameter. All these oak discs can be cut easily from a piece of timber 8in × 5in (203mm × 127mm). The three discs of veneer are 2in (51mm) in diameter (*see* Fig 1.6). It is best to ensure that the grain of all the oak discs runs in the same direction, though the grain of the mahogany veneer should be at right angles to this, as in plywood.

Glue the discs together and clamp until dry. As you see from Fig 1.7, I had only 4in (102mm) capacity clamps available, so I glued up the 4in × 2in (102mm × 51mm) discs (with veneer inserts of course) in one set, and the 5in × 1½in (127mm × 38mm) discs as another set. After an hour I removed the two sets and glued them up together in the lathe using the tailstock centre as a clamp. I left the assembly overnight so the glue could set.

The third variation is a simple inlay or banding of veneer, applied after turning. This one was white ash, inlaid with Rio rosewood. First, turn, shape and finish (including waxing if you wish) a standard skittle, but do not part off yet. With a parting tool, cut a flat-bottomed groove, preferably at the greatest diameter of the skittle, deep enough for your veneer (most standard veneers are 0.024in (0.6mm) thick.

Cut a strip of veneer just wide enough to fit snugly within the recess you have cut around the periphery of the skittle, preferably with the grain of the veneer across the strip. This will make it easier to bend around the curve. If the strip breaks whilst cutting or gluing in, don't worry; just butt the two ends and continue. Use PVA white glue, and hold the strip in position with masking tape.

When dry, sand, or *gently* skim with a flat-ended

Fig 1.9
Base and pillar completed.

scraper so that the surface has a smooth curvature. If your recess was too deep, you will skim the skittle's timber down to the veneer; if the veneer is proud, its thickness will be reduced to meet the main timber. Repolish, part off, and drill the base for its peg.

Skittle Stand
This is just like a cake stand, with a disc base bearing nine pegs and a central turned pillar; it also features a crosspiece for easy carrying, and a dished top to hold a wooden ball which, when the outfit is carried, is held in place by the palm of the hand.

The arithmetic worked out quite neatly; with a 2in (51mm) wide skittle and a ⅛in (3mm) gap between each, the radius for the pegs (that is, the distance between the centre of the base and the centre of a peg) is 3in (76mm) exactly. The radius from centre to rim is 3¾in (95mm) making the diameter 7½in (191mm), which matches the bases of the nine skittles.

Mount a disc of timber 7½in (191mm) in diameter (or slightly larger to allow for truing), and ½in–¾in (13mm–19mm) thick, on your 3in (76mm) screw chuck. Don't worry if your screw goes right through, as the centre will be drilled for the stub of the pillar. True the rim and face, and cut a dovetail recess to take an expanding chuck. The cross-sectional shape is a matter of personal taste; you can see in Fig 1.10 that I cut a flat base. Sand, polish and reverse into your expanding dovetail chuck in order to finish the top surface which is again to your personal taste. I just left a

Fig 1.8
The three variants (left to right): oak/ ebony (vertical join); ash with rio rosewood inlay; oak/mahogany (horizontal layers).

132%

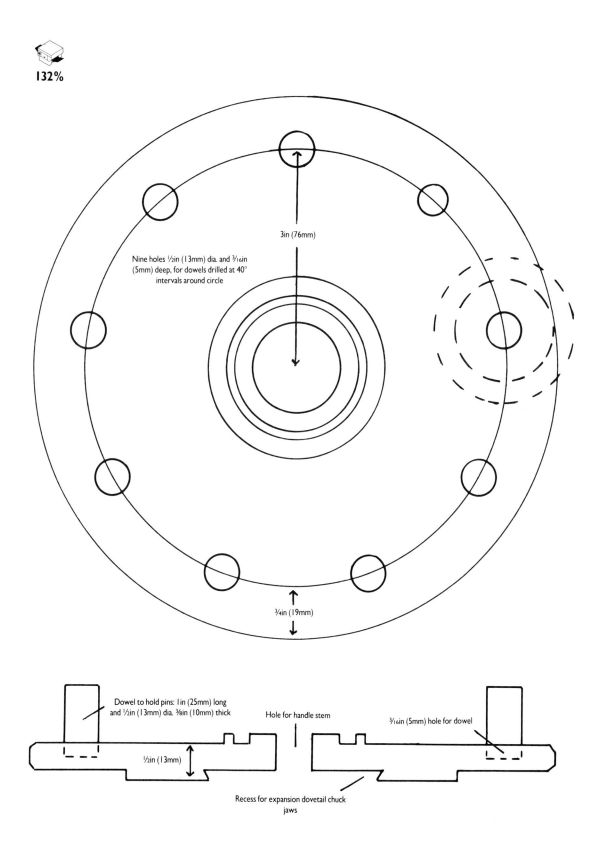

3in (76mm)

Nine holes ½in (13mm) dia. and ³/₁₆in (5mm) deep, for dowels drilled at 40° intervals around circle

¾in (19mm)

Dowel to hold pins: 1in (25mm) long and ½in (13mm) dia. ³/₈in (10mm) thick

Hole for handle stem

³/₁₆in (5mm) hole for dowel

½in (13mm)

Recess for expansion dovetail chuck jaws

Fig 1.10
Skittle stand: base disc.

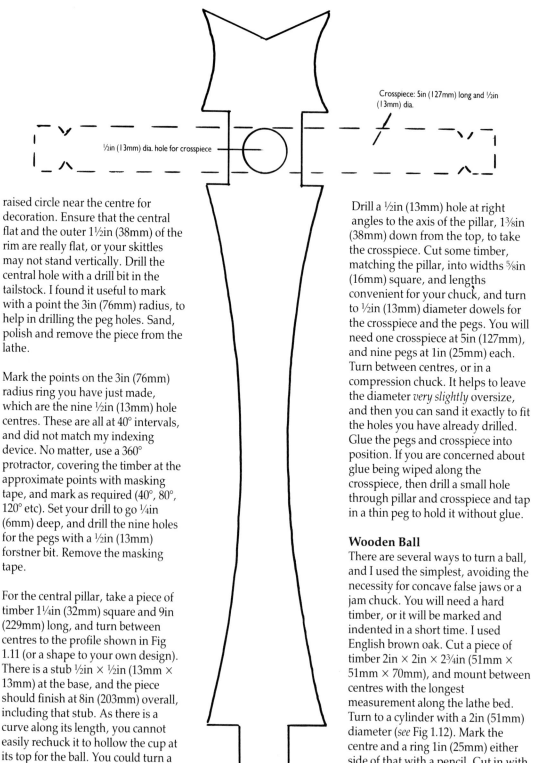

Crosspiece: 5in (127mm) long and ½in (13mm) dia.

½in (13mm) dia. hole for crosspiece

raised circle near the centre for decoration. Ensure that the central flat and the outer 1½in (38mm) of the rim are really flat, or your skittles may not stand vertically. Drill the central hole with a drill bit in the tailstock. I found it useful to mark with a point the 3in (76mm) radius, to help in drilling the peg holes. Sand, polish and remove the piece from the lathe.

Mark the points on the 3in (76mm) radius ring you have just made, which are the nine ½in (13mm) hole centres. These are all at 40° intervals, and did not match my indexing device. No matter, use a 360° protractor, covering the timber at the approximate points with masking tape, and mark as required (40°, 80°, 120° etc). Set your drill to go ¼in (6mm) deep, and drill the nine holes for the pegs with a ½in (13mm) forstner bit. Remove the masking tape.

For the central pillar, take a piece of timber 1¼in (32mm) square and 9in (229mm) long, and turn between centres to the profile shown in Fig 1.11 (or a shape to your own design). There is a stub ½in × ½in (13mm × 13mm) at the base, and the piece should finish at 8in (203mm) overall, including that stub. As there is a curve along its length, you cannot easily rechuck it to hollow the cup at its top for the ball. You could turn a cup separately if you wish, or just part off with the parting tool angled in at 45° as I did. The central nubbin, left at the bottom of the cup, was simply drilled out afterwards having marked its centre with a point to accept the spur of a wood drill bit, which did not then wander.

Fig 1.11
Ninepin holder: pillar and crosspiece.

Drill a ½in (13mm) hole at right angles to the axis of the pillar, 1⅜in (38mm) down from the top, to take the crosspiece. Cut some timber, matching the pillar, into widths ⅝in (16mm) square, and lengths convenient for your chuck, and turn to ½in (13mm) diameter dowels for the crosspiece and the pegs. You will need one crosspiece at 5in (127mm), and nine pegs at 1in (25mm) each. Turn between centres, or in a compression chuck. It helps to leave the diameter *very slightly* oversize, and then you can sand it exactly to fit the holes you have already drilled. Glue the pegs and crosspiece into position. If you are concerned about glue being wiped along the crosspiece, then drill a small hole through pillar and crosspiece and tap in a thin peg to hold it without glue.

Wooden Ball
There are several ways to turn a ball, and I used the simplest, avoiding the necessity for concave false jaws or a jam chuck. You will need a hard timber, or it will be marked and indented in a short time. I used English brown oak. Cut a piece of timber 2in × 2in × 2¾in (51mm × 51mm × 70mm), and mount between centres with the longest measurement along the lathe bed. Turn to a cylinder with a 2in (51mm) diameter (*see* Fig 1.12). Mark the centre and a ring 1in (25mm) either side of that with a pencil. Cut in with a parting tool on the outside of the outer lines to define the length of the sphere's axis, matching the diameter.

You can either shape the sphere by eye or use a template to achieve the true shape. I found it just as easy to go by eye only, using the central line (its equator) as a guide. The main shaping can be done with a 1¼in (32mm) skew chisel or a ½in (13mm) spindle gouge, turning it on its side so that its open face is toward the point of support of the workpiece (that is, toward the headstock or tailstock).

stub. Sand and polish, remove from the lathe, and part off the waste with a handsaw (I used an X-Acto saw blade with 56 tpi). Final sanding of the ends can be done with the ball held gently against a 400 grit 2in (51mm) velcro sanding disc mounted in a Jacobs chuck in the headstock.

Fig 1.12
Ball: blank trued to a 2in (51mm) diameter.

Fig 1.14
The completed set of ninepins.

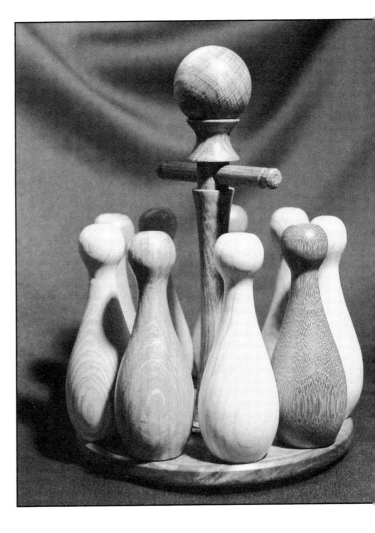

Fig 1.13
Ball: ready to part off.

As you refine the curve, you can reduce the diameter of the supporting ends. Final shaping can be done with a heavy, flat-ended scraper. Because the surface of the sphere is convex, only a minute portion of the cutting edge of the scraper is in contact at any one time. You will end up in a surprisingly short time with an almost perfect sphere, supported left and right by a ⅛in (3mm)

CHAPTER 2

Colourmix Tops

The idea behind this project is to produce one or more spinning tops which will demonstrate to children in a simple fashion the practice of colour mixing. It is one thing to read that yellow and blue make green or to arrive at new colours by messing about with paints, but with these tops you only need to spin to see the mixing.

You may choose to make tops which show one mix only; indeed the simplest would be a semicircle of, say, red, and a semi-circle of blue. I chose to design disc inserts for the tops which show not only the full strength of the mixed hue, but also lighter and darker shades at the same time.

Each disc is divided into six segments, and each segment is further divided by three concentric rings. Each of the six segments contains 15° of white in the smallest central ring, giving a lighter shade, and each contains 15° of black in the outer ring, giving a darker shade of the mixed hue in the centre ring.

I have designed three little spinning tops, all with recesses in their upper surfaces, so that the colourmix discs will fit into any of the tops. You don't need a really close fit; indeed, it is better if you are able to remove the disc just by up-ending the top.

This is a nice easy project, where you can see finished results the same day as you start. If you are worried about the difficulty of painting the discs, later in the chapter I will give you examples of how you can simplify that.

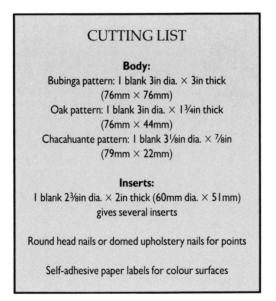

CUTTING LIST

Body:
Bubinga pattern: I blank 3in dia. × 3in thick
(76mm × 76mm)
Oak pattern: I blank 3in dia. × I¾in thick
(76mm × 44mm)
Chacahuante pattern: I blank 3⅛in dia. × ⅞in
(79mm × 22mm)

Inserts:
I blank 2⅜in dia. × 2in thick (60mm dia. × 51mm)
gives several inserts

Round head nails or domed upholstery nails for points

Self-adhesive paper labels for colour surfaces

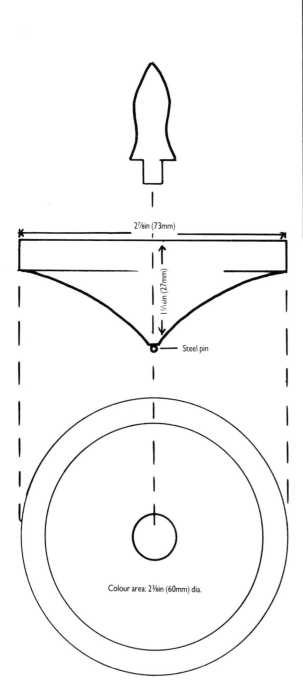

2⁷⁄₈in (73mm)

1¹⁄₁₆in (27mm)

Steel pin

Colour area: 2⅜in (60mm) dia.

Fig 2.1
Bubinga top: shape and dimensions.

Fig 2.2
**Bubinga blank on screw chuck. Recess cut
for colour disc, and housing being cut for
expanding dovetail chuck.**

CONSTRUCTION

Wooden Tops

I have made three tops for this project. Although
you will probably wish to design your own
shapes, those I offer are recommended because
they all have a low centre of gravity, which helps
the stability in motion. The higher the centre of
gravity, the more wobble about the axis at low
speeds.

I have also used three different woods (all quite
dense): bubinga from Cameroun (this top has a
sharply pointed base); chacahuante from Yucatan,
Mexico (this has a rounded base); and brown oak
from England (which is hemispherical in shape).

Finally, I have used three different methods of
turning: with a screw chuck; with a dovetail
housing and reversal on the chuck; and plain
mounting in a contracting chuck. There are more
of course: glue chucking, jam chucking, false jaws
etc, but for those of you who are new to turning, it
might be best to try one of the methods described
below.

Method 1

The first top was made from a blank of bubinga
3in (76mm) in diameter and 3in (76mm) thick,
with the grain running across the face. Drill a
shallow central hole and mount on your screw
chuck, using a scrap wooden spacer to prevent the
screw from going deep. This is of course so that
you can get two tops from the same blank.

Turn to a diameter of 2⅞in (73mm) and true the face of the workpiece. With a ³⁄₁₆in (5mm) drill bit in a Jacobs chuck mounted in the morse taper of your tailstock, drill a central hole in the workpiece to a depth of ³⁄₁₆in–⅜in (5mm–10mm). Now, with the tool rest at right angles to the lathe bed, and using a ⅛in (3mm) parting tool or a narrow square-ended scraper, cut a recess in the face of the timber with an outside diameter of 2⅜in (60mm), leaving a raised ring at the centre of ½in (13mm) diameter. With its central hole, this will later accept the axle. The depth of the 2⅜in (60mm) recess should be ³⁄₁₆in (5mm), which will be the thickness of the disc inserts. Ensure that the base of the recess is flat and sand the side and top surfaces. Finish with polish if you wish, but do not allow wax polish into the central ³⁄₁₆in (5mm) hole, or the glue will not adhere.

Now, using the tip of a skew chisel, recess the side of the cut (that is, the side of the 2⅜in (60mm) circle) to provide a dovetail housing. I used a Multistar chuck with size 'C' jaws in expansion mode, which fitted the recess exactly. If your chucking system is different then simply adjust the diameter (of the recess, and consequently the colour disc inserts).

Part off the top body from the workpiece, to give a thickness of 1¹⁄₁₆in (27mm). Mount this piece on the lathe using your expanding dovetail chuck and, at about 1500rpm, shape the base with a gouge or wide round-nosed scraper. Leave a small flat at the centre, which will accept a nail for the top to spin on (*see* Fig 2.3). Sand and finish the surface, drill a hole to take the nail. (I used a 0.031in (0.8mm) drill, to accept a 0.039in (1mm) diameter round-headed pin – the sort used for tacking a picture frame hook to a plaster wall.)

All that is needed now is a central stem or axle. Mount a piece of matching timber ½in (13mm) square or a little larger in cross section, and about 4in (102mm) long, in the compression jaws of your chuck (or turn between centres if you prefer). Shape the stem to the profile you prefer, leaving a little stub ³⁄₁₆in–⅝in (5–10mm) long and tapering slightly to fit the central hole of the top. Sand, finish and glue into place. Ensure that the maximum diameter of the stem does not exceed ½in (13mm), or the discs will not fit over it.

Method 2

Cut a blank disc of oak 3in (76mm) in diameter from a plank 1¾in (44mm) thick. This method requires no holes to be drilled in the blank, so you can use almost all the thickness. Mark the centre point and mount between centres, with a four-

Fig 2.3
Reversed onto expanding chuck, and base shaped.

Fig 2.4
Oak blank reversed into compression jaws.

prong drive dog at the headstock, and a revolving centre at the tailstock. Check that the workpiece is squarely mounted by turning the lathe by hand. If it flutters when you turn, adjust the point of contact of the tailstock centre. Now, at about 1000rpm, true the diameter to 2⅞in (73mm), and the right hand face flat, and cut a dovetail on the outboard end to accept compression chuck jaws (I cut the dovetail with a maximum diameter of 2⁹⁄₁₆in (65mm) to fit Multistar 'D' jaws). Remove the workpiece and remount on your compression dovetail chuck (*see* Fig 2.4). At about 1500rpm, true the end face, cut the recess for the colour disc, and drill a ³⁄₁₆in (5mm) central hole for the stem. Sand and finish the upper surface. To avoid wax polish entering the central hole you can plug it with a stub of ³⁄₁₆in (5mm) diameter dowel.

Remove the workpiece and reverse it into 3in (76mm) compression jaws. As there is no dovetail

Fig 2.6
**Reversed into compression jaws, base
shaped and hole drilled for pin.**

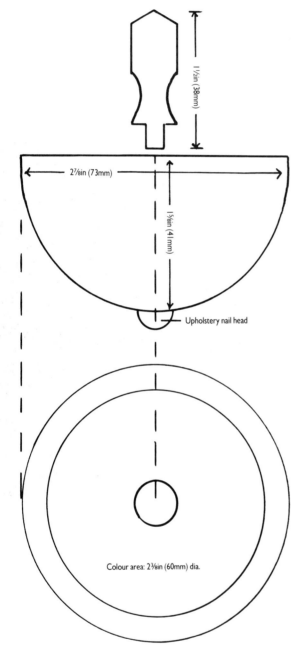

1½in (38mm)

2⅞in (73mm)

1⅝in (41mm)

Upholstery nail head

Colour area: 2⅜in (60mm) dia.

Fig 2.5
Oak top: shape and dimensions.

on the timber, the jaws might mark the
circumference of the piece, so first protect the rim
with a winding of masking tape. You can now
shape the underside; for this particular design I
gave it an almost hemispherical shape, as you will
see from Fig 2.5. Sand, finish and mark the centre
for a pin (*see* Fig 2.6). In this case I used a bronze
dome-headed upholstery nail.

Mount a short length of square section oak
½in–⅝in (12mm–16mm) and turn the stem to
your preferred shape, again leaving a slightly
tapered stub to fit into the central hole of the top,
and ensuring that the finished diameter of the
stem does not exceed ½in (13mm).

Method 3
This method avoids screw chuck holes and also
dovetail housings. Cut a blank disc 3⅜in (79mm)
in diameter from a plank of chacahuante ⅞in
(22mm) thick, using a scroll saw, and mount it in
the size 'E' jaws of your chuck in compression
mode (*see* Fig 2.8). True the circumference with
light scraper cuts and cut the 2⅜in (60mm) recess
for the colour discs as before, leaving the same
½in (13mm) central raised portion. Drill a ³⁄₁₆in
(5mm) hole centrally, sand and finish. Reverse
into the same chuck, protecting the rim of the
timber with masking tape. Now shape the base,
mark for a central pin, sand and polish
(*see* Fig 2.9). Turn a stem as before of matching
timber (*see* Fig 2.10) and glue its stub into the
central hole after tapping the pin into the centre of
the underside.

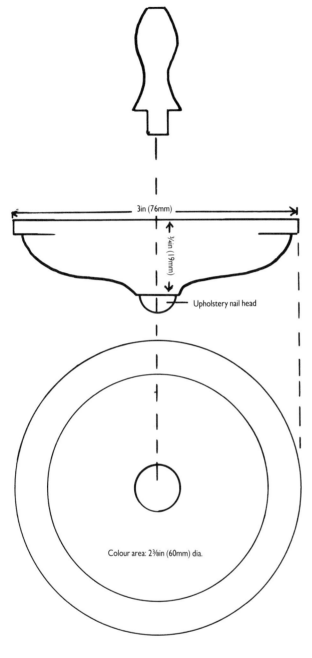

3in (76mm)

¾in (19mm)

Upholstery nail head

Colour area: 2⅜in (60mm) dia.

Fig 2.7
Chacahuante top: shape and dimensions.

Fig 2.8
Chacahuante blank cut on scroll saw and mounted in compression jaws. Note: no dovetail.

Fig 2.9
**Reversed into chuck; base shaped and pin
inserted.**

Colour Discs

First decide the material you wish to use for the
discs, of which you will need at least three. You
can use plywood, cardboard, plastic sheet or even
paper. I used ³⁄₁₆in (5mm) thick discs of lime
wood, parted off from a 2³⁄₈in (60mm) diameter
blank on the screw chuck.

You can paint the discs, preferably with craft
enamel colours (Humbrol ½oz (14g) pots are
ideal), in which case an undercoat of white is
advisable. I found it easiest to paint the designs,
using Rotring liquid watercolours, on to self-
adhesive paper labels (the size of which should be
at least 3in (76mm) square). I then removed the
backing paper and stuck the finished circles on to
the wooden discs. If you do this, it is best not to
cut the 2³⁄₈in (60mm) periphery or the centre ½in

Fig 2.10
**Stem turned from a ½in (13mm) square
blank in compression jaws. Note: no
polish on stub.**

(13mm) circle until after it is stuck onto the wood.
Trim them after application with a craft knife or
scalpel, with the disc face down on a cutting mat.

The following colour mixes are demonstrated,
each with a disc of two colours:
Red and Yellow = Orange; Red and Blue =
Purple; Yellow and Blue = Green. There are, as I
mentioned above, three concentric rings, which
show at the same time light and dark shades of the
orange, purple and green.

An advantage of using self-adhesive labels is that
a mistake is not costly in time or materials. Also it
allows you to experiment with variations of hue.
For example, I found that with the Rotring
colours, the red and blue were fine straight from
the bottle, so my purple colourmix disc was
effective from the start. With the red/yellow mix, I
found that the more intense pigmentation of the
yellow/gold was more effective than lemon
yellow. In the case of the yellow/blue disc it is as
difficult to achieve a proper green as it is when
mixing paint. It is partly a matter of colours on
paper differing from colour in the form of light,
and partly a matter of proportions in the mix.
However, you will find that cyan (a blue-green
colour nearer to turquoise than cobalt) and lemon
yellow, in equal proportions, will give you three
shades of green on the spinning disc.

I have shown at Figs 2.13 and 2.14 how to lay out
the circle before painting. Lines A/A, B/B and C/C
are drawn at 60° intervals. Lines d/d, e/e and f/f are
also at 60° intervals, but these three are all 15°
clockwise from the first three. I suggest you use a
4H or 6H pencil to draw these, so that the lines do
not show through the pigments.

The radii of the circles are at ⁵⁄₁₆in (8mm) intervals,
starting with the centre hole at ¼in (6mm) radius,
and going up to 1³⁄₁₆in (30mm) for the rim – ¼in,
⁹⁄₁₆in, ⁷⁄₈in, 1³⁄₁₆in (6mm, 14mm, 22mm, 30mm).
You can see from Fig 2.14 which lines or parts of
lines can then be erased before painting.

Now glance at the colour progression paintings in
the colour section between pages 92 and 93. You
will see that the three alternating yellow segments
are painted first. Each is a 'V' shape with a little
block on one side. It does not matter if the colour
goes into the middle of the disc, or beyond the
2³⁄₈in (60mm) diameter rim; just let the
brushstrokes flow, and start the stroke at or close
to the centre of the circle. Use a No.1 artist's
brush. You don't need to spend a lot of money on
a Kolinsky sable brush; a Pro-Arte synthetic
filament is ideal. Next, after the yellow is dry (if it

Fig 2.11
**The three tops: bubinga, chacahuante and
brown oak.**

Fig 2.12
View of bases of spinning tops.

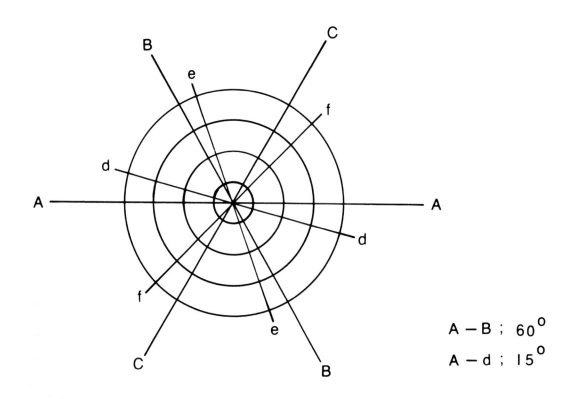

$$A - B \; ; \; 60^{O}$$
$$A - d \; ; \; 15^{O}$$

Fig 2.13
**Setting out the divisions for painting
(Step 1).**

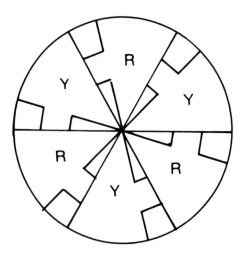

R — red

Y — yellow

Fig 2.14
**Setting out the divisions for painting
(Step 2).**

is damp, the colours will bleed at their junction), paint the red sectors, and finally, the 15° black segments in the outer circle.

Remove the backing, place the disc face down, then place the 2⅜in (60mm) wooden disk on to the sticky side of the painted paper label. By looking down through the central hole of the wooden disc, you can see the little hole at the centre of the paper where you used your compass point to draw the circles, and this will help you

place the disc accurately. Then with a scalpel, trim the excess paper from rim and centre, and the disc is complete. If you wish, you can protect its surface with a covering of self-adhesive transparent plastic, such as Tackiback.

I have also shown in the colour progression paintings the colours used for the other two discs, before and after trimming, to give you an idea how neat your work will look after trimming away any excess brushed colour.

Fig 2.15
**The tops, with interchangeable colour
disc inserts.**

CHAPTER 3

Mobile Radiolaria

It is commonly known that the white cliffs of Dover are made of chalk, formed from countless billions of minute shells of foraminifera. But hardly anyone seems to know much about the other major microscopic marine protozoan order called radiolaria.

The dictionary describes a radiolarian as having 'a silica shell with radiating pseudopoda'. What the dictionaries usually fail to mention is that radiolaria are often very beautiful, and that there are over 4,000 species – which gives a lot of scope for anyone who wishes to model them.

I decided to make a small collection of models, which are now hanging from my lounge ceiling. They look attractive as a set, and as a bonus, in a slight draught of air, they rotate on their nylon filaments, each at a different speed, and create a pleasant mobile. You can either suspend them singly, in separately suspended groups, or create Calder-type mobiles, with three or more suspended on cross-wires (I will suggest how to do that

later in the chapter). Also, for those who are not lovers of marine animals, they could be painted more brilliantly and used as rather up-market festive decorations. All I suggest is that you make sure of your knots, and that you don't place them above where you or your guests may sit.

Very little in the way of materials is required. Most of the pieces of timber which I used came from the scrap box, beyond which only a few bits of dowel, cocktail sticks, paint and nylon monofilament fishing line (5 pound breaking strain) were needed. You can buy little test pots of emulsion or vinyl paint from your DIY store, but it is cheaper to use a spoonful of emulsion paint in an old jam jar lid, mixed with a few drops of liquid artist's watercolour or a little tempera.

To save using Latin names for these little models, I have given them simple descriptive titles. It is easier to say 'urchin', for example, than *Actinosphaerium Eichornii*.

CUTTING LIST

Sputnik
Body: 1 piece 4in × 4in × 4in (102mm × 102mm × 102mm)
Aperture rings: 1 piece 1½in × 1½in × 12in (38mm × 38mm × 305mm)
Spines: ³⁄₁₆in (5mm) dowel: 4ft 6in (1,372mm)

Yellow Peril
1 piece 2½in × 2½in × 4in (64mm × 64mm × 102mm)
Spines: ³⁄₁₆in (5mm) dowel: 4ft 4in (1,321mm)

The Bomb
1 piece 2⅝in × 2⅝in × 4⁵⁄₁₆in (67mm × 67mm × 110mm)
Spines: ³⁄₁₆in (5mm) dowel: 2ft 6in (762mm)

Urchin
1 piece 3in × 3in × 3½in (76mm × 76mm × 89mm)
2 spikes ³⁄₁₆in (5mm) dowel: 9in (229mm) total
Spines: (if black spines long) 168 cocktail sticks
(if black spines short) 126 cocktail sticks

Jellyfish
1 piece 5¼in dia. × 2in thick (127mm × 51mm)
Spines: ³⁄₁₆in (5mm) dowel: 6ft 0in (1,829mm)

Nylon monofilament fishing line for suspension

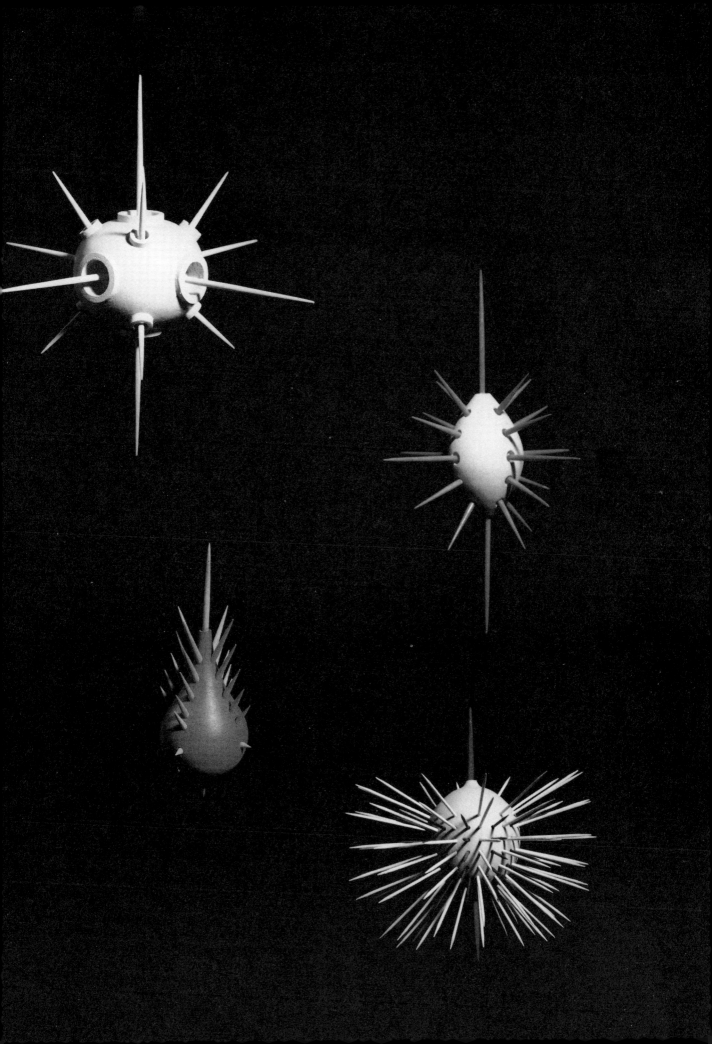

Fig 3.1
Sputnik: drilling the first major hole. Note rubber glove for better grip – a vise would be preferable, and safer.

There is of course no special order of presentation, as I have tried to give as wide a variation in shape, colour and design as possible to stimulate your own ideas. I will describe them in the order in which they were designed. I found it convenient, as you might do, to design and make only one piece per day. In that fashion, my sub-conscious worked out variations for me whilst I slept, so that the next one was ready for me in the morning without my actually having to think!

CONSTRUCTION

Sputnik
This is the largest piece, and it was turned from a piece of ash 4in (102mm) in diameter. The finished model weighs 9½oz (269g), so you may prefer to use a lighter wood, or a smaller piece. Indeed, you may well wish to reduce the size of all the models.

Turn the block of timber to a sphere between centres. Don't worry about the marks made by the headstock drive dog and the tailstock point, as these marks will be drilled out later. There are six large holes to be drilled in the sphere: at its north and south poles, and also at 0°, 90°, 180° and 270° around its equator. With a 1¼in (32mm) forstner or sawtooth bit, drill these holes to a depth of ½in (13mm).

Turn a cylinder of wood to an external diameter of 1¼in (32mm) to match the hole, and drill out the centre of the cylinder with a 1in (25mm) Forstner bit, to give a tube with a wall thickness of ⅛in (3mm) (*see* Fig 3.2). This tube is turned in exactly the same way as the cylinders for the locomotive *King Billy* (*see* page 73), except that you do not round off the inboard end, but part off ⅝in (16mm) lengths as required, after the centre of the cylinder has been drilled out. When you have produced six short lengths of tube, each ⅝in (16mm) long, set them aside for later assembly.

At the centre of the base of each of the six 1¼in (32mm) holes you have made in the sphere, drill a hole ¼in (6mm) deep with a ³⁄₁₆in (5mm) drill bit. These holes will accept the stub ends of the pseudopods (spikes). There are eight more holes to be drilled into the sphere in a similar fashion, and these are at 45° to the main ones, as you see from Figs 3.3 and 3.17. Use a ¾in (19mm) bit for these, and turn a cylinder ¾in (19mm) in diameter drilled out with a ⅜in (10mm) bit to make the inserts for these smaller holes. Again, drill central holes ³⁄₁₆in (5mm) diameter at the bases to take the spikes. Glue the cylinders into the holes to give the raised rim appearance you see in Fig 3.17.

Fig 3.2
Sputnik: cutting one of the rings for insertion into holes.

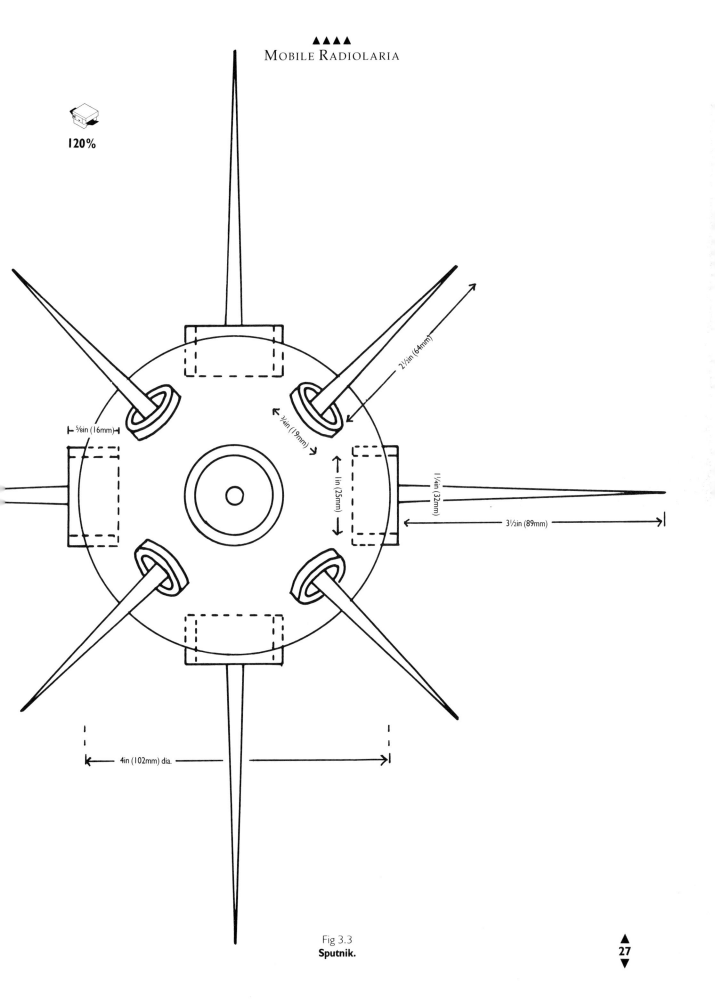

120%

⅝in (16mm)

2½in (64mm)

¾in (19mm)

1in (25mm)

1¼in (32mm)

3½in (89mm)

4in (102mm) dia.

Fig 3.3
Sputnik.

You now need six long and eight short spikes, made from ³⁄₁₆in (5mm) ramin dowel. There is 3½in (89mm) showing when the large spikes are in place, and allowing ½in (13mm) for the hole depth and ¼in (6mm) for the stub which is glued in, the total length of the long spikes is 4¼in (108mm). The overall length of the small spikes is 3¼in (83mm), which will leave 2½in (64mm) showing. These dowel lengths may be tapered by hand using sandpaper, or on the lathe held in a Jacobs chuck on the headstock at 1500rpm or so, and tapered with a ½in (13mm) skew chisel.

The body of this radiolarian was painted with two coats of sea green matte vinyl emulsion, with the spikes painted matte white before assembly (except, of course, for the ¼in (6mm) stubs which were glued in. One of the long spikes was drilled with a 0.02in (0.5mm) drill bit, 1in (25mm) down from its point, and a suitable length of nylon monofilament was firmly knotted on for suspension from a small ceiling hook. I have mine all at different heights so that, whilst fairly closely grouped, all can rotate freely.

141%

Fig 3.4
Yellow Peril.

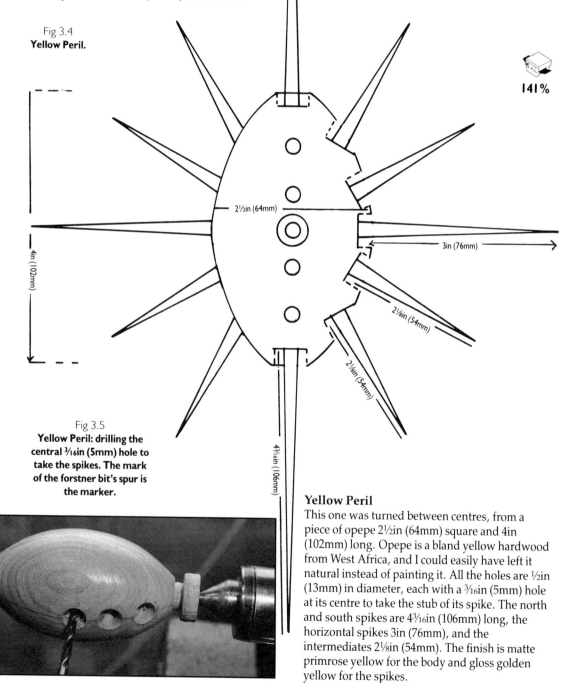

2½in (64mm)

3in (76mm)

2⅛in (54mm)

2⅛in (54mm)

4in (102mm)

4³⁄₁₆in (106mm)

Fig 3.5
Yellow Peril: drilling the central ³⁄₁₆in (5mm) hole to take the spikes. The mark of the forstner bit's spur is the marker.

Yellow Peril

This one was turned between centres, from a piece of opepe 2½in (64mm) square and 4in (102mm) long. Opepe is a bland yellow hardwood from West Africa, and I could easily have left it natural instead of painting it. All the holes are ½in (13mm) in diameter, each with a ³⁄₁₆in (5mm) hole at its centre to take the stub of its spike. The north and south spikes are 4³⁄₁₆in (106mm) long, the horizontal spikes 3in (76mm), and the intermediates 2⅛in (54mm). The finish is matte primrose yellow for the body and gloss golden yellow for the spikes.

The Bomb

Whereas the other designs have all their pseudopods radiating from the centres of their bodies, this piece relies for its impact on having all the main spikes parallel at 60° from the horizontal. Stubs at its waist and base balance the shape. Again, this piece was made from a piece of opepe, with ramin spikes all left in the natural wood. The body was turned between centres from a piece of timber 2⅝in (67mm) square and 4⁵⁄₁₆in (110mm) long, with an application of melamine as a sanding sealer before finishing with a series of grits of sandpaper, ending with 240 grit. All holes were drilled ³⁄₁₆in (5mm),

ensuring that they were angled 30° off the lathe bed. This was done with the lathe stopped but the piece still mounted and locked at 0°, 90°, 180° and 270° in turn. I filed a small 'V' cut on the end of the top of my small tool rest to rest the shank of the drill bit (ensuring that there was a dab of grease to reduce friction, and also that there was only a length of smooth drill shank in contact). You will note that the spikes increase in length as they ascend to the apex: ¼in (6mm) stubs at the waist, followed by ¾in, ⅜in, 1⅛in, 1¼in and 1½in (19mm, 22mm, 29mm, 32mm and 38mm) with the vertical one at 2¼in (57mm) long.

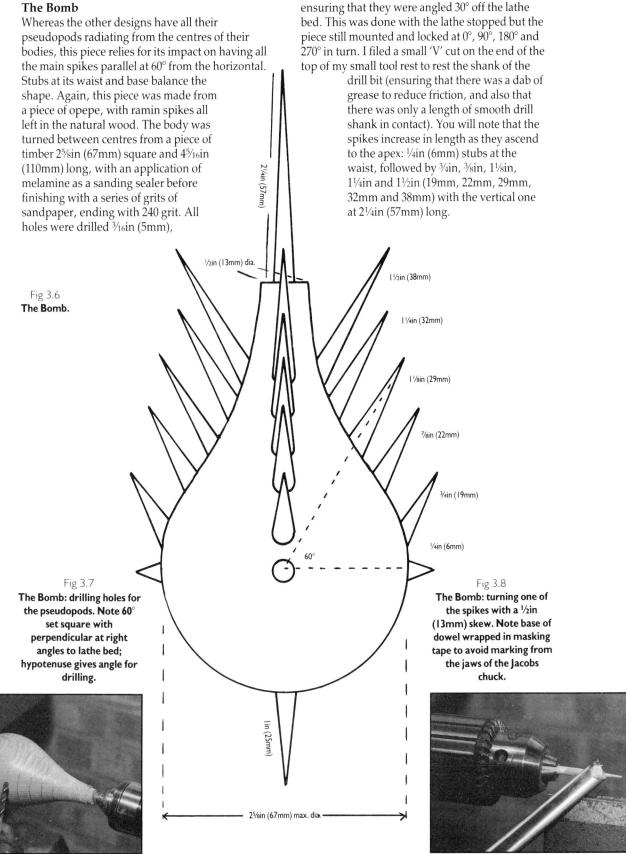

Fig 3.6
The Bomb.

½in (13mm) dia.

2¼in (57mm)

1½in (38mm)

1¼in (32mm)

1⅛in (29mm)

⅞in (22mm)

¾in (19mm)

¼in (6mm)

60°

Fig 3.7
The Bomb: drilling holes for the pseudopods. Note 60° set square with perpendicular at right angles to lathe bed; hypotenuse gives angle for drilling.

Fig 3.8
The Bomb: turning one of the spikes with a ½in (13mm) skew. Note base of dowel wrapped in masking tape to avoid marking from the jaws of the Jacobs chuck.

1in (25mm)

2⅝in (67mm) max. dia.

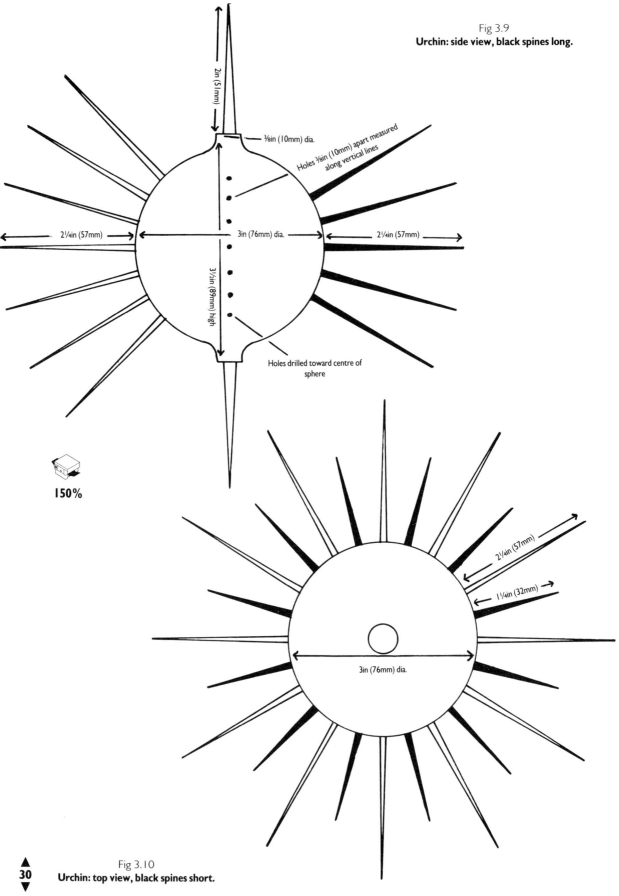

Fig 3.9
Urchin: side view, black spines long.

2in (51mm)

⅜in (10mm) dia.

Holes ⅜in (10mm) apart measured along vertical lines

2¼in (57mm)

3in (76mm) dia.

2¼in (57mm)

3½in (89mm) high

Holes drilled toward centre of sphere

150%

2¼in (57mm)

1¼in (32mm)

3in (76mm) dia.

Fig 3.10
Urchin: top view, black spines short.

Urchin

I have simplified this little beast, but even so it has 12 vertical rows of seven white spines, alternating with 12 vertical rows of five black spines.

Apart from the actual drilling, this is a simple piece as all the spines are made from cocktail sticks with the point cut off their bases and painted before assembly. Only the two vertical spikes bear colour (a rich gloss crimson), whilst the almost spherical body is matte grey (one teaspoonful of white emulsion plus 4 drops of black liquid watercolour).

The lightest puff of breeze sets this one rotating and the spines are so close that a stroboscopic effect takes place at low revolutions. A set of these in different colours would look good, and move attractively.

I have simplified Figs 3.9 and 3.10 to show merely the drilling stations, as a perspective drawing of a gross of spines would be tedious and unnecessary.

Fig 3.12
Urchin: drilling the holes for spines with a 1/16in (2mm) drill. The drill should always point to the centre of the sphere. Note the cradle for support; made from 4in × 2in (102mm × 51mm) scrap, with the curve cut on the band saw to the same diameter as the workpiece.

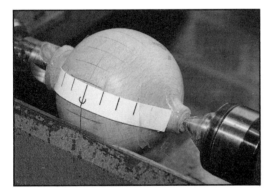
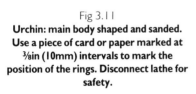

Fig 3.11
Urchin: main body shaped and sanded. Use a piece of card or paper marked at 3/8in (10mm) intervals to mark the position of the rings. Disconnect lathe for safety.

The body is turned from a block of timber 3in (76mm) square and 3½in (89mm) long, to leave a small stub at north and south 3/8in (10mm) in diameter. These stubs are drilled 3/16in (5mm) to take 2in (51mm) spikes. The body must now be marked out with the position of the spines. You can do the marking out and the drilling all on the lathe, but in this case I compromised to save a little time and just marked out on the lathe, removing the piece to be hand-held for the drilling.

All the spines in any one north–south row are 3/8in

(10mm) apart, and the rows rise angularly by 15° increments. With the lathe stopped, mark seven lines around the girth of the workpiece, turning the lathe by hand, each line 3/8in (10mm) from the next, marking the first line central between ends, then three lines either side of that. Using a piece of card, cut to the shape of the spherical workpiece and, resting it on the tool rest horizontally, draw a line parallel to the axis (and, of course, at right angles to the lines around the girth) (*see* Fig 3.11). Repeat this line for every one of the 24 stations of the indexer. Then mark the intersections of the rings and lines with a steel point, taking care to mark only the central five points in alternate rows (i.e. 5, 7, 5, 7 etc.).

Make a small cradle from scrap to hold the sphere, and clamp the cradle to the table of your bench drill, then drill the necessary holes at the marked points with a 1/16in drill bit (*see* Fig 3.12). Support the workpiece and guide it with your hand. Just remember that each hole should point toward the centre of the sphere.

Procure a packet of cocktail sticks. These are

Fig 3.13
**Jellyfish: top turned to profile and sanded.
To hold the piece when reversed on the
screwchuck, turn a small washer of 2in
(51mm) diameter, the hollow of which fits
the top small raised portion.**

Fig 3.14
**Jellyfish: drilling the rim holes using a
notch on the tool rest to guide the drill.
Allow only the smooth shank to touch
tool rest, and use a spot of grease.**

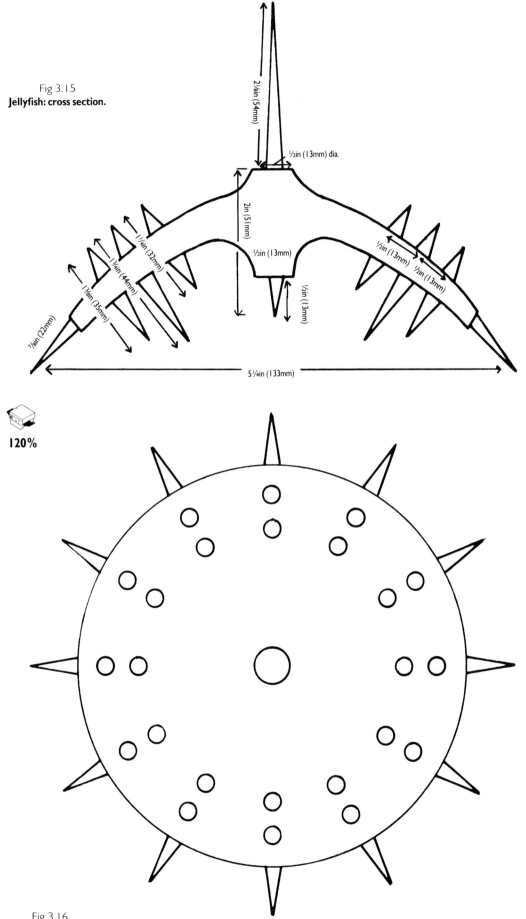

Fig 3.15
Jellyfish: cross section.

2⅛in (54mm)

½in (13mm) dia.

2in (51mm)

½in (13mm)

½in (13mm)

½in (13mm)

½in (13mm)

1¼in (32mm)

1¾in (44mm)

1⅜in (35mm)

⅞in (22mm)

5¼in (133mm)

120%

Fig 3.16
Jellyfish: top view.

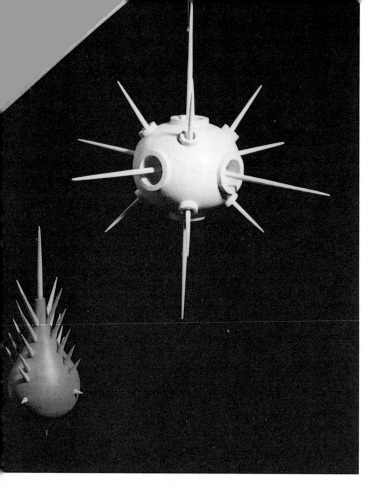

Fig 3.17
**A mobile featuring Sputnik
and the Bomb.**

The three circles of spikes are alternately black and white, whilst the central and rim spikes are black, tipped with white. (I tried black alone for the rim spikes, but they were invisible in shadow, which ruined the proportions of the finished beast.)

As you can see from Fig 3.16, there are 12 drilling stations 30° apart, and the sets (along the radii) alternate two and three spikes: white/black/white and white/black. All the holes are drilled ³⁄₁₆in (5mm) right through the body. The spikes, turned to points at each end, are painted or stained before assembly. You can make them a little longer if you wish, but I suggest that you do not increase their number as the view from below would become very cluttered. As it is, the model creates an unusual effect when rotating slowly on its monofilament, rather like the moving mouth parts of a crustacean.

ASSEMBLY OF A MOBILE

To display the radiolaria in the form of a mobile, first decide what material you intend to use for the support arm or arms. It is usual to use stiff wire which can be obtained from a model supplies store. It is called piano wire, and is normally cut and supplied in straight 36in or 1 metre lengths. It is available in various thicknesses and you will find one to suit you in the range 12SWG to 24SWG (SWG stands for standard wire gauge, and the thicknesses of these two are 0.104in (2.64mm) and 0.022in (0.56mm)). Normally you would solder (or spot-weld) little lugs on to the wire from which to suspend the objects, once you have ascertained the points of balance and decided upon a harmonious arrangement. However, as a simple alternative, you can use a dab of superglue or epoxy.

If you wish, you can use a length of wooden dowel; I used a length of ³⁄₁₆in (5mm) ramin dowel (wiped with black boot polish to tone with the background). It does help to paint or dye the dowel to match or tone with the intended background of wall or ceiling paper. An advantage with dowel is that when you have found the points of balance – from which are supported (a) the whole mobile and (b) the individual elements – you can cut a little groove or notch in the dowel to tie the supporting filament of thin wire or nylon fishing line. (Monofilament fishing line is better than the woven surfcasting type, as it shows up less against a background.) With the notches cut, the pieces will not slide along the dowel and spoil the balance.

Figs 3.17 and 3.18 show examples of mobile suspended radiolaria groups. You can add more if

usually 3in (76mm) long and ¹⁄₁₆in (2mm) in diameter. Cut the point off one end of each of 84 sticks so that they are about 2¾in (70mm) long, and paint them (except for the blunt ends) with white emulsion paint. You can either have your 60 black spines the same length as the white ones, or half length as I have on my model (the two alternative lengths are shown in Fig 3.10). If you decide on the shorter ones, then cut 30 cocktail sticks in half and paint all 60 pieces black (I dipped mine in black ash wood dye and left them on blotting paper to dry). With the ¼in (6mm) stubs glued into place, the short black spines will be 1¼in (32mm) long on the finished model. Paint the body light grey, the two large spikes crimson, and when all are dry, glue the spikes and spines into place with white PVA glue.

Jellyfish

This is the final piece of my set (so far), and it was turned from a piece of ash 5¼in (133mm) in diameter and 2in (51mm) thick, mounted on a screw chuck. Drill the central hole right through, as the piece will be reversed on the chuck to finish the second side. The hole will be filled later by the central spike, which will protrude on both sides of the saucer-like turning. I left this piece in the natural wood, with a wax finish only.

Fig 3.18
Urchin, Jellyfish and Yellow Peril.

you wish; you can change the colours; you can have them all the same colour, or combinations of colours – Sputnik, Urchin and Yellow Peril all painted blue, for instance, with green spines. You can suspend one (preferably the heaviest) at one end of the arm, and two others on another smaller arm, which itself is suspended from the other end of the main arm, so that the pair balance the weight of the first piece. It is not necessary for the

arms to be horizontal in repose; they can rest at an angle, provided that there is free movement laterally for the radiolaria to rotate on their individual filaments.

Well, that's all, and I hope that the set will stimulate your imagination. After all, with over 4,000 to choose from, who is to say that yours is not one previously unknown to science?

CHAPTER 4

The Extraterrestrial Calculator

'O Lorenz,' said the Magistraler, 'you have been accused of bringing this fiendish device to the public. What steps will you take?' 'Rather large ones,' I replied, and slid out of the court to avoid retribution.

The device was the Calculator, and the incident was some time ago; to be precise, the Fothday before the last conjunction of our two moons, Danis and Crepolon.

Today, of course, commercial calculators are available, small enough to put in your pocket, and with organic power cells, but I thought that you might like to build a model of the original, psychic-powered one. It is made wholly of organic materials, with the exception of the four satellite chevron pivots.

If the bronze of these, which are evenly balanced around the circle, upsets the aura, then it is easy to substitute wood.

Left and right of centre there are nine symbols (three times three), and a null area where the calculator can be held. The null has an area of uncertainty to its left and right. This will give you a clue as to its operation. It will calculate, of course, according to the values and names which you personally assign to the symbols; it will predict, but only for you, which will give you high standing in your group; and it has another, secret purpose, which you must discover for yourself.

Now follow the instructions to make your own personal model.

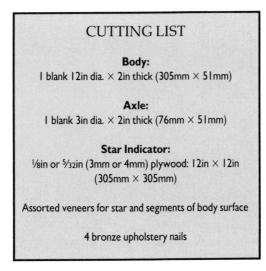

CUTTING LIST

Body:
1 blank 12in dia. × 2in thick (305mm × 51mm)

Axle:
1 blank 3in dia. × 2in thick (76mm × 51mm)

Star Indicator:
1/8in or 5/32in (3mm or 4mm) plywood: 12in × 12in
(305mm × 305mm)

Assorted veneers for star and segments of body surface

4 bronze upholstery nails

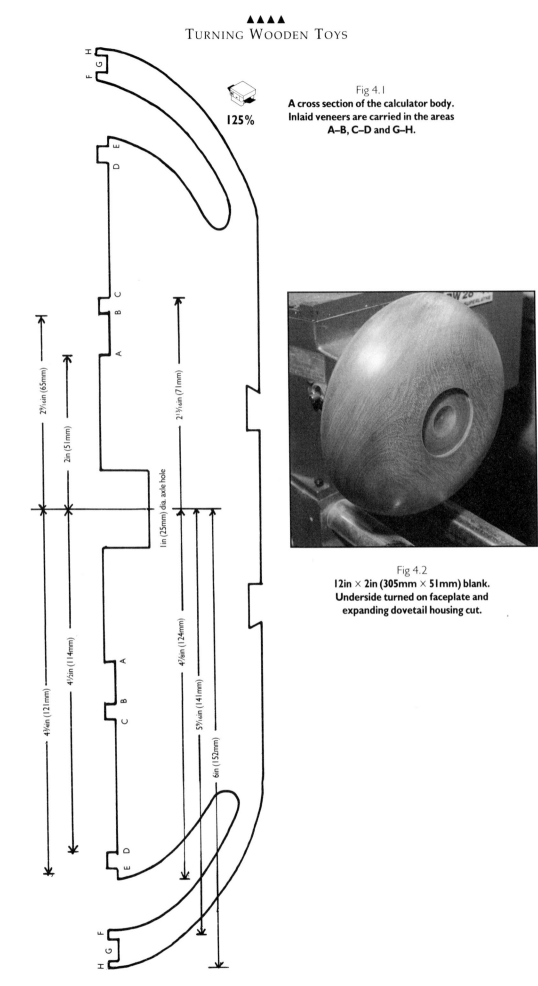

125%

Fig 4.1
**A cross section of the calculator body.
Inlaid veneers are carried in the areas
A–B, C–D and G–H.**

Fig 4.2
**12in × 2in (305mm × 51mm) blank.
Underside turned on faceplate and
expanding dovetail housing cut.**

CONSTRUCTION

Calculator Body

This was turned from a blank of English elm, 12in (305mm) in diameter and 2⅛in (54mm) thick. Mount the blank onto a suitable faceplate, 6in (152mm) in diameter or over. It is convenient to have the screw holes at just over 5in (127mm) radius (10in (254mm) diameter), so that they are turned away when you hollow out the valley between symbol face and rim. If this is not convenient, don't worry, provided you don't drill where the raised rings will be. You can later plug any holes you may have to make on the symbol face, and when the surface is flattened the plugs will be covered by the marquetry veneers.

True up the blank at low revolutions, say 500rpm, and shape the edge to the profile shown in Fig 4.1. Cut a recess for a suitable expanding dovetail chuck (I cut a 3in (76mm) diameter recess to take the 'D' jaws of a Multistar chuck in expansion mode). Sand the surface of the workpiece, i.e. the side and base of the piece (*see* Fig 4.2). Reverse the piece on to your expanding chuck, true the face and mark the necessary rings in pencil. There is a centre hole 1in (25mm) in diameter, which can usefully be drilled on the lathe with a Forstner bit in a Jacobs chuck mounted in the morse taper of your tailstock. Drill to a depth of about ¾in (19mm) or a little more; it is not critical.

Now, with the lathe turning, mark circles at the following radii: 2in (51mm), 2½in (64mm), 2¾in (70mm), 4½in (114mm), 4¾in (121mm), 5¹⁹⁄₃₂in (142mm), 5¹¹⁄₁₆in (144mm), and 5¹⁵⁄₁₆in (151mm). Look at Fig 4.1. These points are marked alphabetically, starting with 'A' at 2in (51mm)

radius, and ending with 'H' at 5¹⁵⁄₁₆in (151mm) radius.

Between rings A and B, recess the surface to a depth of ⅛in (3mm to 4mm) and the same between rings C and D. You can use a ⅛in (3mm) parting tool and flat-nosed scraper for this, ensuring that the surface is flat. The two areas so defined will carry the marquetry inlays. Recess similarly – and carefully – the band between rings G and H. This will give a circle ⁹⁄₃₂in (7mm) wide between the two thin raised rings each ¹⁄₁₆in (2mm) wide. This recess will accept the calibrations, again in veneer.

Between rings E and F, starting ⅛in (3mm) outside ring E, you should now hollow out as shown in Fig 4.1. I found that a ⅜in (10mm) round-nosed scraper was an acceptable tool for this operation; you don't need to spend serious money on a special tool (*see* Fig 4.3). Sand the surface, but note that if you are using a dense, close-grained timber (rosewood, for example), do not make too smooth the areas which you will later cover with veneer. These should be left a little rough, to give tooth to the adhesive. Remove the piece from the lathe. You can leave the timber natural if you wish, or dye it to suit your own tastes. If you do decide to dye the wood, it is not necessary to do so where the veneers will be applied, but do ensure that you dye the top and sides of the raised rings which you have cut on the top surface, and also brush the dye right into the recess between E and F.

Before starting the veneering, you may as well make the other parts.

Fig 4.3
**Hollowing between rim and main area
with a ⅜in (10mm) round-nosed scraper.**

Centre Axle

This was made from a 3in (76mm) diameter piece of cherry wood. You can either turn this in one piece, as shown in Fig 4.4, with its 1in (25mm) plug integral, or you can turn plug and domed top separately. You will then, of course, drill a 1in (25mm) hole on the underside of the dome to accept the plug. It depends what pieces of timber come readily to hand.

You will need two washers, preferably of soft leather. I used belly hide from a Charolais cow, as it was thick and soft (like the cow). Two washers are required, both with a 1in (25mm) central hole. The lower one, which is fitted between the main turning and the star indicator, can be up to 3in (76mm) in diameter, and is fitted suede side down. The other washer, cut to a 2in (51mm) diameter, will fit suede side up, just under the dome of the centre axle. You will then have adequate support for the star, which can rotate freely between the smooth surfaces of the leather washers.

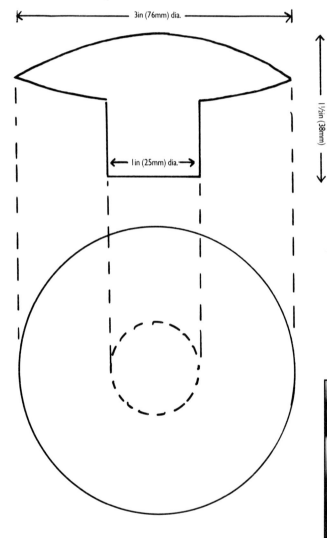

Fig 4.4
The centre axle turned as one piece.

Fig 4.5
Checking centre axle stem with calipers to ensure a 1in (25mm) diameter.

Star Indicator

This is cut from ⁵⁄₃₂in (4mm) birch ply. The width across points is 12in (305mm) and it has a central hole 1in (25mm) in diameter

(*see* Fig 4.6). You can sand the sides of the hole slightly, with sandpaper wrapped around a dowel, just enough to give free movement on the axle.

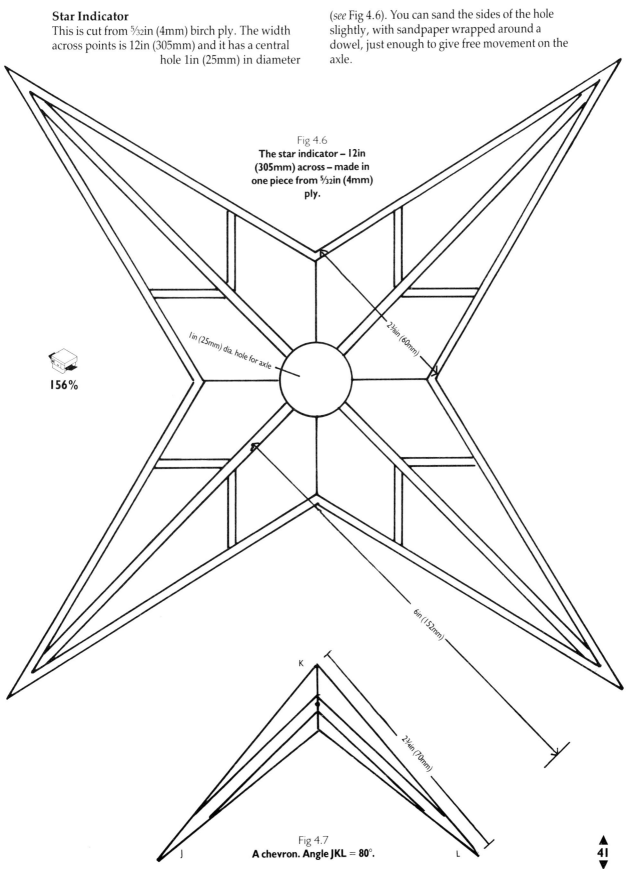

Fig 4.6
The star indicator – 12in (305mm) across – made in one piece from ⁵⁄₃₂in (4mm) ply.

1in (25mm) dia. hole for axle

2³⁄₈in (60mm)

6in (152mm)

2³⁄₄in (70mm)

156%

K

J   L

Fig 4.7
A chevron. Angle JKL = 80°.

You could use MDF (medium density fibre-board), but my stockist at least only stocks ¹⁄₁₆in (2mm) and ¼in (6mm) thicknesses of sheet. The thinner one is too flimsy, and the other is too clumsy. Cut out the star on a scroll saw, sand the edges if necessary, and dye those edges to match the calculator body.

Cut four of the 'V' shapes, again from ⁵⁄₃₂in (4mm) birch ply. Note that the outer edges do not form a right angle; the angle is actually 80° (see Fig 4.7). These chevrons will fit on the arms of the main star, as shown in Fig 4.8, with the pivot points 2in

Calculator/Predictor Segments

As I mentioned in the introduction, there is a null area; that is, a sector where there is no response (rather like an area outside the lobes of a radio aerial, where signals cannot be picked up). On this device, the null is the plain triangular-shaped area, bounded on either side with inlaid triangles, which indicate areas of uncertainty. Look at Fig 4.9, and hold the book with the null nearest you. There is a dividing bar furthest from you at 12 o'clock, with nine defined areas either side of it at 18° intervals. (If there were no null, there would be 20 equal divisions.)

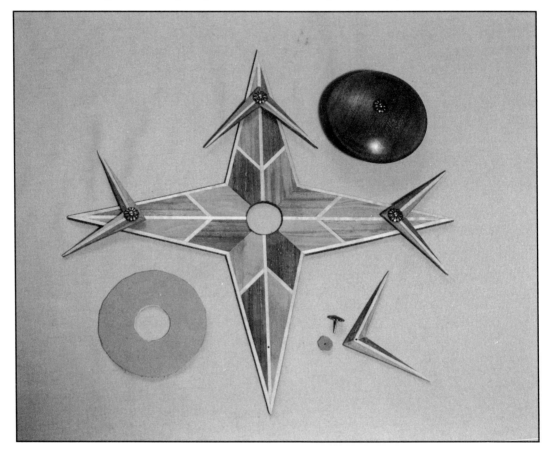

Fig 4.8
**Star indicator, inlaid, plus centre axle,
fine-tuning chevrons, and leather
washers.**

(50mm) in from the points. Dye the edges to match the star edges. The pivots for these fine-tuning chevrons are fancy bronze upholstery nails with little leather washers between chevron and star indicator arm. Snip off any excess length of the nail shanks, so that they will not scratch the finished inlaid surface. I used another of these nails, just for decoration, at the centre of the axle dome, pushed into a pre-drilled hole and held with a dab of epoxy.

It is for you to assign values and names to these 18 segments. You can even design your own symbols, if you do not wish to copy mine. You will, however, find it useful to alternate light and dark areas. For example, the first segment clockwise from 12 o'clock is a dark half-sunrise on a light background; the second segment has light lozenges on a dark background, and so on. Don't go too wild on varieties of timber for the veneers. I found that dark backgrounds were conveniently cut from the mahogany family and light backgrounds from aspen, which has a much more silky sheen than, say, sycamore. Dividing staves were cut from walnut, and the null from Castello boxwood. It is, of course, entirely up to you which veneers you use, and it is fun selecting them. All my veneers came from a reputable supplier (Art Veneers Co. Ltd of Mildenhall), and all were 0.024in (0.6mm) thick, which simplifies final sanding of the surfaces.

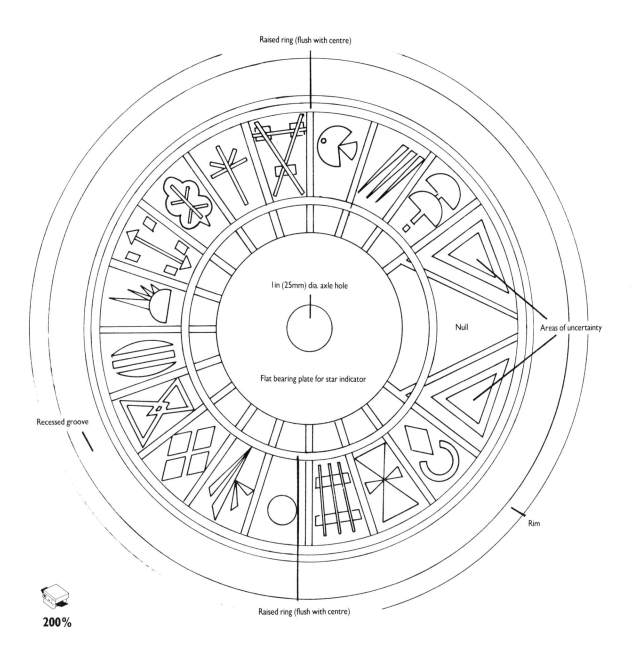

Raised ring (flush with centre)

1in (25mm) dia. axle hole

Flat bearing plate for star indicator

Null

Areas of uncertainty

Recessed groove

Rim

Raised ring (flush with centre)

200%

Fig 4.9
The calculator body, showing the null area and areas of uncertainty (totalling 72°), and the 18 predictor segments (18° each to the centres of the dividing strips).

Marquetry Inlays

If you haven't done any marquetry before, don't worry. There is nothing difficult with the shapes in the design, and you need little in the way of equipment. I cut my veneers on a plastic cutting mat, which is self-healing, but if you only want to use veneers on this occasion, a mat is not worth the expense. Use a piece of ¼in (6mm) MDF, or the smooth side of a piece of hardboard (masonite). When the surface gets scored by knife cuts, then just sand it smooth again, and throw it away after the job is finished. For cutting, a Swann-Morton scalpel is ideal: a No. 3 handle with a No. 10A blade (obtainable from stationers and craft shops). For glue, any white PVA is acceptable; Bostik Wood Adhesive Rapid sets quicker than most. You can hold down little pieces with ordinary masking tape while the glue sets.

First cut out all the dividing strips, which are 5/32in (4mm) wide. The main ones are 2½in (64mm) long (cut to 2⁹/16in (65mm) and they can be trimmed exactly when gluing into place). Cut templates from card, one small one to match the segment areas between rings A and B, and another to match the segment areas between rings C and D. You can cut around these when laid over a piece of veneer to speed up the making of the background pieces for each segment. Incidentally, it looks neater if the grain of these segments runs radially, i.e. from centre to rim.

Glue the first divider into place at 12 o'clock. For the first segment clockwise, cut around the template and lay on a piece of cream-coloured aspen veneer. Glue the cut piece next to the divider, and its matching piece below it between rings A and B. Cut a semicircle of veneer (half of a ¾in (19mm) circle of mahogany), place it over the aspen background, and lightly cut around it with the point of your scalpel. When you remove the mahogany, you can see the outline cut in the surface. Deepen the cut and remove the waste. Glue into its place the semicircle of mahogany, then do similarly for the four elongated triangles which form the rays of the rising sun, one ray at a time.

You will find that each piece of waste will lift quite readily as the glue below it may be set, but not hard dry. If you go off for dinner halfway through a segment, don't worry. You can make a miniature chisel at almost no cost, to lift the dry waste. Take a large masonry nail (3½in (89mm) Obo pin), and a 6in–8in (152mm–203mm) length of ¾in (19mm) dowel. Drill a hole into the end of the dowel to take the masonry nail and tap it in, point first, for at least ¾in (19mm), preferably 1in (25mm). If it is

loose, then squeeze a little epoxy glue into the hole first. Now grind the head of the nail flat and square-ended, and facet one side of the end. This gives a tiny chisel which you can grind from 1/16in to 3/16in (2mm to 5mm) wide. With the facet almost flat on the wood, this tool will lift little waste pieces of veneer from the ground timber (see Fig 4.10).

Back to the construction: lay in another dividing bar and cut the dark background for the next segment using the template. Inlay the little squares of light wood and the arrow (easiest in three pieces; shaft and two points separately).

It will probably help you to mark with a pencil the proposed positions of the segments. At the very least mark the quadrants. The centre of the first strip should be at 12 o'clock. The centre of the 5th strips should be at 3 o'clock and 9 o'clock. If you find as you proceed that you are not spot-on, but your strips are accurately cut at 5/32in (4mm) wide, then there is a tiny error in the width of your template (half a millimetre on each would give an error of 5/32in (4mm) by the time you reach the areas of uncertainty). Adjust this error, if it exists, either by shaving a minute strip from the side of a segment (use a steel ruler, not wood or plastic), or by cutting a slightly oversize segment, to compensate.

Proceed in this fashion all the way round the surface of the calculator.

Rim

As you see, I have not drawn all the rim calibrations on Fig 4.9, but you can see clearly from Figs 4.13 and 4.14 what has been done. Starting at 12 o'clock and going clockwise:

First section (36°, equivalent to two segments) 12 half triangles with ¼in (6mm) bases next to the inner edge of the rim.
Second section (again 36°) 20 white oblongs ⅛in (3mm) wide.
Third section repeat of first section.
Fourth section repeat of second section.
There is then a black square to indicate that you are entering the area of uncertainty.

Anticlockwise calibrations are similar, as you see, and start to the left of 12 o'clock with the pattern of white oblongs. The whole null area is white, with only three central markers at 12° intervals.

These calibrations are laid in one at a time and, although it sounds tedious, is quite quick if you cut your veneers into strips of the correct width first, and cut off the pieces required as you

Fig 4.10
Using a miniature chisel (made from a masonry nail) to remove the centre waste, ready to inlay a mahogany triangle.

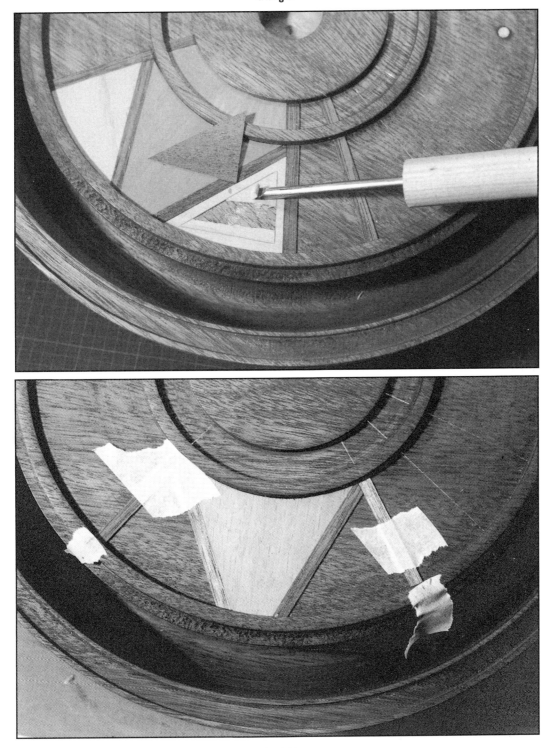

Fig 4.11
Null area glued into place with dividing strips.

Fig 4.12
**Segment No. 8, inlaid with padauk, ready
for its second semicircle inlay. Note card
templates for the inner and outer
segment veneer pieces.**

Fig 4.13
**The first segment (36°) of the rim
calibration inlaid. Note the aspen and
ebony pieces on the side, cut and ready to inlay.**

proceed. I must mention one point to watch: I had no black veneer in stock at the time and thought I'd save time by dyeing some sycamore veneer with black ash wood dye. I found that when it was laid in and I tried to sand its surface, the white turned grey with the dust from the black-dyed wood. You should use ebony or, if that is too hard and brittle for you, a dark walnut. When veneering is complete, sand the surface smooth by hand, or by remounting on the lathe. If the latter, use only the finest sandpaper – it doesn't take long to sand through 0.024in (0.6mm) of veneer! Veneer the star indicator and its four chevrons to

the pattern shown in Figs 4.6 and 4.7, or to your own preferred design. Note that the edge and centre strips on my design are $\frac{1}{10}$in (2.5mm) wide. Drill for the mounting pins, making the hole smaller than the shank of the nail.

You can now assemble the whole device. If the 1in (25mm) axle stub is too loose, then wrap a single winding of plastic insulation tape around it. This will give a gently forced fit, which can be disassembled if required in the future.

You are now ready to amaze your friends with your uncanny powers!

Fig 4.14
**The Extraterrestrial
Calculator**

CHAPTER 5

Gamesphere

Well, to be honest, not a true sphere – more like a ripe puffball or a hot-air balloon, but you see what I mean. It is not in any case your quick bit of turning, polished off before dinner, but it *is* a project that is great fun to build, and which will produce a nice family heirloom. It took me three weeks to design and build, so think in terms of about 75 hours work if you include the marquetry and make all the games pieces. I doubt that you would want to knock off a dozen to flog at your local craft fair.

The sphere comprises seven pieces, five of which carry game boards. Reading from the base upwards, we have noughts and crosses, solitaire, ludo, chess/draughts and Chinese chequers. Above that is a hollowed layer in which to store the games pieces, and finally a lid. You need not be limited to those games, of course – you can make many alternative games within the circular boundary of a board. Lots of other suitable games can be found in

Jeff and Jennie Loader's *Making Board, Peg and Dice Games* (GMC Publications, 1993). Also, if you choose to make false jaws, rather than the expanding dovetail jaws of the Multistar chuck which I used, you can have different games on the top and the bottom of each piece.

The timber I used is English oak. You can, of course, use almost any hardwood you wish, but do ensure that it is really dry, as the whole thing could be spoiled if the slices start curling up like dry toast. Mine was kiln dried to 12% moisture content, and there was slight movement even then.

You will see from the plans that you will need timber in two thicknesses, 1¼in (32mm) and 1¾in (44mm), and the maximum width required is 8½in (216mm). This was decided upon because I was able to obtain those sizes easily, because that width offered a reasonable size of game board (7in (178mm) for the chess board), and because it would enable the whole set to be turned on

CUTTING PLAN

I have drawn a cutting plan (*see* Fig 5.1), on the assumption that you have access to a band saw. From this it can be seen that you will need the following timber for the main construction: (A) one piece 8½in × 26in × 1¾in thick (216mm × 660mm × 44mm) and (B) one piece 8½in × 24in × 1¼in thick (216mm × 610mm × 32mm). Do keep the offcuts as they can be used for the games pieces.

You will also need veneers to cover five surfaces (not lid or storage piece.)

If you are purchasing turning blanks you will need the following in oak:

1 blank 7¼in dia. × 1¼in thick (185mm × 32mm)
1 blank 8³⁄₁₆in dia. × 1¼in thick (208mm × 32mm)
1 blank 8¼in dia. × 1¼in thick (210mm × 32mm)
2 blanks 5⅛in dia. × 1¾in thick (127mm × 44mm)
1 blank 7⅝in dia. × 1¾in thick (210mm × 44mm)
1 blank 8⅜in dia. × 1¾in thick (213mm × 44mm)

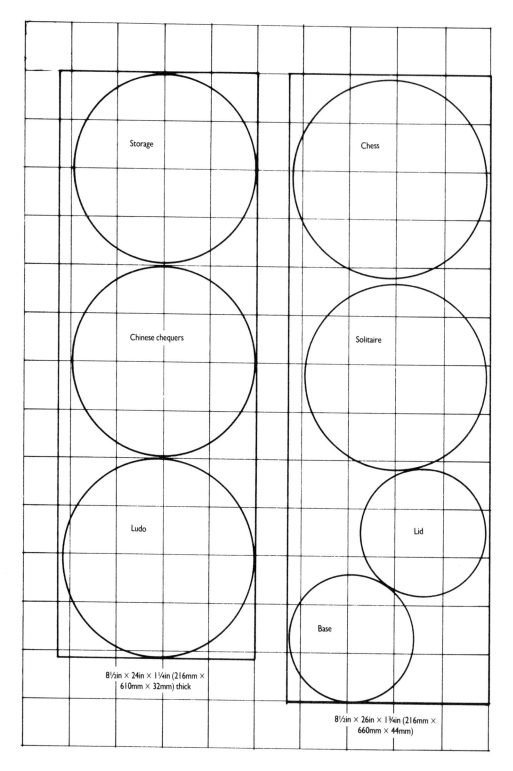

Fig 5.1
Cutting plan.

almost any lathe with a swing of 9in (229mm) or more.

You should decide, before starting, how you will make the actual game board surfaces. As you can see from the photographs, I decided to use simple marquetry, and I will describe that below, but you can draw, paint, burn with a pyrography point, leave as plain timber (in the case of solitaire or Chinese chequers), or insert painted card, etched or scratched perspex, or even inlay strip metal. (Imagine a rosewood sphere, inlaid with brass or silver – imagine is all I can afford to do!)

There are a few general points to bear in mind before we get down to the construction of the sphere and the games pieces. First, as you will see, the pieces interlock by means of a raised ring ⅛in high by ¼in wide (3mm × 6mm) on the top of each piece except the lid, and a recess of the same dimensions (well, a few thousandths of an inch greater) underneath each piece. When marking and cutting these, it is very easy to forget whether it is supposed to be a ring or a groove, so either be careful and ensure that you know which you are supposed to be doing, or keep the workshop door closed to prevent ripe language from disturbing the neighbours.

Secondly, make templates in thin card for the edge of each piece, and check each piece for edge curvature with the piece below by mounting, say, the finished base on the chuck and, with the lathe stopped, placing the solitaire board on it. Any discrepancy in diameter or curve can be rectified then by light cuts with a scraper whilst the pieces are turned together with a blank disc of scrap wood between the right-hand piece and the tailstock.

Thirdly, I suggest that you do not make the game board surfaces (marquetry or otherwise) until you have completed the seven pieces of the sphere. Wait until the whole thing is assembled, you are satisfied with the curvature, and you have stained and polished all the pieces.

MAIN CONSTRUCTION

BASE Noughts and Crosses
Mount a 5⅛in (130mm) diameter 1¾in (44mm) thick blank on a screw chuck, using a wood disc if necessary to limit the screw penetration to ½in (13mm) or less. This is the only piece which can be completely finished on the screw chuck. All the others will need to be reversed onto an expanding

Fig 5.2

**Lid and storage piece removed to show
Chinese chequers, with playing pieces.**

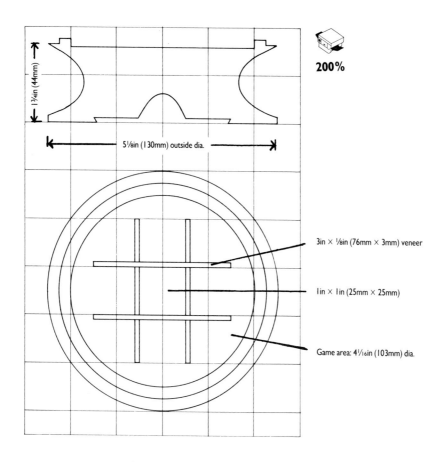

200%

3in × ⅛in (76mm × 3mm) veneer

1in × 1in (25mm × 25mm)

Game area: 4¹/₁₆in (103mm) dia.

1¾in (44mm)

5⅛in (130mm) outside dia.

Fig 5.3
**Seventh layer and base
piece: noughts and crosses.**

dovetail chuck, so you might as well get into practice with this one too and, by slightly dishing the base, avoid any possible wobble of the finished sphere.

Turn to profile with a ½in (13mm) gouge, ½in (13mm) scraper and a card template traced from the plans. Cut a shallow ⅛in (3mm) dovetail housing in what will be the top of the piece. The diameter is not critical, but I used a Multistar with size 'D' jaws 2⅞in (73mm) diameter for all pieces. Remove from the lathe, mount your chuck on the spindle, and secure the piece in the chuck jaws with the base towards the tailstock. Turn another shallow dovetail housing in the base, the same size as the one now holding the workpiece on the lathe, and in the centre turn a little hollow to remove all signs of the screw chuck hole. Slightly dish the circle of the base, so that the outer rim is, say, ¹/₃₂in (½–1mm) proud of the inner circle. The finished sphere will now sit steadily on the base. Sand the base, then reverse it on the chuck in

order to finish the top surface. With the lathe at 1000–1200rpm (not critical) mark with a pencil the two rings ¼in (6mm) apart, which define the sides of the locking ring that will fit into the groove in the bottom of the next piece. Use a square-ended scraper to remove the timber outside the larger ring, to a depth of ⅛in (3mm). Then remove the timber from within the inner ring to a depth of ¼in (5–6mm), checking the flatness of this area as you go with a flat edge of about 3½in (89mm) in length. The depth of this flat inner area, being greater than the edge of the piece, will allow for the thickness of the marquetry surface to be applied later, and will still be deep enough to prevent the base of the next piece from touching or scratching the game surface. Sand the piece all over, stain if required, and finish with a wax polish of your choice, ensuring that no wax goes on the flat game surface, if you intend to glue veneer on to it later. (Use masking tape if you feel you need to.)

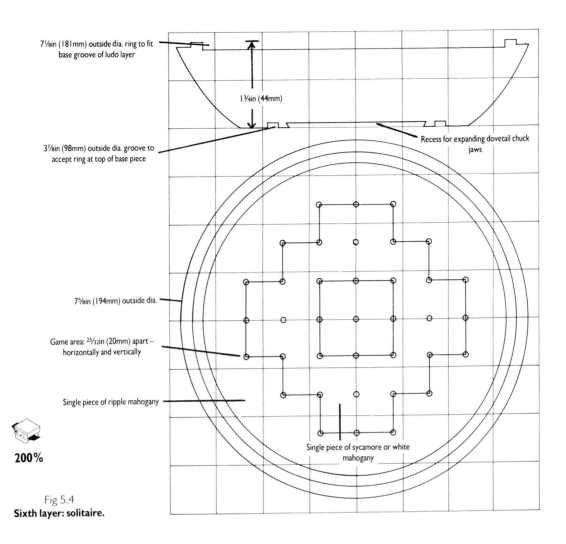

7¹⁄₈in (181mm) outside dia. ring to fit base groove of ludo layer

1³⁄₄in (44mm)

3⁷⁄₈in (98mm) outside dia. groove to accept ring at top of base piece

Recess for expanding dovetail chuck jaws

7⁵⁄₈in (194mm) outside dia.

Game area: ²⁵⁄₃₂in (20mm) apart – horizontally and vertically

Single piece of ripple mahogany

Single piece of sycamore or white mahogany

200%

Fig 5.4
Sixth layer: solitaire.

PIECE 2 Solitaire

This is made in exactly the same was as the base, but using a blank of 7⁵⁄₈in (194mm) diameter, 1³⁄₄in (44mm) thick. With the locking ring set in ½in (13mm) from the edge, the game surface is 6⁵⁄₈in (168mm) in diameter.

Check the inner and outer diameters of the locking ring which you have turned on the top of the base and transfer these to the base of the solitaire board, cutting the groove carefully with a parting tool. Check the fit of the two pieces whilst the larger one is still mounted on the lathe. Aim for something reasonably snug, rather than a tight fit.

Having already turned the outside of the disc to shape using a card template, check the curvature of the two pieces together to ensure that they match and that the curve is smooth. If not, place the base on the already mounted solitaire board, place a waste wood disc on the outboard side of the pair, and bring up the tailstock, locking the two snugly together. With the lathe at 800–1000rpm, refine the curve of the two pieces with a scraper, ensuring that, at this stage, you do not reduce the diameter of the upper rim of the larger piece, as this would affect all the others above it.

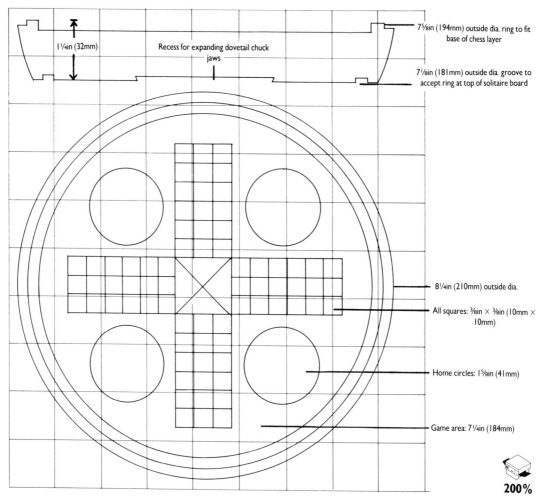

7⅝in (194mm) outside dia. ring to fit base of chess layer

Recess for expanding dovetail chuck jaws

1¼in (32mm)

7⅛in (181mm) outside dia. groove to accept ring at top of solitaire board

8¼in (210mm) outside dia.

All squares: ⅜in × ⅜in (10mm × 10mm)

Home circles: 1⅝in (41mm)

Game area: 7¼in (184mm)

200%

Fig 5.5
Fifth layer: ludo.

PIECE 3 Ludo

This is turned from a piece of timber 8¼in (210mm) diameter by 1¼in (32mm) thick, and worked exactly as Piece 2, except that, as the outer curve is lessening, the upper retaining ring can be set only ¼in (6mm) from the rim, rather than ½in (13mm), yielding a larger game board area with a diameter of 7¼in (185mm).

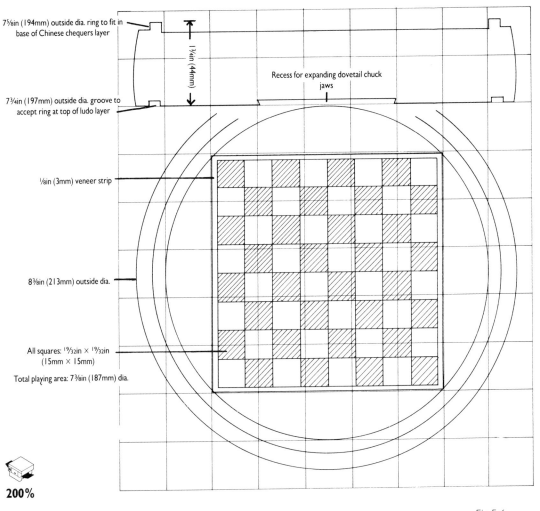

7⅝in (194mm) outside dia. ring to fit in base of Chinese chequers layer

1¾in (44mm)

Recess for expanding dovetail chuck jaws

7¾in (197mm) outside dia. groove to accept ring at top of ludo layer

⅛in (3mm) veneer strip

8⅜in (213mm) outside dia.

All squares: ¹⁹⁄₃₂in × ¹⁹⁄₃₂in (15mm × 15mm)

Total playing area: 7⅜in (187mm) dia.

200%

Fig 5.6
Fourth layer: chess.

PIECE 4 Chess or Draughts

This is deliberately the largest piece, as it is likely to be the most used and, as it is also the heaviest, it will rest solidly and will be fully stable. It is turned from a disc 8⅜in (213mm) in diameter by 1¾in (44mm) thick, and if made of oak, will weigh 2¼lb (just over 1 kg). The game surface is 7⅜in (187mm) in diameter, which allows a chess board of 5in (127mm) square, with individual squares of 1⁹⁄₃₂in (15mm). This makes for pretty easy marquetry, as I will describe later.

Don't forget to continue checking the outer curve of the sphere as you go, as outlined for the base, though of course you must not mount more than two pieces together on the lathe when refining the curve. Any slackness in the locking rings would play havoc with the circularity of the pieces, if three pieces were to spin together.

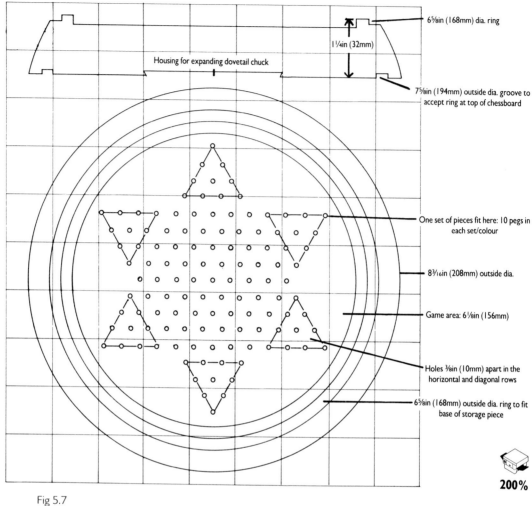

6⅝in (168mm) dia. ring

1¼in (32mm)

Housing for expanding dovetail chuck

7⅝in (194mm) outside dia. groove to accept ring at top of chessboard

One set of pieces fit here: 10 pegs in each set/colour

8³⁄₁₆in (208mm) outside dia.

Game area: 6⅛in (156mm)

Holes ⅜in (10mm) apart in the horizontal and diagonal rows

6⅝in (168mm) outside dia. ring to fit base of storage piece

200%

Fig 5.7
Third layer: Chinese chequers.

PIECE 5 Chinese Chequers

We have now passed the halfway stage, and the curve of the sphere is now lessening the diameter toward the lid. The upper retaining ring of this piece, however, should be set ¼in (6mm) in from the rim, giving a game area 6⅛in (156mm) in diameter.

The piece is turned from a blank of 8³⁄₁₆in (208mm) diameter by 1¼in (32mm) thick. A point to

remember here is that the finished piece will have 121 holes ½in (13mm) deep drilled in the top, and seven of these are grouped around the centre of the board. As those holes will be above the spot where you have drilled initially for the screw chuck, and then turned out a hollow, you could penetrate right through the piece. To avoid this, ensure that the hole for the screw chuck is not much more than ¼in (6mm) deep.

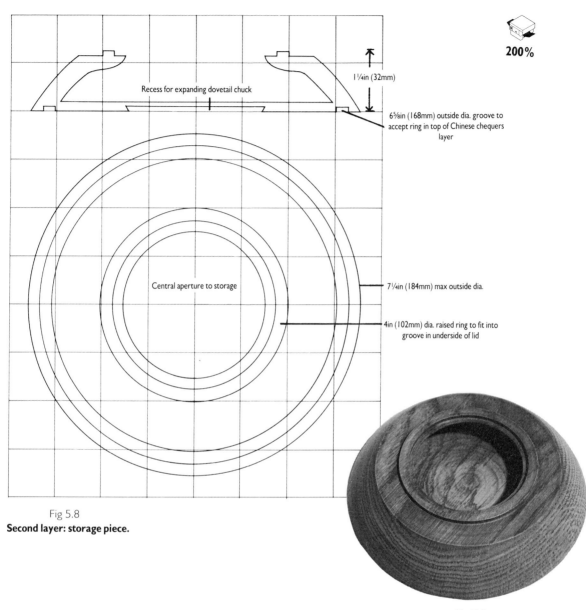

200%

Recess for expanding dovetail chuck

1¼in (32mm)

6⅝in (168mm) outside dia. groove to accept ring in top of Chinese chequers layer

Central aperture to storage

7¼in (184mm) max outside dia.

4in (102mm) dia. raised ring to fit into groove in underside of lid

Fig 5.8
Second layer: storage piece.

Fig 5.9
Storage piece, empty.

PIECE 6 Storage for Games Pieces

This penultimate piece should be large enough to contain all the games pieces, provided that you utilize the Chinese chequers pieces (there are 60 of them) for the solitaire game, as you are unlikely to be playing both simultaneously. For the purposes of the photography, I have made a separate set for solitaire, and I would need to hollow this piece more than I have, if I wished to store the lot.

This piece is turned from a disc 7¼in (185mm) in diameter by 1¼in (32mm) thick, and the retaining ring should be set ¼in (6mm) in from the ring. Open out a hole in the centre of the top surface 3¼in (82mm) in diameter and 1in (25mm) deep,

relative to the top of the retaining ring. *Do not exceed this depth*, and check carefully as you go, because you are getting close to the top of the dovetail housing which now holds the piece on the lathe. As you see from the plans, you still have ⅛in (3mm) thickness, which you will need for strength.

Using a round-nosed, side-cutting scraper (or a Stewart Hooker, if you have one lying about) hollow out the sides of the hole to get a reasonable storage volume. I have left the sides ⅜in (10mm) thick (*see* Fig 5.8), but you can take it thinner, provided you leave enough wood to support the rim, which in turn bears the lid.

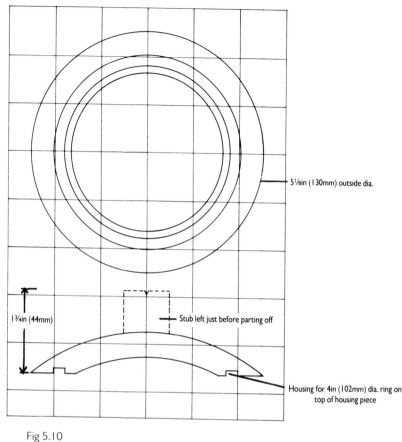

200%

5⅛in (130mm) outside dia.

1¾in (44mm)

Stub left just before parting off

Housing for 4in (102mm) dia. ring on
top of housing piece

Fig 5.10
Gamesphere lid.

PIECE 7 Lid

You will, no doubt, have your favourite method of making this deceptively simple little bit, which is only 5⅛in (130mm) in diameter by ¹³⁄₁₆in (20mm) thick. Like that American crooner, I did it my way.

Starting with a disc 5⅛in (130mm) in diameter by 1¾in (44mm) thick, mounted on a screw chuck, true up and cut the retaining groove of what will be the base of the lid, matching it with the locking ring on the top of the storage piece. Then gently hollow out, as per Fig 5.9, to a depth of ¼in (6mm) at the centre. Sand smooth, though it is not necessary to stain or polish at this stage as it can be done by hand later. With the piece still mounted on the screw chuck, start cutting in on the left of what will be the rim of the lid using a parting tool or whatever you like, until you reach the intermediate shape shown in Fig 5.9.

Remove the piece from the lathe and mount the storage piece on the chuck, open side toward the tailstock, of course. Place the part-finished lid on to it, engaging the locking ring of the storage piece with the groove on the underside of the lid. Now bring up your tailstock gently (force might crack the rim or sides of the hollow piece), and you will be able to finish the domed top of the lid, with the exception of a small central area, which is still supported by the tailstock centre. Stop the lathe, secure the lid to the storage piece with masking tape, then turn off the remaining waste and sand the surface. Remove the lid, stain and wax polish by hand.

The main construction is now complete. Assemble the seven pieces, aligning the crossgrains to avoid colour variations, smile a satisfied smile, and proceed to phase two, the game board surfaces themselves.

200%

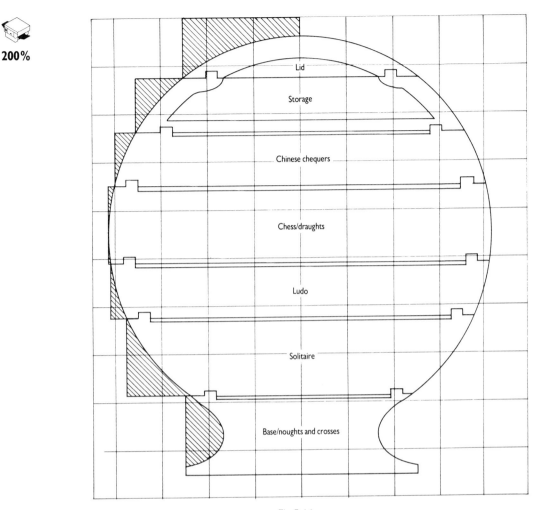

Lid

Storage

Chinese chequers

Chess/draughts

Ludo

Solitaire

Base/noughts and crosses

Fig 5.11
**The gamesphere: a cross section of all
seven pieces showing the interlocking
rings/grooves.**

GAME BOARD SURFACES

All the marquetry within the sphere is simple
geometrical stuff, and you only need two
contrasting woods for any of the games. I have
used mostly ripple mahogany and gaboon, except
for the Chinese chequers where I have inlaid a
disc of rippled walnut. You don't need to spend
much on veneers – a bag of offcuts will scarcely be
depleted for this project. A good source if you
need it is the Art Veneers Co. of Mildenhall (*see*
page 170).

Apart from the veneers, you will need a cutting
board, which need only be a square of hardboard,
a fine-bladed craft knife, a steel ruler and a fairly
quick-drying glue. I used to use balsa cement, but
now find Bostik Wood Adhesive Rapid very
suitable. A small 100ml bottle will be ample.

Fig 5.12
**The gamesphere: seven
tiers, all in English oak.**

Noughts and Crosses

Let us start with the easiest. Your base piece has a flat area within the locking ring of 4$\frac{1}{16}$in (103mm) diameter. Ensure that it is clean and free of wax polish by scraping with a knife blade if necessary. Select a piece of dark veneer, protect the centre with a piece of scrap held down with masking tape, and with compasses describe a circle of just over 4$\frac{1}{16}$in (103mm) diameter, that is about $\frac{1}{96}$in ($\frac{1}{4}$mm) oversize. Cut carefully with a craft knife, and offer it to the base piece. With fine sandpaper you can reduce the edge to get a perfect fit. Draw on the disc of veneer the position of the four strips to be inlaid later; each parallel pair is 1in (25mm) apart. Apply glue to the base, not the veneer and lay down the veneer disc. Place a scrap disc of wood on it, clamp it all together, and leave for an hour. The reason for this is that the veneer will expand as soon as it is wetted with the glue, and you could end up with bubbling and distortion if you do not clamp it firmly.

Fig 5.14
Solitaire board. The surface comprises only two pieces of veneer.

Solitaire

The flat surface is 6$\frac{5}{8}$in (168mm) in diameter, and I prepared and fitted (without applying glue) a disc of rippled mahogany. In this case the centre hole mark was allowed to show as it will be drilled later. The whole game board comprises only two pieces of veneer. I glued the 6$\frac{5}{8}$in (168mm) disc to the base first, and then inlaid the roughly cross-shaped piece of gaboon after lifting out the waste, but you will probably find it easier to cut out before gluing.

The centres of the holes on the finished game are all $^{25}\!/_{32}$in (20mm) apart, which will make it easy for you to draw or trace the shape of the white veneer on to the main disc. Remove the centre square on the white piece and, with that piece held in its correct position on the mahogany disc with masking tape (or sellotape), cut all round with your craft knife. It is sufficient merely to score it, then remove the white veneer and complete the cuts with the aid of a straightedge. Retain the centre square of mahogany, and assemble all three pieces of veneer checking for snug fit all round. With a pencil arrow, mark all pieces to show their final position, just in case there are any discrepancies. Apply glue to the base, and quickly apply the outer mahogany circle, the white cross shape, and finally the centre mahogany square. Cover with greaseproof paper or clingfilm, and a scrap wooden disc, and clamp until dry. The clingfilm, of course, is to stop any excess glue from securing the waste wood disc to the game surface.

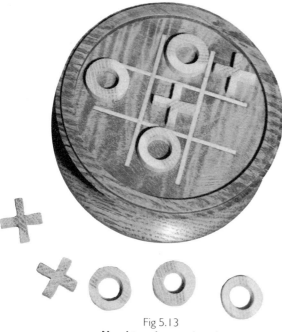

Fig 5.13
Noughts and crosses board.

With the disc glued flat to the base, use a steel straightedge to cut out the strips you have marked as per Fig 5.3. Cut strips of a contrasting wood of the same width and length, glue and insert at once, pressing down gently with a smooth knife handle or something similar. It does not matter if the thickness of the veneers do not match because after 15 minutes you can mount the piece on the lathe and at, say, 1000rpm, sand the surface smooth and apply a wax finish to the game surface.

Remove the clingfilm and the disc, mount the

squares; these can then be inlaid separately with their dividing strips. You will find it convenient to use either the point of your craft knife or a pair of tweezers to handle the small pieces. Don't be too mean with the glue, and you will not need to hold down any of the pieces, once glued into position.

Fig 5.15
Ludo board, inlaid using white and rippled red mahogany.

piece on the lathe, and sand and polish. Remove from the lathe and mark the positions of the 37 holes with a steel point. It is useful to have a bench drill press for this job, to ensure verticality. Drill the holes to a depth of ⅜in (10mm) with a ³⁄₁₆in (5mm) wood drill bit. The centre spur is a guide as you let the drill down into the marked points.

Ludo

This may look a little more complicated, but in fact the board comprises only four triangles, four circles (1⅝in (41mm) in diameter) and 72 small ⅜in (10mm) squares divided by thin strips of a contrasting wood. You will probably find it easiest to make up the disc of veneer from four quadrants and, if you do, it looks neater if the grains all run in the same direction.

For reference, mark the turned oak base piece with the centre point, and also north, east, south and west. As you will see from the plan, the lines which form the junctions of the centre triangles, if produced, will run through the centres of the circles.

Start with one quadrant of background veneer glued onto the base. Cut a circle of contrasting veneer 1⅝in (41mm) in diameter, place in position with masking tape and cut around it. (By the way, pencil marks on the surface do not matter at this stage.) Remove the marked circle by lifting it out before the glue has set, and inlay the contrasting piece. Mark up and cut away the excess to make way for the main cross, which is made up of small

Fig 5.16
Chess/draughts board, made with the same veneers as the ludo board.

Chess or Draughts

Cut 32 light and 32 dark squares, ¹⁹⁄₃₂in × ¹⁹⁄₃₂in (15mm × 15mm), from strips ¹⁹⁄₃₂in (15mm) wide cut from the veneers. Mark the vertical and horizontal axes on the base piece and, starting at the centre, glue the small squares on to the base in normal alternating colours. Keep the grain all in the same direction. Cut four arcs of light wood to fit between the locking ring of the piece and the actual chessboard, drawing the curve on the veneer with compasses set to the exact radius. Check for fit – it does not matter if the straight edge of the cut piece of veneer does not exactly match the side of the chessboard (provided the curved edge is snug to the locking ring) as you will next inlay a narrow strip around the chessboard. Repeat with the other three arcs. Sand and polish on the lathe as with the other game boards.

Fig 5.17
Chinese chequers board.

Chinese Chequers

As described for noughts and crosses, cut a disc, from one piece of veneer if possible, to the diameter of the inside of the locking ring, i.e. 6⅛in (156mm) and sand its edge very gently if necessary until it fits snugly. Glue the base, lay in the veneer disc, immediately clamp using a waste disc of wood a little smaller than the veneer, as before. Leave for half an hour, and then check that it has dried flat. Mark with a pencil, or by tracing from the plans, the positions of the six triangles (which are equilateral with sides of 1³⁄₁₆in (30mm)). Now cut six triangles from contrasting veneer – they can all be of the same wood, or made from six different veneers. Place in position, cut around the edges, remove the waste from the board surface, and inlay the triangles.

This game is made or ruined by the neatness of your drilling. All 121 holes are ⅜in (10mm) apart, which helps, but you will find it easiest to make up a full-size template on tracing paper, with the drilling points marked on it accurately. Place the template in position on the board, ensuring that the points of the drilling pattern match the apexes of the six inlaid triangles. Now mark through the paper with a steel point, and then drill the holes ¹⁹⁄₃₂in (15mm) deep, with a ³⁄₁₆in (5mm) wood drill. Mount on the lathe, and sand and polish to complete.

THE PLAYING PIECES

Noughts and Crosses

Take a piece of scrap wood about 5in (127mm) long and ⅞in (22mm) square, with the grain running lengthwise. Turn between centres to ²⁵⁄₃₂in (20mm) diameter, finishing with a paring cut with a skew chisel.

Reduce the diameter at one end from 2in (51mm) to ½in (13mm) and mount this in a Jacobs chuck on the headstock. Alternatively, you can reduce the diameter to suit the mini-jaws of a Multistar chuck. You can now hollow out the end with a ¼in (6mm) gouge to leave the walls of what is now a tube, about ³⁄₁₆in (5mm) thick. Part off from this five rings, each about ³⁄₁₆in (5mm) thick, and these will be your noughts. The crosses are simply (but very carefully) cut by band saw or scroll saw from a slice of scrap wood ³⁄₁₆in (5mm) thick. It would be safer to use a scroll saw or a fret saw if you have one.

Ludo

As you can see from Fig 5.20, I adopted a helmet shape for these pieces, identical to the pawns in the chess game. You can use eight of these ludo pieces in the chess, and reduce the overall number of pieces for the sphere. I used short lengths of ⅜in (10mm) diameter scrap, again held in a Jacobs chuck.

Fig 5.18
Five tiers of the sphere.

Mark a length of 25⁄32in (10mm) from the end, after truing up, and shape the piece with a ½in (13mm) skew chisel, which will yield a surface that requires no sanding. Part off and repeat, but don't leave less than a 1in (25mm) stub in the chuck. I left four pieces in plain white oak, and stained the remaining three sets of four in golden pine, mahogany and black. Of course, you may choose other shades or colours. If the latter, liquid watercolour is useful; see the section on Chinese chequers pieces below.

Solitaire

These pieces can be made in the same way as the Ludo pieces, from ⅜in (10mm) diameter rod. Again, mark off a 25⁄32in (20mm) length and, with a parting tool, reduce the top end to ⅛in (3mm) diameter and the bottom end to 3⁄16in (5mm) diameter, then finish the slightly tapering body with a skew. You need 36 pieces, which will leave the centre hole of the game board empty when you start. I stained these pieces in rosewood dye.

Chinese Chequers

To make life easy, I cut these from 3⁄16in (5mm) ramin dowel, cut into 5in (127mm) lengths, and held in a Jacobs chuck. The end of the dowel was initially pushed into the chuck as far as it would go, to reduce whipping of the outer end. For these

pieces, and indeed some of the chess pieces too, I found it useful to make up a couple of miniature turning tools. These were very simple, and comprised a handle 7in (178mm) long of 1in (25mm) dowel, drilled ⅛in (3mm) at one end to a depth of 1¼in (32mm), and a 3½in (89mm) obo masonry nail pushed firmly into the hole, point first. The head of the nail was then ground to the required shape. I used a point, a skew and a ⅛in (3mm) scraper; you may find it worthwhile making up a parting tool in miniature as well, but try the point first for this task, as it is effective for small diameters.

The Chinese chequers pieces are 1in (25mm) long and, as you see from Fig 5.22, have a small rounded head and a gently pointed base end. With a small skew you can make these in under a minute each, so don't worry about the fact that there are 60 of them.

You need 10 each of six colours. I used yellow, orange, red, green, blue and black. Using tweezers, I dipped each piece in the appropriate colour and then left all the pieces, not touching each other of course, to dry on a sheet of blotting paper. I use Rotring Artists colour, a liquid watercolour, the pigments of which never separate out (except for white, but I would use ordinary emulsion or gloss for that). When the pieces are dry (left overnight preferably) lightly wax by hand.

Chess

The miniature set I designed for this board may best be described as a heavily modified Staunton. (Incidentally, I discovered that Mr Staunton did not design the set which bears his name. It was designed by an unknown artist in 1839, and registered at the British Patent Office in 1849 by Howard Staunton, who was the English chess champion at the time.)

For this miniature set, the pawns use the helmet shape as made for the ludo, so you need make only eight of these. I left the white pieces in unstained white oak, and the black were of the same wood, dyed with black ash wood dye. This dries with a faint white blush which, when polished off with a dry cotton cloth, is all the finish necessary.

The rook, or castle, is a symmetrical piece ½in (13mm) in diameter and 1¹⁄₃₂in (26mm) high, with two crosscuts in the top rim. The hollow in the top can be achieved with your miniature scraper, and the waist with a ¼in (6mm) gouge.

The knight was the most interesting piece to design and make. Standard commercial chess sets always have the knight in two pieces, a turned base and a carved head with a stub glued into the base. I wanted to achieve a one-piece design, as you see in Fig 5.25. Turn a cylinder ²⁵⁄₃₂in (20mm) diameter and mount in a Jacobs chuck, or the plain bore of a Multistar mini chuck. Mark off the positions of the base and stub as per Fig 5.25 and turn these to size, leaving the section which will be the horse's head alone. Remove from the lathe, still in the chuck, which can be held for the next operation. Draw a vertical centre line for guidance, and carefully band saw or scroll saw the top section as shown in Fig 5.25. This will give an intermediate shape which is almost square, with its thickness tapering toward the top (the horse's ear). Using a paper or thin card template, draw the outline of the horse's head on the piece, and cut away the waste, leaving a generous margin. Part off the piece from the wood stock. Mount a 2in (51mm) velcro sanding pad, with 120 grit, on the lathe. Holding the knight in your fingers you can finish the outline and sand the sides of the piece quite easily. All that remains is to drill the eye (if you wish).

The bishop is a simple turning of ½in (13mm) diameter and 1¼in (32mm) high. Turn to the

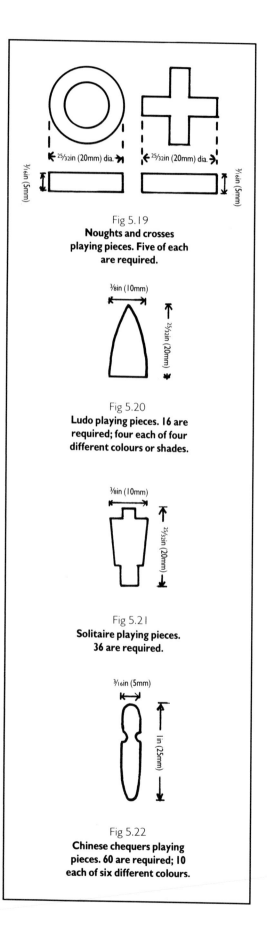

Fig 5.19
Noughts and crosses playing pieces. Five of each are required.

Fig 5.20
Ludo playing pieces. 16 are required; four each of four different colours or shades.

Fig 5.21
Solitaire playing pieces. 36 are required.

Fig 5.22
Chinese chequers playing pieces. 60 are required; 10 each of six different colours.

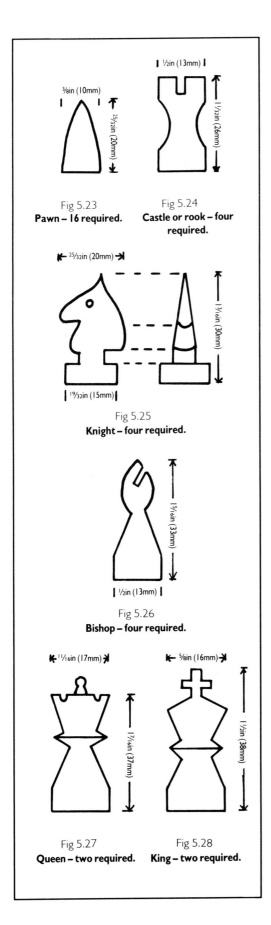

Fig 5.23
Pawn – 16 required.

Fig 5.24
Castle or rook – four required.

Fig 5.25
Knight – four required.

Fig 5.26
Bishop – four required.

Fig 5.27
Queen – two required.

Fig 5.28
King – two required.

profile shown in Fig 5.26, sand and part off. The angled saw cut in the mitre shape at the top is most safely done by hand with a tenon saw with the piece held in the wood-lined jaws of your vice. If you use your band saw to make the cut, use a piece of scrap below it (a piece of ¼in (6mm) MDF is ideal) and offer it to the blade very gently.

The queen, at 1⁷⁄₁₆in (37mm) high by ¹¹⁄₁₆in (17mm) diameter, is almost the same size as the king, and is made from ¹¹⁄₁₆in (17mm) rod, mostly using a ½in (13mm) skew. The centre top is cut first with a parting tool, then with the rest at right angles to the lathe bed, the queen's head is hollowed with a miniature tool to a depth of ¹⁄₁₆in (2mm), leaving a rim as shown in the drawing, with four indentations made by hand with a needle file.

The king, made from ⁵⁄₈in (16mm) rod, is 1½in (38mm) high, and is made similarly to the queen, except that the cross at the top is left in the round initially. When the piece is otherwise finished, part off and, with the 2in (51mm) velcro pad on the lathe, sand off the left and right of the topknot to leave a cross ¹⁄₁₆in (2mm) thick.

CHAPTER 6

King Billy

When my editor suggested that I design a train, my first thought was of the film *The General* which Buster Keaton made in 1926, a little before my time (but only a little!). *The General* was a locomotive, typical of the American type of 4-4-0 locos. Over 25,000 were built, with many variations. Mine is halfway towards a real model, and retains favourite features such as the bell, huge lantern, large woodburning smokestack and cowcatcher.

Its appearance, compared with many simple children's toys, is enhanced by a smooth increase in the diameter of the boiler at the firebox end, a properly counterbalanced wheel pattern, and couplings between the drive wheels. I originally intended to carica-

ture the design, but I found that, as it grew, it became more and more true to the original designs which inspired it. Those American engineers of the 1850s just naturally built in the beauty of steam, so why spoil the proportions?

I decided this time to use timber a little more exotic than my usual native hardwoods, and chose padauk for the main coloured components. It came from Cameroun, rather than the Andaman Islands (Pterocarpus Soyauxii rather than Dalbergioides), but it is still beautiful, and pleasant to work with. The steam safety valve and dome are in tulipwood, and the stack is in rare violet rosewood. The rest will not strain your wallet.

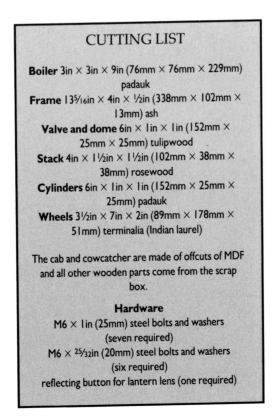

CUTTING LIST

Boiler 3in × 3in × 9in (76mm × 76mm × 229mm) padauk
Frame 13⁵/₁₆in × 4in × ½in (338mm × 102mm × 13mm) ash
Valve and dome 6in × 1in × 1in (152mm × 25mm × 25mm) tulipwood
Stack 4in × 1½in × 1½in (102mm × 38mm × 38mm) rosewood
Cylinders 6in × 1in × 1in (152mm × 25mm × 25mm) padauk
Wheels 3½in × 7in × 2in (89mm × 178mm × 51mm) terminalia (Indian laurel)

The cab and cowcatcher are made of offcuts of MDF and all other wooden parts come from the scrap box.

Hardware
M6 × 1in (25mm) steel bolts and washers (seven required)
M6 × 25/32in (20mm) steel bolts and washers (six required)
reflecting button for lantern lens (one required)

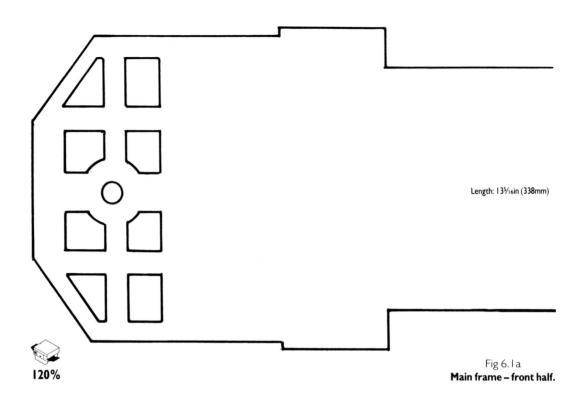

Length: 13⁵⁄₁₆in (338mm)

120%

Fig 6.1a
Main frame – front half.

CONSTRUCTION

The general proportions of this type of locomotive based on the measurements I made of eight different variants, appear to be:

● **boiler** half the total length
● **drive wheels** one and a half time the boiler diameter
● **bogie wheels** two-fifths the diameter of the drive wheels

By selecting initially a boiler length of 9in (229mm), the other dimensions followed, but it did mean that the frame came later in the design process than it should have done, and this proved a little awkward. You, however, will find construction straightforward, if you start with the frame, on which all else hangs.

Frame

This is cut from one piece of ½in (13mm) thick ash, and the shape is given in Figs 6.1a and 6.1b. ¼in (6mm) holes are drilled at the front for the bogie bolt and at the rear for a tender. The piercings at the front end of the frame are optional, but they do lighten the appearance considerably. Drill ³⁄₁₆in (5mm) holes horizontally as shown, centrally through the thickness, to a depth of ¹⁹⁄₃₂in–²⁵⁄₃₂in (15mm–20mm). It is important that the distance between centres of these holes is 3¾in (95mm). They will take ¼in × 1in (6mm × 25mm) axle bolts which will cut their own threads in the timber when screwed into the

³⁄₁₆in (5mm) holes. You could, if you wish, use axles fitted at right angles to the frame's longitudinal axis, but bolts are easier. I used black ash wood dye to finish the frame.

Boiler

This is a simple turning between centres of a block of timber (padauk in this case), 9in (229mm) long and 3in (76mm) square in cross section. Don't worry about the marks which will be made at the ends by the four-prong drive dog and the tailstock point, as both will be hidden on assembly. Do make sure that you true the ends flat. Turn the piece to a round section, then reduce the diameter for part of the length, as shown in Fig 6.2. The first 1½in (38mm) (measured from the cab) is 2¾in (70mm) in diameter, which reduces to 2⁵⁄₁₆in (59mm) for the rest of its length, with a smooth curve in transition between these two dimensions. Sand the surface whilst still on the lathe with your usual series of grits (I use 2in (51mm) velcro sanding discs, 120, 180, 240 and 400 grits). Originally I intended to leave this boiler as it was, with a cut-out in the frame to accept the bulge at its rear end, but I found that the cut-out seriously weakened the frame, as it was almost the same width. It is therefore necessary to flatten the bulge at its base, where it will be glued to the frame. Carefully cut this section off (as shown by the dotted lines on Fig 6.2) a little at a time if you prefer caution. The band saw is suitable for this operation. Sand the cut flat.

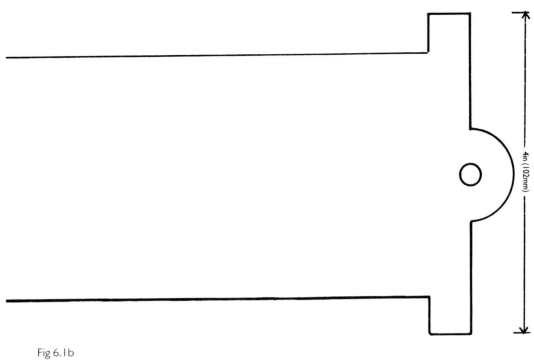

Fig 6.1b
Main frame – rear half.

170%

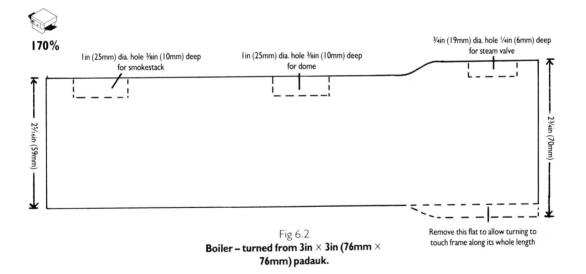

Fig 6.2
Boiler – turned from 3in × 3in (76mm × 76mm) padauk.

Remove this flat to allow turning to touch frame along its whole length

For the front door of the boiler, mount a disc of timber, say 2¾in (70mm) in diameter and 1in (25mm) thick on to your screwchuck with the grain running across the disc and the screw hole shallow. Turn the front door to the profile shown in Fig 6.3, exactly to the diameter of the front of the boiler. The centre boss and the circular groove are optional. I wanted just a little contrast so I used bubinga for this piece, but padauk looks good too.

With the boiler placed with its flat down on the table of your bench drill, drill the holes in the top for the smokestack (1in (25mm) in diameter), dome (1in (25mm) in diameter) and safety valve (¾in (19mm) in diameter). Use Forstner bits at low speeds and a low rate of feed in order to preserve a crisp edge to the holes. You are drilling into a convex surface so take the bit down, say, ¼in (6mm) as measured at the left or right side of the holes. Set aside the boiler for later assembly.

Fig 6.3
Boiler with smokestack, dome and steam valve assembled, plus front door.

Fig 6.4
**One drive wheel with its card template.
Note ¼in (6mm) hole at centre, and ³⁄₁₆in (5mm) hole on thick spoke.**

Drive Wheels

There are four drive wheels, arranged as two coupled pairs, and it is worth cutting a template of card, as shown in Fig 6.4. It is important, for the appearance of the assemblies, to get the cut-out right. You will see that one spoke is thickened (½in (13mm)) wide as compared with ¼in (6mm) for the others), as it will be drilled ³⁄₁₆in (5mm) to accept a ¼in × ²⁵⁄₃₂in (6mm × 20mm) bolt for the connecting rod. The opposite side of the wheel is counterbalanced by a thickened rim.

You can turn two wheels from one block of timber 3⅜in × 3⅜in × 2in (86mm × 86mm × 51mm), mounted on the screwchuck, with the

Turn the wheel block to 3⅜in (86mm) diameter and true the face, on which you should mark a circle ¼in (6mm) in from the edge, and also mark a circle at the centre ¹⁹⁄₃₂in (15mm) in diameter (or the diameter of your bolt head, whichever is the greater). Between these two circles, recess the face ¹⁄₁₆in (2mm) with a flat scraper or parting tool. This defines the rim and boss. Sand, mark the centre point (for later drilling) and, with a thickness at the rim of ⁷⁄₁₆in (11mm), part off the wheel. (You could make it a little thicker if you wish.) Repeat with the same blank, and the second blank, to give four wheel blanks.

Using the card template, mark the holes between the wheel spokes,

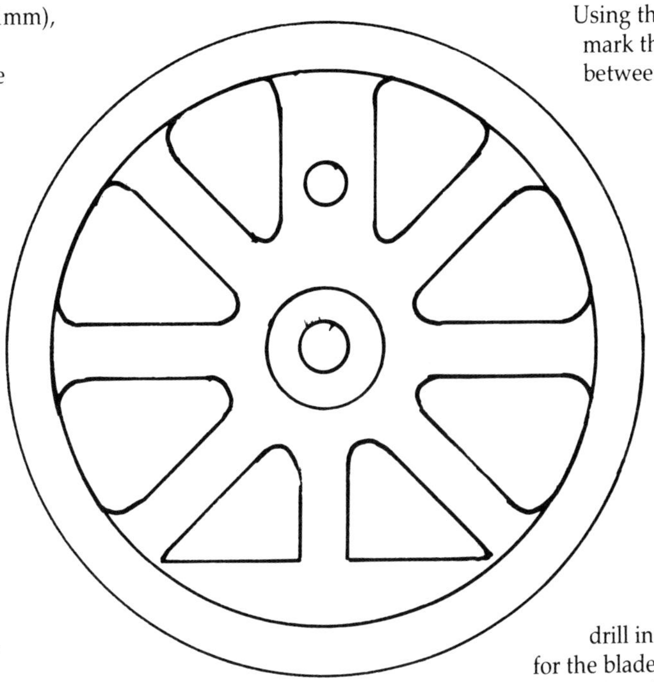

Fig 6.5
Drive wheel (four required).

3⅜in (86mm) dia.

grain across the disc. I used Indian laurel (terminalia, though I hate the name – it suggests some horrible illness to me!) and I found it quite acceptable, as it has enough elasticity to be tapped with the ¼in (6mm) bolt in its connecting rod hole.

You may find that very hard woods like dalbergias (rosewoods) and diospyros (ebonies) will split when so tapped, so be careful. You can, of course, still use the hardest woods, but you may have to drill ¼in (6mm) instead of ³⁄₁₆in (5mm) for the connecting rod bolt hole, and then glue the bolt in place with epoxy.

drill inside those markings for the blade, and cut out on the scroll saw (or with a hand fret saw). Mark the position of the hole for the connecting rod bolt (halfway between rim and centre) and drill it ³⁄₁₆in (5mm); then drill the wheel's centre hole ¼in (6mm) for its axle bolt. Repeat for all four wheels.

I found the Indian laurel rather dull in colour and it detracted from the richness of the padauk, so I dyed the wheels cinnamon, which toned very well.

Smokestack, Dome and Valve

There is a tremendous variety in the shapes used in the 1850s for the woodburner's stack. Mine is quite modest in diameter, and is turned from a piece of violet rosewood 1½in (38mm) square and 4in (102mm) long (finished). Turn between centres to the profile shown in Fig 6.6. The base diameter must be exactly 1in (25mm) to fill without any gap the hole you have drilled for it on top of the boiler. Reverse into a compression chuck (I used the plain bore of a Multistar chuck with 'A' jaws in compression mode) protecting the rosewood with a winding of masking tape (*see* Fig 6.7). Bring the tool rest across the lathe bed, close to the end of the workpiece, and hollow it out with a ¼in (6mm) gouge, the hole being ¾in (19mm) in diameter at the top. You could use a ¾in (19mm) Forstner bit in a Jacobs chuck mounted in the tailstock to clear most of this if you wish, finishing off with a small side-cutting scraper. I achieved a smooth inner surface just with the gouge, as the wood is so hard and dense.

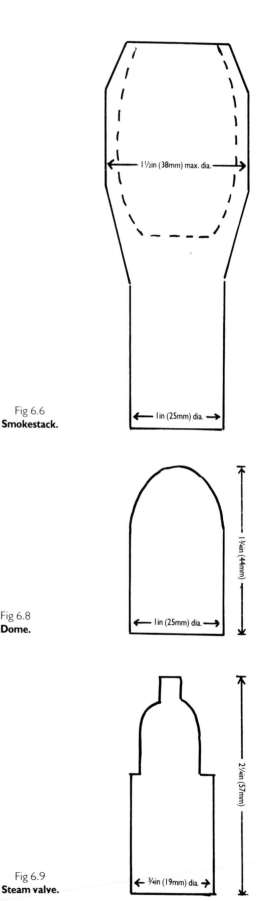

Fig 6.6
Smokestack.

1½in (38mm) max. dia.

1in (25mm) dia.

Fig 6.8
Dome.

1¾in (44mm)

1in (25mm) dia.

Fig 6.7
Hollowing out the (violet rosewood) smokestack.

The steam safety valve (⅞in (22mm) in diameter) and dome (1in (25mm) in diameter) are both turned from a length of tulipwood, first between centres to a 1in (25mm) diameter, then in the same chuck as the stack, to finish off the top ends. Sand very lightly and with fine sanding paper on discs so as to maintain the full diameter, which again must fit into the holes without gaps. Also, note that fierce sanding of these woods can cause splitting or surface checking due to friction heat.

2¼in (57mm)

¾in (19mm) dia.

Fig 6.9
Steam valve.

Cylinders

The cylinders (the padauk horizontal tubes fixed to the front sides of the frame) are turned in the same way. They must finish at 2½in (64mm) long with a 1in (25mm) outside diameter, and be drilled ⅝in (16mm) to a depth of 1⅞in (48mm), as you will see from Fig 6.11.

The depth of drilling is to allow the full movement of the piston connecting rod as the front drive wheel rotates. (The actual movement from fully forward to fully aft is 1¾in (44mm).) I have cheated here, because there is actually no piston or gudgeon pin. It is much more complicated to make and is invisible when assembled. All you need to see is the connecting rod moving with the wheels.

Repeat for the second cylinder and sand a flat along the exterior of each, to assist gluing to the frame.

Bogie

The bogie is the section carried by the four small wheels, which are represented by the first digit of the '4-4-0' classification of this type of locomotive. It comprises two oblongs of ½in (13mm) thick timber (ash, in my case), the dimensions of which are shown in Fig 6.13. For added strength, I used two 1in (25mm) black screws to hold these pieces together, screwed up through the larger base piece of the bogie assembly. Drill horizontally four holes ³⁄₁₆in (5mm) in diameter for the wheel axle bolts. Drill centrally down from the top ¼in (6mm) for the pivot bolt which attaches the bogie

Fig 6.10
Turning the cylinders – first stage.

Fig 6.11
Cylinder drilled and surface sanded.

To save on wood, I turned a length of padauk to just over 1in (25mm) in diameter, and with a parting tool and a ½in (13mm) skew chisel tip, cut two dovetails (as shown in Fig 6.10) adjacent to one another, but in opposite directions. The size of dovetail should fit suitable jaws of your chuck.

Part off, and mount one of the two blanks in the chuck (in this case, Multistar 'A') jaws in compression mode. At low speed, drill the blank with a ⅝in (16mm) Forstner bit mounted on the tailstock. Use a piece of masking tape wrapped around the shank of the bit with a pencil depth mark on it. Reduce the outside diameter of the cylinder to 1in (25mm), and sand to a smooth surface (*see* Fig 6.11). Shape the closed end to the curve shown in Fig 6.12, sand again and part off, finishing the remaining end nubbin by hand.

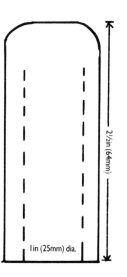

1in (25mm) dia.

2½in (64mm)

Fig 6.12
Cylinder (two required).

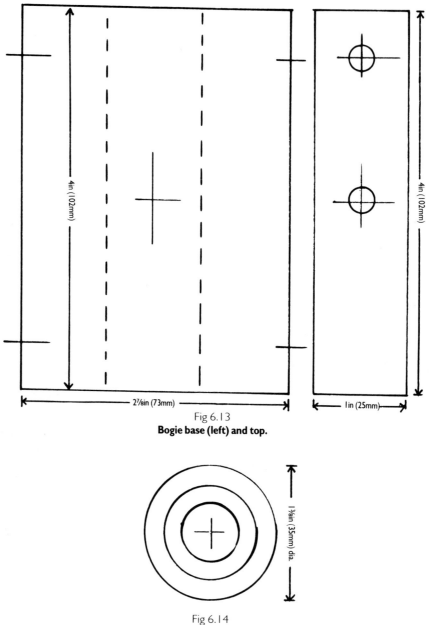

Fig 6.13
Bogie base (left) and top.

Fig 6.14
Bogie wheel (four required).

to the frame, and also a ⁹⁄₃₂in (7mm) diameter hole ½in (13mm) back from the leading edge, which will accept the little tow post; you can turn the tow post from scrap and glue into place. Dye the assembly black, as for the frame, and whilst it is drying you can turn the wheels.

The four small wheels were again made from Indian laurel, dyed cinnamon to match the drive wheels. Turn a cylinder of timber 1⅜in (35mm) in diameter, and mount in the compression chuck. With the tool rest at right angles to the lathe bed, push a ⅛in (3mm) parting tool into the timber, ⅛in (3mm) in from the rim, to a depth of

¹⁄₁₆in–⅛in (2mm–3mm). This creates the rim and centre boss. Mark the centre point, return the tool rest to its usual position, and part off the wheel to give it a thickness of ⅜in (10mm). Repeat until you have four wheels, then drill their centres ¼in (6mm) right through, for the axle bolts. Dye if required, and when dry assemble on to the bogie frame.

You may find it easiest to mount the frame first in the wood-lined jaws of a vice and create the tapped thread inside the holes at the sides of the bogie, by screwing the ¼in × ²⁵⁄₃₂in (6mm × 20mm) bolts in first without the wheels. You can then see that the bolts are going in straight. Then remove the bolt, push it through the wheel centre, and reassemble.

Connecting Rods

These are simply cut from thin strips of timber on the scroll saw. The rod with a hole at each end joins the front and rear drive wheels. The rod with one end plain fits on to the front drive wheel on the same bolt as the double-ended rod. The plain end of the longer rod fits loosely inside the cylinder. Use ¼in × ²⁵⁄₃₂in (6mm × 20mm) bolts to attach the connecting rod to the rear wheels, with washers (or a spare ⁵⁄₁₆in (8mm) nut) to keep the

Fig 6.15
Bogie assembly – exploded view.

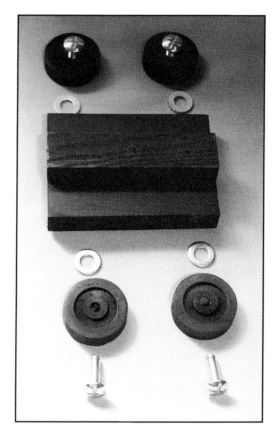

Fig 6.17
Wheels, bogie and linkage assembled on to frame.

Fig 6.18
Frame, wheels and boiler assembled.

Fig 6.16
Connecting rods (two of each required).

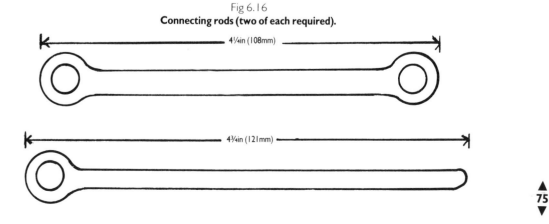

4¼in (108mm)

4¾in (121mm)

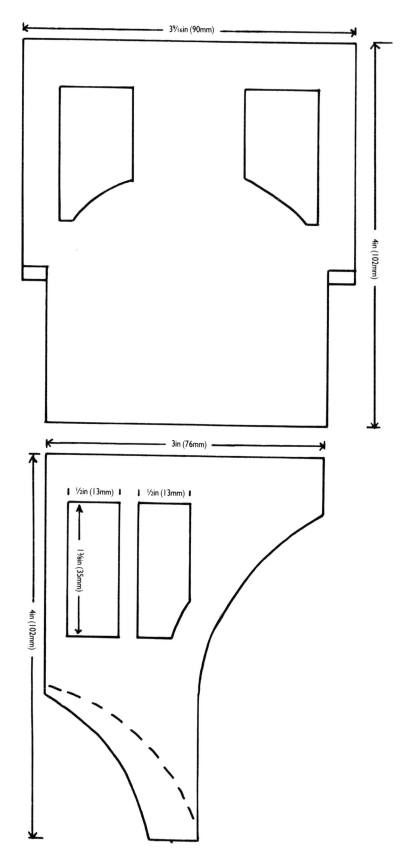

Fig 6.19
Cab front (top) and sides (two required).

rod proud of the axle bolt head and rim. Use ¼in × 1in (6mm × 25mm) bolts for the connecting rods on the front wheel, and also for the axles of all four drive wheels. You will find it necessary to keep the linkage slack, so drill the holes in the connecting rods at a ⁹⁄₃₂in (7mm) diameter. I cut my connecting rods from Indian laurel strip ⅛in (3mm) thick, dyed black to match the frame.

Test Assembly

It is convenient now to assemble the wheels, bogie and linkage to the frame (*see* Fig 6.17), holding the cylinders temporarily in place with adhesive tape.

Check, by pushing the assembly along, that there is room within the cylinders for the connecting rods to move freely back and forwards without either falling out in the rear position or hitting the end of the cylinder when in the forward position. If one falls out, either make a slightly longer one, or move the cylinder back a bit (you would have to cut the frame for this). If too long, remove the rod, and cut a bit off the end.

When all is well, you may now carry out the basic assembly. The bogie assembly is mounted on the frame by its screw, which gives 15° of steerability (much better than the full-sized loco!) The drive wheels are assembled with their linkage in place. Any squeaking caused by the wheels rotating on their bolts can be cured by rubbing candle wax into the wheel's centre hole.

One point to raise here is traction. Wooden wheels, apart from being rather noisy on some floors, have a poor grip on the surface. If you are going to give this locomotive to your child as a pull-along toy, I suggest you get some large wide rubber bands and fit them to the rims of the wheels. This increases friction and reduces noise. There is ample room between the two drive wheels on each side to accept the thickness of a couple of rubber bands. (Actually, I suspect that many of you will prefer the model as a display on a shelf, and it won't be getting too many hard knocks.)

Now glue the smokestack, dome and valve into their holes on top of the boiler. Glue the boiler front door into place, and then glue the whole assembly on to the frame. The rear of the boiler is located 1⅝in (41mm) in front of the rear flat of the frame (ignore the semicircular tender mount).

You may be interested to know that I did not use my usual white PVA glue on this project. In view of the hardness and lack of porosity of many of the timbers, I used only epoxy two-part resin glue (Araldite Rapid, which sets in 5–10 minutes).

Cab

This is basically a front, two sides and a lid, all cut from ¼in (6mm) MDF, sanded, glued and stained black. You could use slices of padauk to match the boiler, or veneer the cab with padauk veneers, but I wanted to create a balance between red and black, even though the full-sized locos usually had cabs painted to match their boilers.

Cut out the four main parts, using a scroll or fret saw to pierce the windows in the front and side panels. Glue the sides to the front panel, ensuring that they are at 90° to the front. When the glue is set, cut and try the top piece. Round off the front and side edges of the roof piece, as shown in Fig 6.19, and glue into place.

Cut the two quadrant shapes for the wheel arches (*see* Fig 6.20). You will observe that they do not carry the same curve as the one you have cut in the side panels. This is partly because of the overlap required in the gluing up, and partly because the arch panels have to curve right to the rear of the cab assembly. Anyway, don't worry – it looks fine when made up.

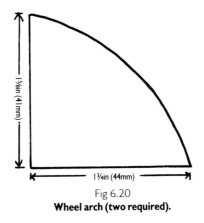

Fig 6.20
Wheel arch (two required).

Glue the wheel arches into place, sand the assembly all over, and dye black. If you do not sand all over, the normal MDF surface will finish glossy, and the edges of the roof – which you have sanded to a curve – will finish matte. Glue the cab assembly into place on the frame, looking down on it to ensure that it is central, i.e. its outer edges match the sides of the frame.

Nameplates

I called this one *King Billy* (the name of a certain Australian pine) because the Americans usually used male names for their locomotives, just as the English usually use female names for their boats. Call yours what you like – it's your model!

Fig 6.21
Cab assembly in ¼in (6mm) MDF. Note wheel arches: outer curve matches rear wheel.

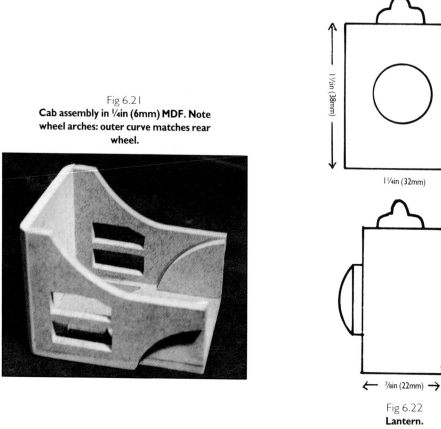

1½in (38mm)

1¼in (32mm)

⅞in (22mm)

Fig 6.22
Lantern.

Fig 6.23
Full basic assembly, with cab stained black and in place, plus cylinders, lamp and boiler flanges.

Fig 6.24
**Cowcatcher – first stage of
assembly in MDF.**

The plates are made from thin white acetate sheet (used in railway modelling). The letters are dry-transfer letraset, in Helvetica 12 point capitals. The plates were cut out from the sheet (with a scalpel) after the lettering had been applied as it was easier then to keep the lettering central. The corner cut-outs are quadrants of a $\frac{5}{32}$in (4mm) diameter circle, drawn first in pencil on the plastic. The plates were fixed on to the cab with Araldite.

Lantern

This is a simple block of padauk, 1½in (38mm) high, 1¼in (32mm) wide and ⅞in (22mm) thick with the grain running vertically. It is drilled at the front to take a $\frac{19}{32}$in (15mm) diameter reflecting button (from a dressmaking shop). I turned a little finial or knob for the top from a scrap of matching timber. The lantern is held on to the boiler door by a short length of $\frac{3}{16}$in (5mm) dowel, which is glued into holes in the door (top rim) and the lantern (bottom rear centre).

After a single application, with a brush, of Danish oil to all untreated wooden parts, we have now reached the stage I call 'full basic assembly' (*see* Fig 6.22). This means that it looks like a locomotive, but as a model it has no fragile bits on it which might get knocked off by a boisterous child. If you intend to cherish your model, there are a few more bits you can add.

Cowcatcher

This is a difficult assembly to make accurately. It would be better to use metal rather than wood (or MDF as I did). The real thing is a series of curved rods or bars of steel, all with different curvatures. As you see from Fig 6.23, I have simplified the frame of this piece into two triangles at right angles, the lower one slotted to accept curved rails. Cut nine of the curved rails all to the same length and glue into place in the slots, starting with the centre one. Trim all the ends, top and bottom, after the glue has set, and dye the assembly black. The flat on the back is then glued to the centre front of the bogie assembly, with a packing piece temporarily under it to keep the cowcatcher $\frac{11}{32}$in (9mm) off the ground. To increase weight and stability, I have added a block

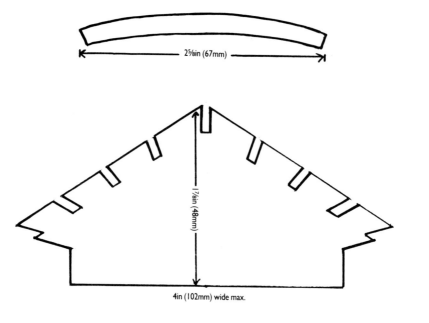

2⁵⁄₈in (67mm)

1⁷⁄₈in (48mm)

4in (102mm) wide max.

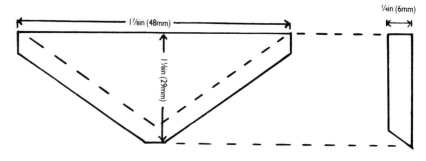

1⁷⁄₈in (48mm)

1¹⁄₈in (29mm)

¹⁄₄in (6mm)

Fig 6.25
Cowcatcher.

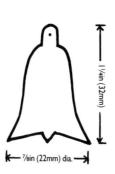

1¹⁄₄in (32mm)

⁷⁄₈in (22mm) dia.

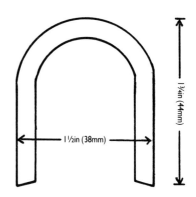

1¾in (44mm)

1½in (38mm)

Fig 6.26
Bell plus frame.

Fig 6.27
**The complete locomotive,
with cowcatcher, bell, side
steam tubes and ash
box below.**

of padauk below the frame between the drive wheels, to represent the ash box.

Two strips of ³⁄₁₆in (5mm) dowel, rounded at each end, are glued to the sides of the boiler to represent external steam tubes (you could use real brass rod for this). Finally, the bell, turned from a scrap of padauk, and mounted with fuse wire in a little inverted 'U' frame, is glued to the top of the boiler between stack and dome.

I have not fitted out the cab with the necessary levers, piping and gauges; let that be an extra labour of love for you.

CHAPTER 7

Castle Crécy

This stronghold was already built for John of Wessex when he was called to France in 1346 by Edward II. He and his archers supported the Black Prince at Crécy and the battle was such a great victory for the English that John renamed his castle after it on his return. It was not until the Black Death had finished its ravages that the French-style roofs were added to what were crenellated bastion towers and keep. It is an interesting example of a 14th-century symmetrical castle where special attention was paid to defence in the form of a barbican, a drawbridge, and machicolation on all outer walls. (Machicolation is an overhanging parapet supported by corbels; there were usually holes between the corbels, used to drop stones on attackers.)

The model is made mainly of English ash, with roofs of Nigerian iroko and Brazilian mahogany, and with the ring courses of the keep in Mexican chacahuante for contrast. The bastion towers are of American oak, because I had that timber in stock in the required dimensions. You will, of course, choose your own timbers and type of finish.

CUTTING LIST

1. Bastion towers
3in × 3in (76mm × 76mm): 1ft 8in (508mm)

2. Gate and barbican towers
1¾in × 1¾in (44mm × 44mm): 3ft 0in (914mm)

3. Tower parapets
1⁵⁄₁₆in × 5in (33mm × 127mm): 4ft 0in (1,219mm)

4. Walls and steps
¾in × 3¾in (19mm × 95mm): 6ft 0in (1,829mm)

5. Machicolation
½in × 1⁵⁄₈in (13mm × 41mm): 3ft 0in (914mm)

6. Barbican walls, drawbridge and gate curtain wall
½in × 2½in (13mm × 64mm): 2ft 3in (686mm)

7. Bailey floor (and veneer to cover)
¼in (6mm) ply or MDF: 13¼in × 10in (337mm × 254mm)

8. Keep parapet
1 disc 6⅛in diameter × 1¾in (156mm × 44mm)

9. Motte
1 disc 8in diameter × ¾in (203mm × 19mm)

10. Bastion tower roofs
4 discs 4in diameter × 4in (102mm × 102mm)

11. Keep roof
1 disc 6⅛in diameter × 2⅝in (156mm × 67mm)

12. Gate tower roofs
2 discs 1¾in diameter × 2in (44mm × 51mm)

13. Barbican tower roofs
4 discs 1½in diameter × 1⅞in (38mm × 48mm)

14. Keep rings
1 disc 5⅛in diameter × 2⅝in (130mm × 67mm)

I have included allowances for cutting flat timber and parting off turned pieces, but none for waste. You can simplify the list by, for example, obtaining 3ft (914mm) of ½in (13mm) thick timber 5in (127mm) wide for items **5** and **6**, and if you are a regular turner, your scrap box will yield all the smaller roofs at least.

CONSTRUCTION

Bastion Towers

These are the towers at each corner of the main structure, and each is 3in (76mm) diameter and 4½in (115mm) high, in two sections; the main base is 3¾in (95mm) to match the height of the walls, and the capping piece is 25/32in (20mm) to bring the height of the tower to match the crenellations. Take a 5in (127mm) length of 3in (76mm) diameter timber, and mount between centres on the lathe. Turn to a circular cross section and finish the surface. I find the 2in (51mm) velcro sanding pad ideal when mounted in the chuck of a hand-held electric drill, and I use grits of 120, 180, 240 and 400. True the base of the tower with a parting tool, making the base very slightly concave so that it will rest on its rim. Mark off 3¾in (95mm) and cut in with a narrow parting tool. Mark and cut in to give another disc of 25/32in (20mm) thickness. Now fully part off the cylinder and disc, the final ¼in (6mm) or so being cut by

hand off the lathe, and the central nubbins removed with the corner of a flap wheel of coarse grit.

Make three more towers to match. It will help if you mark the pairs (cylinder and disc) on their flat surfaces with a number to correspond with the corner location, i.e. mark the tower cylinder and disc for the northwest corner, number one; northeast, number two, etc. This is because the grain of each pair will match and the join will be almost unnoticeable when glued up.

You must now remove a quadrant of each tower base (*not* the discs, which remain whole). Take one

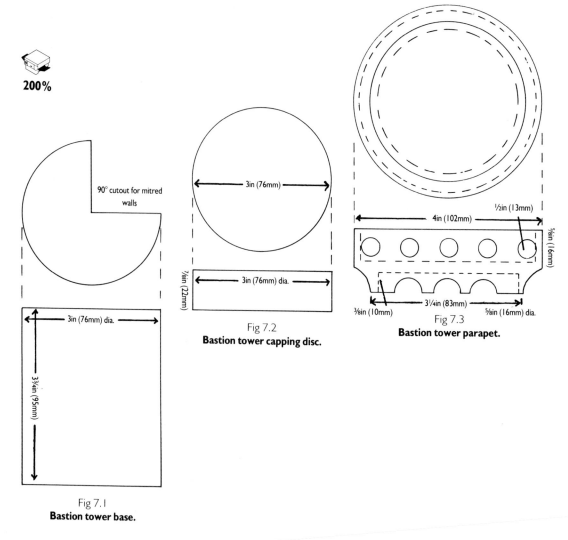

200%

90° cutout for mitred walls

3in (76mm) dia.

3¾in (95mm)

Fig 7.1
Bastion tower base.

3in (76mm)

7/8in (22mm)

3in (76mm) dia.

Fig 7.2
Bastion tower capping disc.

½in (13mm)

4in (102mm)

5/8in (16mm)

3/8in (10mm)

3¼in (83mm)

5/8in (16mm) dia.

Fig 7.3
Bastion tower parapet.

cylinder, select the grain pattern you wish to show on the finished castle, and mark on the flat top two lines from the centre to the circumference, at 90° exactly. Remove the quarter segment using either a band saw or a hand tenon saw. The two faces thus revealed will have the ends of two walls glued to them later. Repeat with the other three tower cylinders and proceed with making the parapets for these towers.

Bastion Tower Parapets

Take a 5in (127mm) disc of timber 1⁵⁄₁₆in (33mm) thick (a little thicker will do no harm) and mount it on the lathe on a suitable screw chuck. The pilot

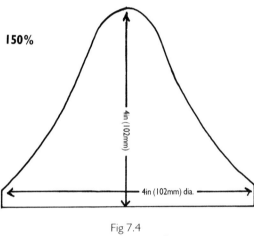

150%

4in (102mm)

← 4in (102mm) dia. →

Fig 7.4
Bastion tower roof.

Fig 7.5
Bastion tower: assembled.

hole for the screw should first be drilled centrally, and it should go right through the timber, which will be reversed later on the chuck. Turn to a true disc and mark on the face two circles: one of 3in (76mm) diameter (which will be hollowed to accept the top of the tower) and one of 3¼in (83mm) which is the inner limit of the curvature of the corbelling. Use a large round-nosed scraper to achieve the curve down to this line, shown in Fig 7.3. Reposition your tool rest across the lathe bed and hollow out the 3in (76mm) circle to a depth of ⅜in (10mm). Reverse the piece on the screw chuck and, leaving an outer wall of ¼in (6mm) thickness, hollow out again to a depth of ⅝in (16mm). True up the circumference if necessary and sand smooth.

Instead of square crenels on the top surface, there are 12 round arrow holes at 30° intervals, and matching curved corbels on the lower edge. These are most conveniently achieved using a simple jig mounted in the cross vice of a bench drill. First

mark the 12 positions on the circumference of the parapet. Draw with compasses a 5in (127mm) circle on a piece of paper, and mark 12 lines from the centre at 30° intervals, extending them beyond the circle. Place the workpiece on the circle and mark it where each line projects. The jig I made comprised only a 3in (76mm) disc of timber nailed vertically on a small block of scrap timber held in the cross vise. The arrow holes are drilled with a ½in (13mm) diameter Forstner (or sawtooth) bit, and the corbels are cut with a ⅝in (16mm) Forstner, all whilst the workpiece is held on the disc of the jig which, of course, fits into the 3in (76mm) diameter hollow on its underside. It is important to remember that although the full arrow holes can be drilled safely with the workpiece hand held, this does *not* apply to the half circles of the corbelling. You must clamp the parapet to the jig for each separate drilling, otherwise you will seriously deface the surface, as the drill bit will not cut true when its central spur is right on the edge of the wood.

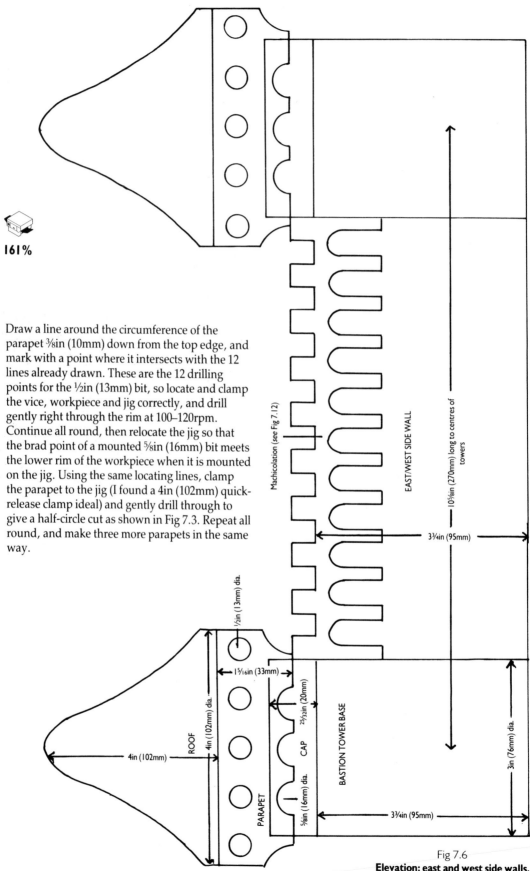

161%

Draw a line around the circumference of the parapet ⅜in (10mm) down from the top edge, and mark with a point where it intersects with the 12 lines already drawn. These are the 12 drilling points for the ½in (13mm) bit, so locate and clamp the vice, workpiece and jig correctly, and drill gently right through the rim at 100–120rpm. Continue all round, then relocate the jig so that the brad point of a mounted ⅝in (16mm) bit meets the lower rim of the workpiece when it is mounted on the jig. Using the same locating lines, clamp the parapet to the jig (I found a 4in (102mm) quick-release clamp ideal) and gently drill through to give a half-circle cut as shown in Fig 7.3. Repeat all round, and make three more parapets in the same way.

Machicolation (see Fig 7.12)

EAST/WEST SIDE WALL

10⅝in (270mm) long to centres of towers

3¾in (95mm)

½in (13mm) dia.

1⁵⁄₁₆in (33mm)

²⁵⁄₃₂in (20mm)

4in (102mm) dia.

ROOF

4in (102mm)

CAP

BASTION TOWER BASE

3in (76mm) dia.

PARAPET

⅝in (16mm) dia.

3¾in (95mm)

Fig 7.6
Elevation: east and west side walls.

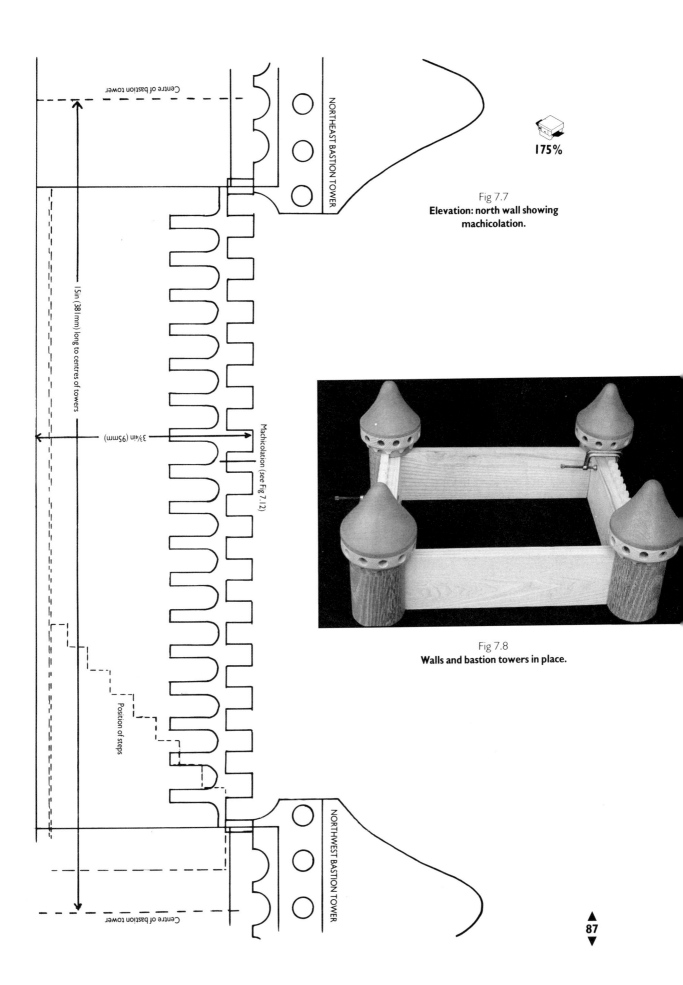

175%

Fig 7.7
Elevation: north wall showing machicolation.

NORTHEAST BASTION TOWER

Centre of bastion tower

15in (381mm) long to centres of towers

3¾in (95mm)

Machicolation (see Fig 7.12)

Position of steps

Centre of bastion tower

NORTHWEST BASTION TOWER

Fig 7.8
Walls and bastion towers in place.

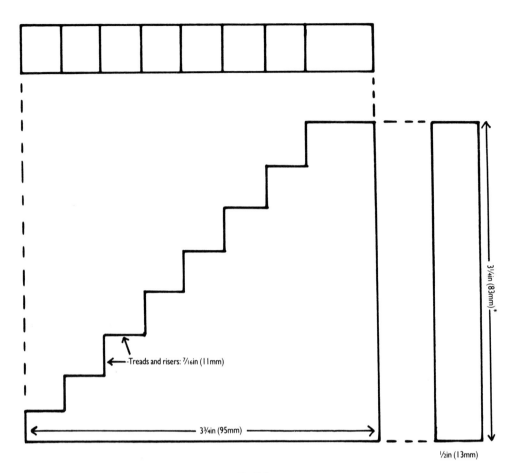

Treads and risers: 7/16in (11mm)

3¾in (95mm)

3¼in (83mm)*

½in (13mm)

Fig 7.9
Steps (four sets required).
*Height should match actual height
between keep floor and base of crenels on
castle walls.

Bastion Tower Roofs

These are made from a timber which contrasts with the main structure. In the prototype castle, I intended to use iroko for all the roofs, but did not have enough in stock. However, I did have some Brazilian mahogany in the right thickness and I found that iroko stained with pitch pine wood dye, and mahogany stained with yellow pine both dried with almost the same hue; also the grain patterns were not dissimilar when mounted with the side grain of all pieces facing the front.

Each roof is a simple turning, to the profile shown in Fig 7.4, of a 4in (102mm) diameter disc mounted on a 3in (76mm) screw chuck. True the base with a parting tool as far as the chuck allows to provide a flat seating when gluing up the whole tower assembly.

Castle Walls

As you can see from Figs 7.6, 7.7 and 7.8, the main

walls are basically simple lengths of timber ¾in (18mm) thick, mitred at each end. The height of the walls exactly matches the bases of the towers. Cut and mitre two pieces 15in (381mm) long, and two pieces 10⅝in (270mm) long. Take one of the longer pieces which will form the south wall (bearing the gate towers). Mark the centre and cut out from its top surface centrally an oblong 2in (51mm) wide and 1³⁄₁₆in (30mm) deep, as shown by the dotted line on Fig 7.11.

You may now glue the walls, with a tower base fitted outside each corner (the corbels, crenels and internal steps will be added later). Now glue on the tower discs, matching the grain with the bases, and then glue the parapets and roofs.

Bailey

A bailey is the courtyard of a castle, and in the case of this model it is merely a floor fitted to cover the space between the four walls you have assembled. I wanted to make this of the same timber as the walls, but as the size is 13¼in × 10in (337mm × 254mm), I would have had to butt join 2 or 3 lengths of timber. The simple solution was to use ¼in (6mm) ply, surfaced with ash veneer 0.024in (0.6mm) thick.

Take a piece of plywood (or MDF if you prefer) slightly larger than the dimensions given above, lay the wall/tower assembly on it, and draw round inside the walls with a finely pointed pencil. Then cut out the required shape; a scroll saw with a no. 5 blade (16.5tpi) is ideal. In fact, I did all my cutting of the flat parts of the castle with a scroll saw using a no. 9 blade (14tpi) for the ½in and ¾in (13mm and 19mm) timber, and a no. 5 blade for the fine detail, like the machicolation.

Check the fit of the cut ply, then veneer its top surface. You may need to butt two or more lengths of veneer to achieve the width of 10in (254mm), but I was easily able to obtain a single leaf of ash veneer large enough. Cut slightly oversize, apply PVA white glue to the ply, and lay on the veneer. Clamp for one to two hours in a veneer press if you have one, or between two sheets of ply with a heavy weight on top (bricks would do). When dry, invert on to a cutting mat, trim the veneer with a craft knife or scalpel, and glue the piece into the base of the castle walls.

Steps

The castle is provided with steps at each corner of the bailey. The castle walls provide sentry walks within the crenellations, and reinforcements from within the castle can ascend quickly to the ramparts from the nearest corner.

Each set of steps is cut from ½in (13mm) thick timber, the height of which matches the height of the wall (3¾in (95mm)), less the floor (¼in (6mm)) – 3½in (89mm). A length of 3¾in (95mm) allows a top step of ¾in (19mm), and ⁷⁄₁₆in (11mm) treads and risers.

Cut four sets of steps, as shown by the dotted lines in Fig 7.7. You may either cut each separately, or draw a pair together with the steps interlocking to save time and effort (see Figs 7.9 and 7.10). Then one cut will provide two sets of treads and risers, but be careful when you turn the piece at each corner. It is best to use the narrowest blade if you want to avoid possible friction burns at the change in direction, which would have to be sanded off.

The four sets of steps may now be glued into position. Note that the two which butt on to the south wall descend to the north, whilst the other two are at right angles to the first pair, and rise to west and east respectively (see Fig 7.15).

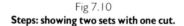

Fig 7.10
Steps: showing two sets with one cut.

Gate Towers

It is now convenient to make the two towers which will bear the drawbridge between them. When finally in position they will also have a crenellated curtain wall between them, but don't worry about this yet.

Each tower is 8⅛in (206mm) long as a finished turning (plus the roof of course) and 1¾in (44mm) in diameter. Turn between centres in the normal way and sand the surface smooth. I like to start with an oversize blank – in this case 8½in × 2in × 2in (216mm × 51mm × 51mm) square cross section. True up each end to give a finished height of 8⅛in (206mm). The towers fit on to the south wall at either side of the 2in (51mm) gap you have already cut, and half the diameter is cut out to the height of the wall, forming a 'D' shaped, semicircular cross-section for the lower 3⅝in (92mm) of each tower, the flat of which is glued to the wall. Before cutting the half section, select the grain on the finished tower and mark out accordingly. The cut can conveniently be made on the band saw. The gate tower roofs are 1¾in (44mm) in diameter by 2in (51mm) and were

turned from iroko to match the bastion tower roofs, on a 1in (25mm) screw chuck to the profile shown in Fig 7.11.

Glue the roofs on to the towers with side grain facing forward, and clamp the towers into position. Do not glue them yet, as you will have to drill a hole in each to take the drawbridge pivot dowel.

Machicolation

It is now time to do a bit of fancy cutting on the scroll saw (or use a hand fret saw if you prefer). First prepare four strips of timber, two at 12⅞in (327mm) and two at 7⅞in (200mm) long, from ½in (13mm) thick wood (1⁹⁄₁₆in (40mm) wide). Cut a chamfer on one side as shown on the cross section given in Fig 7.17, just above the horizontal drawbridge. This section will give the full ½in (13mm) thickness to the crenellation at the top, whilst tapering the corbels down to ⅛in (3mm) at the bottom.

175%

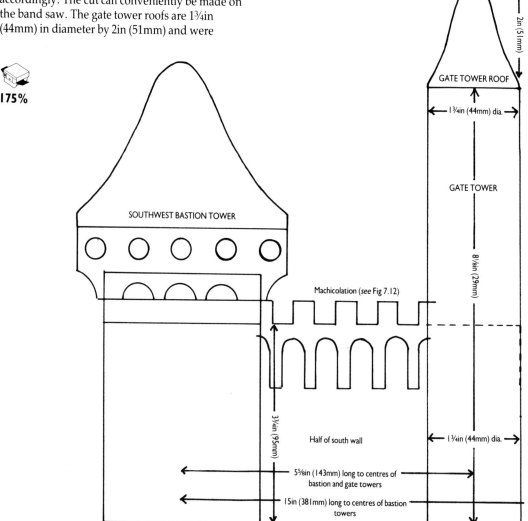

SOUTHWEST BASTION TOWER

Machicolation (*see* Fig 7.12)

GATE TOWER ROOF

1¾in (44mm) dia.

GATE TOWER

8⅛in (29mm)

2in (51mm)

3¾in (95mm)

Half of south wall

1¾in (44mm) dia.

5⅝in (143mm) long to centres of bastion and gate towers

15in (381mm) long to centres of bastion towers

Mark in pencil the centre line of each length of wood. You may either trace or mark out the pattern. I find it easier to mark out fully on each piece, and this is not difficult. The north wall crenellation has a void at the centre, and the side (east and west) walls each have a merlon at the centre, so mark these first. A merlon is the solid upright part of a parapet and the voids between them are called crenels. Each crenellation is ⅜in (10mm) high and ⅜in (10mm) wide. These three walls each have a corbel at the centre of the lower edge, so mark them first. Each corbel is ³⁄₁₆in (5mm) wide with a gap of ⅜in (10mm) between each, and a semicircle of ⅜in (10mm) diameter at the top.

Mark out the fourth strip of machicolation to match the 12⅞in (327mm) north strip if you wish, and you will later cut lengths from it to fit the south wall, between bastion and gate towers.

Alternatively, you can mark out just two short lengths of 3⅜in (96mm) as per Fig 7.12. In all cases be generous at each end, as you will need to tailor the ends (on a small drum sander) to fit the curves of the towers they abut. Cut out the crenels and the waste between the corbels on the scroll saw using a fine blade (no. 5). You can see from Fig 7.13 what the finished strips should look like.

As Fig 7.14 shows, the outside surface of each wall is flush with the centre of each tower; the machicolation strips are therefore shortest on the back face and increase in length as each end follows the curve outward of the tower it joins. Tailoring these end curves is easily done, as I said above, using a small drum sander mounted in a Jacobs chuck in the lathe headstock, with the workpiece resting on the tool rest, brought close to the sanding drum. Mark the end of the machicolation strip with the spot where it will join the tower on its back face, and also the approximate curve required. It is then a matter of gently sanding that curve, frequently checking the fit on the castle, and finishing one end before tackling the other. Take it gently – a coarse sanding drum eats the wood quickly! Glue the strips into position as you finish them, but do not yet glue the gate towers (*see* Fig 7.15).

Fig 7.11
Elevation (south): tower gate.

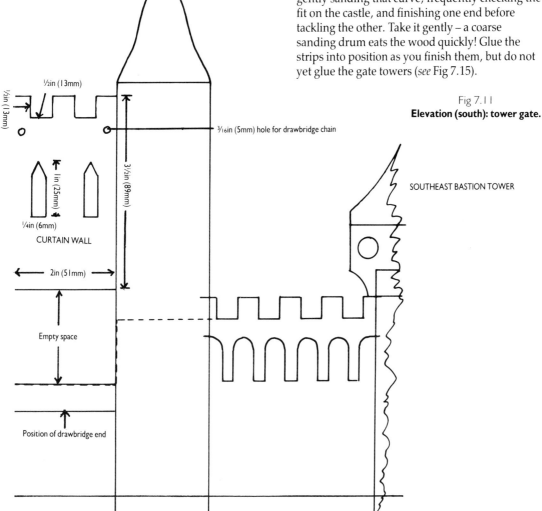

½in (13mm)

½in (13mm)

³⁄₁₆in (5mm) hole for drawbridge chain

1in (25mm)

¼in (6mm)

CURTAIN WALL

3½in (89mm)

2in (51mm)

Empty space

Position of drawbridge end

SOUTHEAST BASTION TOWER

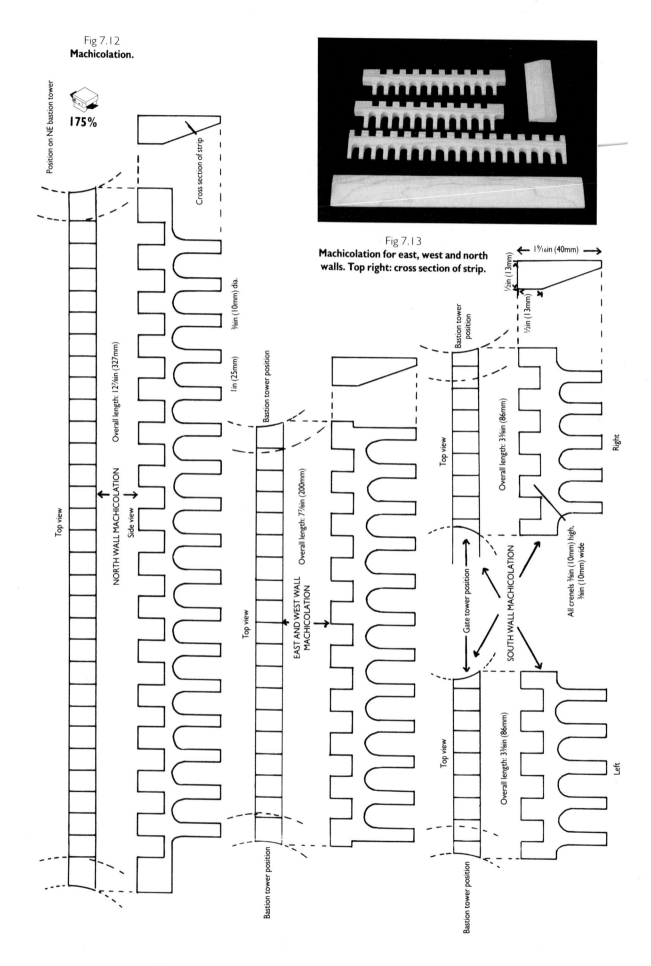

Fig 7.12
Machicolation.

Position on NE bastion tower

175%

Cross section of strip

Top view

NORTH WALL MACHICOLATION

Side view

⅜in (10mm) dia.

1in (25mm)

Overall length: 12⅞in (327mm)

Fig 7.13
Machicolation for east, west and north walls. Top right: cross section of strip.

1⁹⁄₁₆in (40mm)

½in (13mm)

½in (13mm)

Bastion tower position

Top view

EAST AND WEST WALL MACHICOLATION

Overall length: 7⅞in (200mm)

Bastion tower position

Bastion tower position

Top view

Overall length: 3⅜in (86mm)

Gate tower position

SOUTH WALL MACHICOLATION

All crenels ⅜in (10mm) high, ⅜in (10mm) wide

Right

Left

Top view

Overall length: 3⅜in (86mm)

Bastion tower position

Ninepins, complete with
stand and ball.

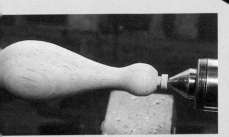

The basic shaping of the
skittle completed.

Set of ninepins. Left to right: white ash,
mahogany, spalted beech, taun, opepe,
brown oak, spalted hackberry,
afrormosia, olive ash.

Bubinga blank on screw chuck, with
recess cut for colour disc.

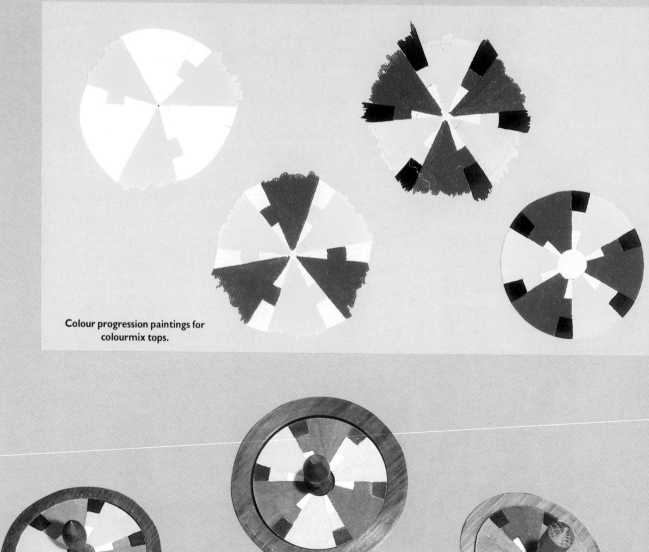

**Colour progression paintings for
colourmix tops.**

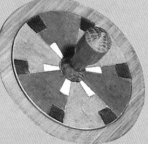

Colourmix tops – the three versions.

Mobile Radiolaria. Clockwise from top: Sputnik, Urchin, Jellyfish, Yellow Peril, the Bomb.

Extraterrestrial Calculator.

Using compasses to draw outer edge of veneer for area of uncertainty on the E.T. Calculator.

Noughts and crosses from the Gamesphere.

Gamesphere partially dismantled to show lid, storage piece, Chinese chequers and chess.

Solitaire and ludo from the Gamesphere.

King Billy.

Hollowing out the violet rosewood smokestack from *King Billy*.

Crécy. Castle gate, showing barbican, drawbridge, walkway and motte.

Castle Crécy.

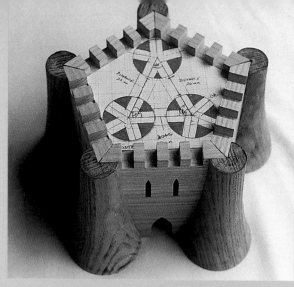

The keep of Castle Quint, with pentagonal drawing to guide placing of towers.

Castle Quint.

Noah's Ark.

Noah's Ark with rondavel main deck.

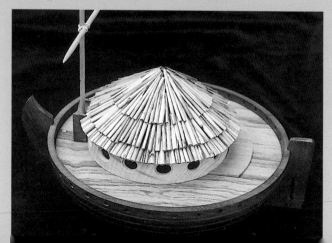

Castle Quint. Blazons of the progeny of Baron Wolfric (1260):

ELINOR Or, bend sinister vert LEOFRIC Gules, canton

OSWALD Orange, gyronny argent

DUNSTAN Vert, chevronny azure

RAINE Per pale, dexter azure, sinister argent, cross azure

Fantasy bridge, viewed from downstream
showing stations 10 to 18.

Drilling the dome portholes of Starship
Moth.

Starship *Moth*. Main deck: control centre
and three compartments lined in plum
suede.

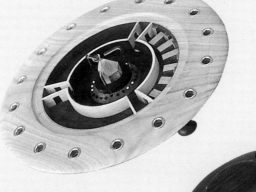

Starship *Moth* completed, with dome
removed.

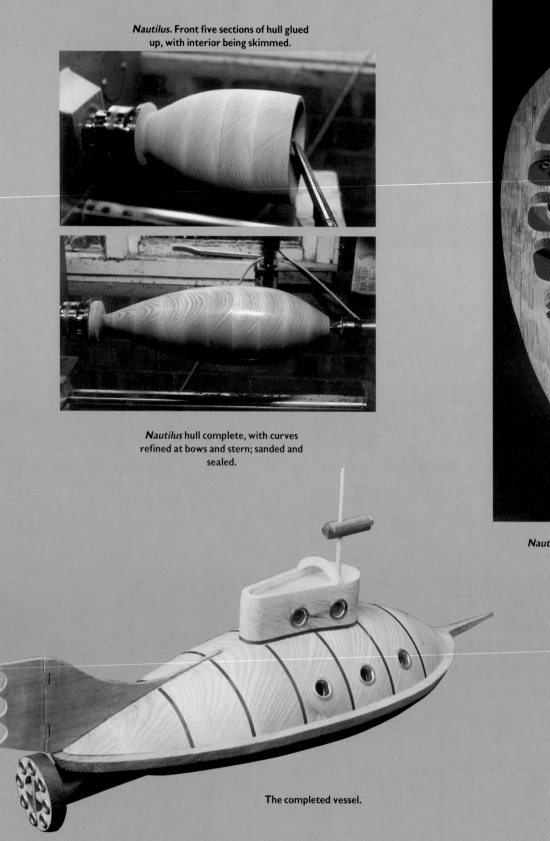

Nautilus. Front five sections of hull glued up, with interior being skimmed.

Nautilus hull complete, with curves refined at bows and stern; sanded and sealed.

Nautilus, with top shell remove

The completed vessel.

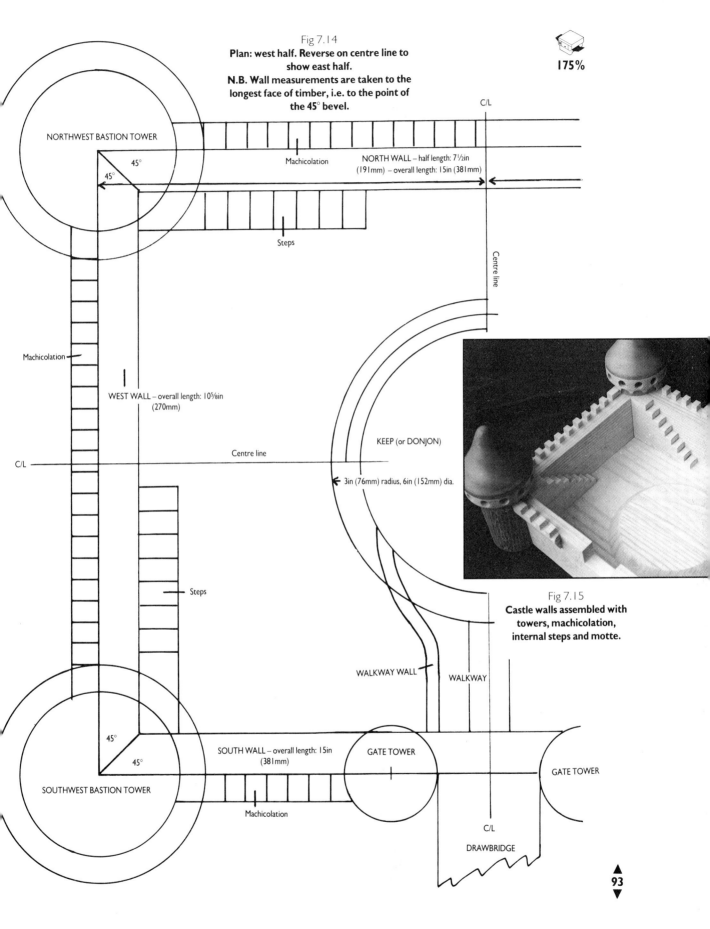

Fig 7.14
Plan: west half. Reverse on centre line to show east half.
N.B. Wall measurements are taken to the longest face of timber, i.e. to the point of the 45° bevel.

175%

NORTHWEST BASTION TOWER

45°

45°

Machicolation

Steps

C/L

NORTH WALL – half length: 7½in (191mm) – overall length: 15in (381mm)

Centre line

Machicolation

WEST WALL – overall length: 10⅝in (270mm)

Centre line

C/L

KEEP (or DONJON)

3in (76mm) radius, 6in (152mm) dia.

Steps

Fig 7.15
Castle walls assembled with towers, machicolation, internal steps and motte.

WALKWAY WALL

WALKWAY

45°

45°

SOUTH WALL – overall length: 15in (381mm)

GATE TOWER

GATE TOWER

SOUTHWEST BASTION TOWER

Machicolation

C/L

DRAWBRIDGE

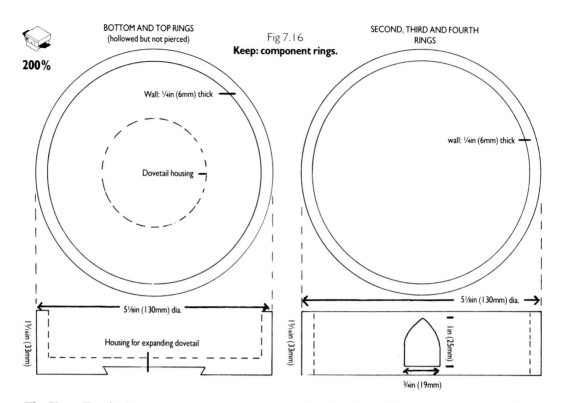

BOTTOM AND TOP RINGS
(hollowed but not pierced)

200%

Wall: ¼in (6mm) thick

Dovetail housing

5⅛in (130mm) dia.

1⁵⁄₁₆in (33mm)

Housing for expanding dovetail

Fig 7.16
Keep: component rings.

SECOND, THIRD AND FOURTH
RINGS

wall: ¼in (6mm) thick

5⅛in (130mm) dia.

1⁵⁄₁₆in (33mm)

1in (25mm)

¾in (19mm)

The Keep (Donjon)

Castle Crécy has a particularly generous keep,
centrally located between the walls. John liked
plenty of space and the lord's living quarters in
the upper floor of the keep provided that, and
privacy too. The keep is 11¹¹⁄₁₆in (297mm) high
and is built of five rings of ash, with the top and
bottom rings closed, and with ¼in (6mm) rings of
chacahuante (or any other contrasting wood you
prefer) between them. There is a parapet of the
same pattern as those of the bastion towers, but
with more arrow holes and corbels, and a domed
roof of mahogany. The five ash rings were turned
from 5¼in (133mm) blank discs cut from a plank
of ash 1⁵⁄₁₆in (33mm) thick. If you use timber of a
different thickness, you will need to adjust the
number of rings and/or the thickness of the motte
(the bevelled base of the keep). A small variation
in height will not destroy the aesthetic balance,
provided you avoid exceeding the 5⅛in (130mm)
finished diameter.

Take one blank disc and mount on the lathe on a
3in (76mm) screw chuck. Turn to a 5⅛in (130mm)
true diameter, true the face and cut a suitable
dovetail recess for your expanding dovetail chuck
(I used a Multistar chuck with size 'C' jaws using a
2⅜in (60mm) recess, but the size is not critical).
Remove the workpiece, mount it on your
expanding chuck and hollow out, leaving the
walls ¼in (6mm) thick or a little more, with the
base the same thickness. Sand smooth, remove
and do the same again with what will be the top

ring of the keep. Check the grain pattern of the
second piece so that it will finish in the same
direction as the base.

Take another blank, mount on the screwchuck,
turn to a 5⅛in (130mm) diameter, true the ends
and sand smooth. Move the tool rest across the
lathe bed, mark ¼in (6mm) in from the
circumference and part off a ring, gently pushing
your parting tool right through the thickness of
the blank at the end of the cut. Cut two more rings
in the same way (see Fig 7.16).

Using the same method, cut four rings ¼in (6mm)
thick and ¼in (6mm) wide from a blank of
contrasting timber. After a trial dry assembly,
select the second and fourth rings from the bottom
and cut one door and three windows in the
second ring and four windows in the fourth ring,
orientating them north, east, south and west. I
first marked the apertures, then drilled a small
hole in each and cut out with a fine-bladed coping
saw. Now, matching the grain patterns (all side
grain facing the same way), you may now glue up
the keep assembly. When fully dry, mount
between centres (on the same expanding dovetail
chuck) and, using a revolving tailstock centre if
you have one, lightly skim true with a scraper at
moderate revolutions, sand to 400 grit and remove
from the lathe.

Keep Parapet

This is 6⅛in (156mm) diameter, giving a ½in

(13mm) overhang above the keep wall, and is cut from a blank disc 6⅛in × 1¾in (156mm × 44mm) (I used American oak to match the bastion towers). The arrow holes are the same size at ½in (13mm) and so are the corbels at ⅝in (16mm), but as the circumference is greater than the towers,

Fig 7.17
Elevation: the keep (donjon).

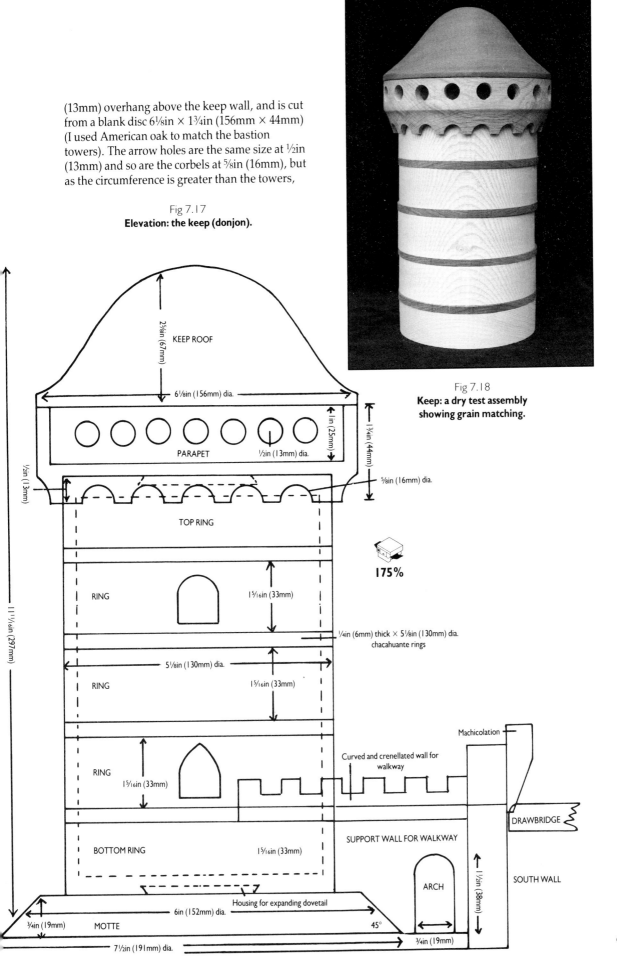

Fig 7.18
Keep: a dry test assembly showing grain matching.

KEEP ROOF

2⅝in (67mm)

6⅛in (156mm) dia.

1in (25mm)

1¾in (44mm)

PARAPET

½in (13mm) dia.

⅝in (16mm) dia.

½in (13mm)

TOP RING

RING

1⁵⁄₁₆in (33mm)

¼in (6mm) thick × 5⅛in (130mm) dia. chacahuante rings

175%

5⅛in (130mm) dia.

RING

1⁵⁄₁₆in (33mm)

11¹¹⁄₁₆in (297mm)

Machicolation

Curved and crenellated wall for walkway

RING

1⁵⁄₁₆in (33mm)

DRAWBRIDGE

SUPPORT WALL FOR WALKWAY

BOTTOM RING

1⁵⁄₁₆in (33mm)

1½in (38mm)

SOUTH WALL

Housing for expanding dovetail

ARCH

MOTTE

6in (152mm) dia.

45°

¾in (19mm)

¾in (19mm)

7½in (191mm) dia.

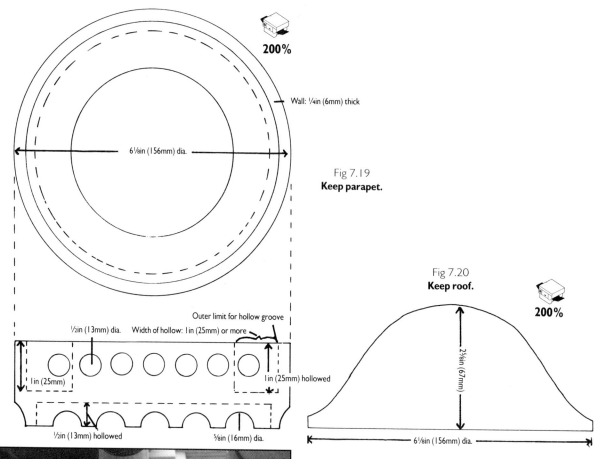

200%

6⅛in (156mm) dia.

Wall: ¼in (6mm) thick

Fig 7.19
Keep parapet.

½in (13mm) dia.   Width of hollow: 1in (25mm) or more

Outer limit for hollow groove

1in (25mm)

1in (25mm) hollowed

½in (13mm) hollowed

⅝in (16mm) dia.

Fig 7.20
Keep roof.

200%

2⅝in (67mm)

6⅛in (156mm) dia.

Fig 7.21
**Castle gate, showing
barbican, drawbridge,
walkway and motte.**

there are more drillings – 18 holes 20° apart. It is useful to draw a 6in (152mm) circle with 18 lines radiating from the centre for use as a marking guide, and to make another jig similar to that described earlier for the bastion tower parapets,

but this time with a 6in (152mm) diameter vertically mounted disc (or slightly smaller, for easy fit). Follow the instructions as for the tower parapets. The bottom of the keep parapet is hollowed to a 5⅛in (130mm) diameter, but all else is similar.

Turn the roof from a blank 6⅛in (156mm) diameter and 2⅝in (67mm) thick to match the profile in Fig 7.20, then glue the parapet and roof to the keep. The keep is set on a motte and to represent this I used a disc of ash ¾in (19mm) thick, cut with a 45° bevel to give a 6in (152mm) circle at the top, increasing to 7½in (191mm) at the base. You can cut this with a scroll saw from two butted 4in (102mm) pieces of timber if necessary.

Walkway
There are now only a couple of jobs within the walls, before you go on to the barbican. One is the walkway, between the drawbridge and the keep main door. Fig 7.21 clearly shows its shape and construction. It is made from a piece of ¼in (6mm) ply, veneered with ash to match the bailey, and the crenellated walls are cut on the scroll saw from ¾in (19mm) timber. It is 2in (51mm) wide at the drawbridge end and widens to meet the curve of the keep.

First cut out the plywood as per Figs 7.14 and 7.17. It may help to use the actual keep wall as a pattern for the curve to match it. Tailor to fit on the drum sander, if necessary and veneer the top. Use the plywood piece as a template to draw the curves of the side walls on the ¾in (19mm) stock, and cut them out using a medium blade on the scroll saw. Be generous at the ends of the curved parts of the walls, which must be sanded to fit the keep. Cut a support piece as shown in Fig 7.17, with an archway. The only difficulty occurs when cutting the crenellations on the walkway walls, which are ⅜in (10mm) wide but only ³⁄₁₆in (5mm) deep: when you cut these out of the curved portions of the walls you will need to rest the end of the workpiece on a piece of scrap timber of a suitable thickness, both for support and to achieve a right-angled cut. An optional piece is the little external staircase at the rear (north) of the keep. I cut this from a spare ring, but you could easily make one up from small vertical strips, or omit it completely.

200%

Drawbridge

Cut this from ½in (13mm) timber 2in (51mm) wide. Round the top of the end (which will be pivoted) and drill a ³⁄₁₆in (5mm) hole centrally through the width to give a horizontal hole ¼in (6mm) from the end and at half the thickness of the piece (*see* Fig 7.22). Fit a length of ³⁄₁₆in (5mm) dowel (sanded slightly to fit) protruding, say, ½in

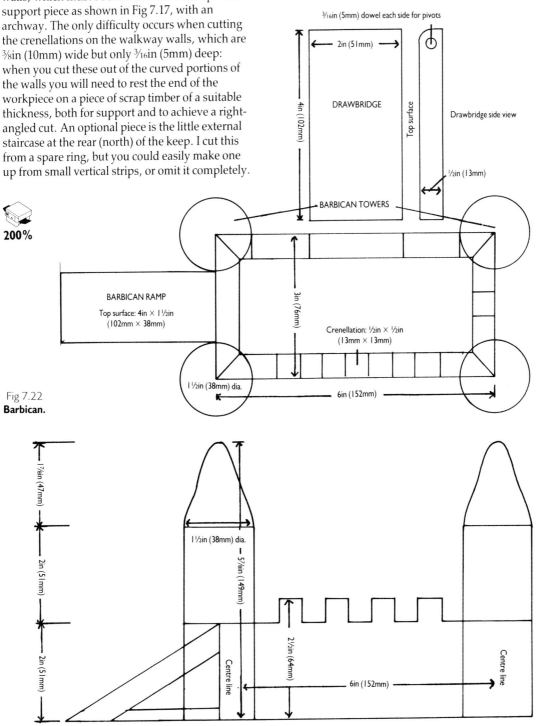

Fig 7.22
Barbican.

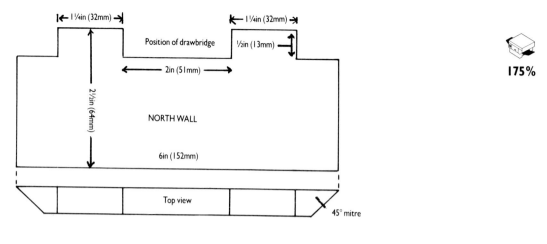

175%

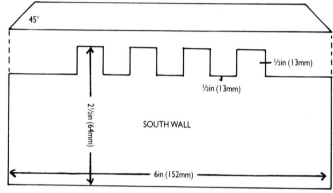

Fig 7.23
Barbican walls.

(13mm) each side, and use this to mark on the gate towers the position of the drill holes for the pivot dowel. Drill these horizontally. Affix two miniature eyelets to the outer end of the drawbridge, fit the pivot dowel into the towers and glue the towers into their final position. The chain, of which you will need two lengths each of 7½in (191mm), has 12 links per inch (or thereabouts) and can be obtained from a model supplies shop. The inboard ends are each fitted with a small wooden bead glued into the bead hole with epoxy. Do this after threading the chain through the curtain wall.

You should now complete the tower gate by fitting a curtain wall between the two towers. Cut this from ½in (13mm) thick timber, 2in (51mm) wide and 3½in (89mm) high. Cut the ½in × ½in (13mm × 13mm) crenellations at the top, and the two arrow slits, then drill the two holes of ³⁄₁₆in (5mm) diameter for the drawbridge chain (*see* Fig 7.11). Now carefully make the two vertical edges concave with a 1½in (38mm) drum sander so that the piece will slide snugly between the towers, and glue it into position.

Barbican

A barbican is an advance fortification from which the gateway to a castle is defended. For Castle Crécy, this comprises a box structure 6in × 3in (152mm × 76mm) plus corner towers (*see* Fig 7.22).

From ½in (13mm) thick timber, cut walls: two at 6in × 2½in (152mm × 64mm), one at 3in × 2½in (76mm × 64mm) and one at 3in × 2in (76mm × 51mm). Mitre the ends and cut crenellations as shown in Fig 7.23: ½in × ½in (13mm × 13mm). The 6in (152mm) wall nearest the castle wall has a gap 2in (51mm) wide, cut to accept the end of the drawbridge.

Fig 7.24
Barbican tower (four required).

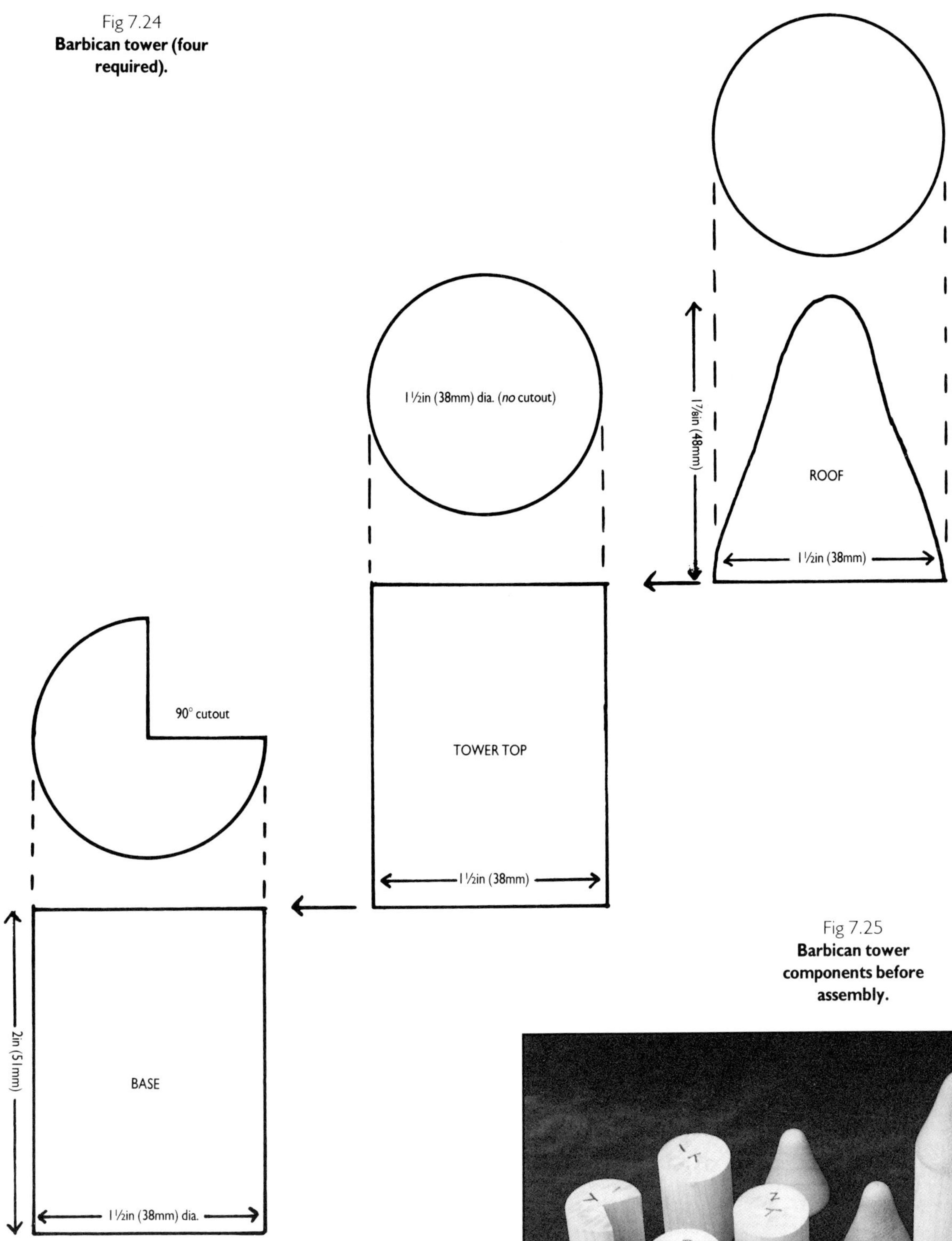

1½in (38mm) dia. (*no cutout*)

1⅞in (48mm)

ROOF

1½in (38mm)

90° cutout

TOWER TOP

1½in (38mm)

BASE

2in (51mm)

1½in (38mm) dia.

Fig 7.25
Barbican tower components before assembly.

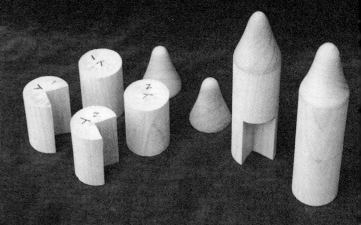

Fig 7.26
Barbican walls assembled, ready for tower tops and floor.

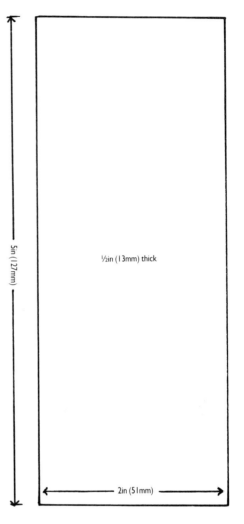

½in (13mm) thick

5in (127mm)

2in (51mm)

Fig 7.27
Barbican floor. To fit flush with base of crenels.

Turn four towers 1½in (38mm) in diameter from 4½in (114mm) lengths of square timber, and part two lengths of 2in (51mm) from each turned and sanded cylinder. Number the pairs, as you did for the castle bastion tower pairs, and cut a 90° quadrant from each lower section. On a 1in (25mm) screw chuck, turn four roofs 1½in (38mm) in diameter and 1¾in (44mm) high from scrap timber to match the other roofs (*see* Figs 7.24 and 7.25). Glue up the whole assembly, as shown in Fig 7.26, and fit a floor piece of ¼in (6mm) ply veneered to match the rest. Glue this floor into place, flush with the bottom of the crenels (i.e. its surface 2in (51mm) above the base of the wall) (*see* Fig 7.27). Cut a ramp as shown in Fig 7.28 from scrap ½in (13mm) wood, angled at 30°, and glue it to the side of the barbican which has no crenellation. You may make this east or west, whichever pleases you – after all, it's your castle, and it is now complete.

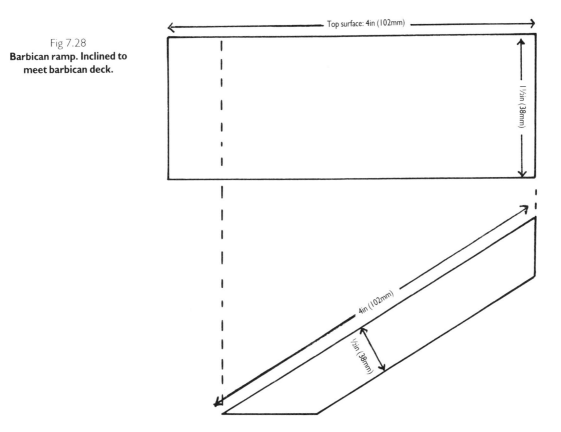

Fig 7.28
Barbican ramp. Inclined to meet barbican deck.

Top surface: 4in (102mm)

1½in (38mm)

4in (102mm)

½in (38mm)

Fig 7.29
Castle Crécy.

CHAPTER 8

Castle Quint

Castle Quint was completed in 1260 for Baron Wolfric. It was designed by Teraille de Laurent, who was brought over from France for this task. The castle takes its name from the five huge buttresses supporting the keep (the old French word for five was 'quinte'). The structure, apart from its Gallic elegance, is unusual for its mathematical principles. De Laurent insisted that all aspects of the castle should be expressed in odd numbers, not even ones. In fact, the whole base is pentamerous: five buttresses, five keep walls, five turrets, and each turret with five piercings.

It is surprising that Wolfric, not noted for his tolerance, should allow his architect so much latitude. However, it was said that de Laurent got his way by naming each turret after one of the Baron's five children, and you can see their individual shields on the model. This apparent frivolity proved useful in later years when the call to arms to, say, Dunstan, sent guards instantly to the south-west turret. Little remains now, but it is believed that the church at Wolfham is built of stone from the Castle Quint.

The model is made mainly from English air-dried ash, with the tower roofs, parapets and rings of iroko. You will, of course, choose your own timbers.

It is a good exercise in between-centres turning, with one or two unusual elements for spice, such as the bolection rings on the towers, details of which are covered in the section on construction.

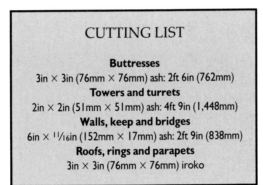

CUTTING LIST

Buttresses
3in × 3in (76mm × 76mm) ash: 2ft 6in (762mm)
Towers and turrets
2in × 2in (51mm × 51mm) ash: 4ft 9in (1,448mm)
Walls, keep and bridges
6in × ¹¹⁄₁₆in (152mm × 17mm) ash: 2ft 9in (838mm)
Roofs, rings and parapets
3in × 3in (76mm × 76mm) iroko

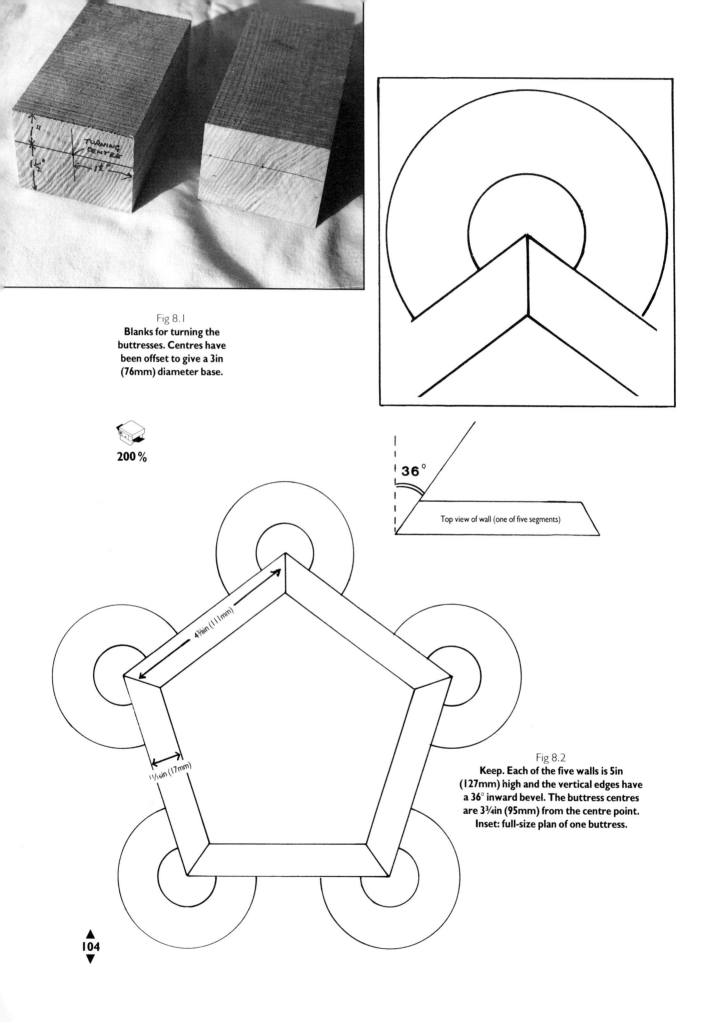

Fig 8.1
Blanks for turning the buttresses. Centres have been offset to give a 3in (76mm) diameter base.

200%

36°

Top view of wall (one of five segments)

4⅜in (111mm)

11/16in (17mm)

Fig 8.2
Keep. Each of the five walls is 5in (127mm) high and the vertical edges have a 36° inward bevel. The buttress centres are 3¾in (95mm) from the centre point. Inset: full-size plan of one buttress.

CONSTRUCTION

Buttresses

The first job is to turn the five buttresses. Straight away I ran into a problem, as I could not easily obtain ash in 3in × 3in (76mm × 76mm) section. "So use another wood", you will say. Well, I had settled on ash because originally I had decided to stain it pale grey (black ash wood dye, diluted 1:10 with white spirit) which would simulate the colour of stone and enhance the simple grain pattern. (In the event, I left the whole thing

Whichever size you choose, 3in × 2½in (76mm × 64mm) or 3in (76mm) square, take a 6in (152mm) length, mark the centres, and mount on the lathe with a four-prong drive centre at the headstock and a live centre (if you have one) at the tailstock. Turn initially at about 500rpm, certainly no more if you are turning eccentrically, until you have roughed out. You can now increase the speed to about 900/1000rpm. With a parting tool, mark the base and top to give a finished height of 5in (127mm), with a 3in (76mm) base diameter, curving down to 1¼in (32mm) at the top, where

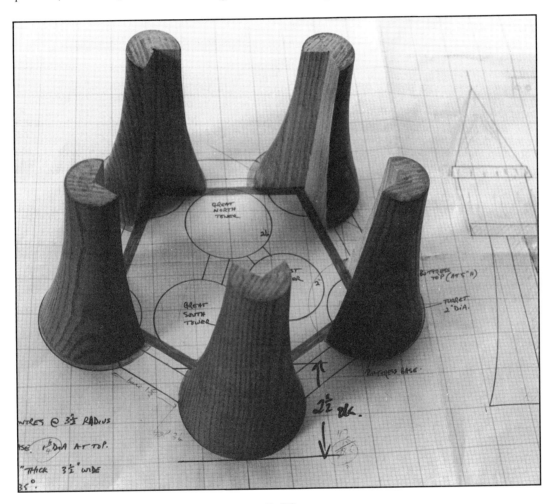

Fig 8.3
**Five buttresses (with 108° cutout) placed
over original working drawing.**

unstained.) I was able, however, to get timber 3in × 2½in (76mm × 64mm), which was cheaper, and proved acceptable for the buttresses, provided you are willing to turn eccentrically. I have marked a piece in Fig 8.1 so that you can see that the centre is offset (at both ends); the resulting flat at the bottom end is lost when the 'V' cut is made to accept the castle walls.

the turret will join. It will assist you to trace and cut from thin card, a template of the curve required for all five buttresses. Dish each end very slightly (i.e. make slightly concave) when parting off, with the point of the parting tool 1° or 2° toward the centre of the piece, so that it will sit firmly on its rim.

When you have turned and sanded smooth all five

200%

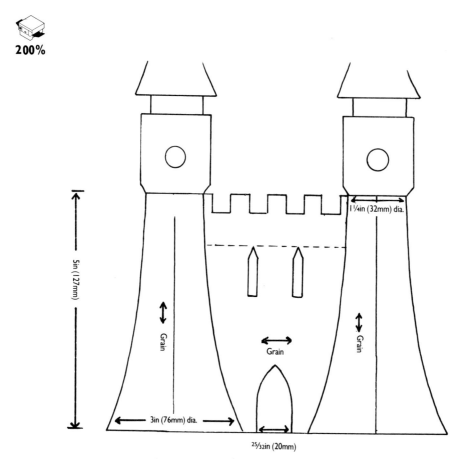

Fig 8.4
Top of keep flush with base of crenellation.

5in (127mm)

Grain

3in (76mm) dia.

1¼in (32mm) dia.

Grain

Grain

²⁵/₃₂in (20mm)

Fig 8.5
Five keep walls, each cut with a 36° bevel, to give an internal angle of 108°.

Fig 8.6
Keep walls and buttresses assembled.

buttresses, it is necessary to cut out vertically the 108° 'V' shape which will accept the butted ends of two adjacent walls. Place the base of one buttress on the full size plan of one of the buttresses shown inset in Fig 8.2. If you used 3in × 3in (76mm × 76mm) timber, you can decide by turning it what grain you wish to show on the finished model (*see* Fig 8.3). (If you used 3in × 2½in (76mm × 64mm) timber, you are committed to cutting out the flat.)

Mark at the base and top the positions of the two cuts to be made. You can join these positions with a pencil line drawn with a flexible ruler following the curve of the wood. I actually made these cuts with a band saw using the full 6in (152mm) depth of cut, and with a piece of ¼in (6mm) MDF larger than the base of the buttress, placed underneath the workpiece to counteract the flexibility of the plastic insert at the centre of the saw table (I must get around to making a solid metal insert for my cheap Taiwanese band saw). I don't really recommend this method as your fingers can get quite near the saw blade. It is safer to mount the piece in a vise and make the two cuts by hand with a tenon saw.

Walls

The timber I used happened to be $^{11}/_{16}$in (17mm) thick. It is not actually critical, provided that the external measurement of $4^3/_8$in (111mm) is maintained, but note that if you change the thickness it will affect the area of the keep top. Thinner walls will increase the area which they enclose, give more space within which to locate the towers, and thus require longer bridges between them. Thicker walls would necessitate a reduction in the base diameter of the towers, which would spoil the aesthetics.

I had an ash plank 6in (152mm) wide, which allowed me to cut the five walls with the grain running horizontally, and also to make the keep top in one piece. I used a small scroll saw to cut the walls and their bevels at the same time. It is difficult to set the saw accurately for the required 36° bevel; in fact I achieved 35°, which left a gap of 2° at each joint, mercifully covered by the turrets. Check your cut on a piece of scrap first.

Fig 8.4 shows the side view (elevation) of the base unit to indicate the wall position, and I found it worthwhile making a card template of the shape between the two buttresses, with two tabs folding back into the crenellations. The arrow slits and gate were cut out from the template and it was used to pencil in the piercings on each of the five walls. (N.B. only one gate is cut; between the south and east towers.) Drill a small hole, wide enough for the saw blade, within each arrow slit position, and cut out with the scroll saw. I used a No. 9 blade (14tpi, 0.019in (0.5mm) thickness), although a No. 7 would be as good (16½tpi, 0.015in (0.38mm) thick). The crenellations at the top of each wall are $^7/_8$in (10mm) wide and $^3/_8$in (10mm) deep, and the arrow slits are $^3/_{16}$in (5mm) wide and 1in (25mm) high. Make sure that the slits do not go above the dotted line as shown on Fig 8.4, as this represents the underside of the top of the keep.

You may now assemble the base. Glue the five walls together, checking that the angles are correct. I used Bison woodglue, a slow white PVA which sets within the hour in a warm atmosphere. Don't leave the assembly in the cold, as the glue will not adhere properly. The five walls can be held together with a couple of strong rubber bands.

Next, glue the five buttresses in position (*see* Fig 8.6). When all is set firm, cut the top of the keep from $^{11}/_{16}$in (17mm) timber, the same as used for the walls (or thinner if you prefer). You may either cut a template of card to fit the aperture, or merely turn the assembly upside down onto the timber

and mark the area to be cut out with a finely pointed pencil. Mark the side of the pentagon which will be above the castle gate in case there is any variation. Glue the pentangle into position, with its top surface flush with the bottom of the crenellation. The base unit is now complete.

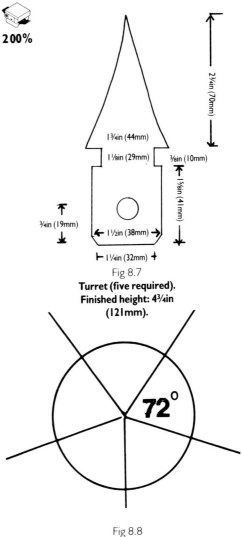

200%

Fig 8.7
Turret (five required).
Finished height: 4¾in
(121mm).

Fig 8.8
Marking guide for the five piercings in the turrets: ½in (13mm) diameter holes.

Turrets

The finished height of each turret is 4¾in (121mm) and it has a maximum diameter of 1¾in (44mm), so it is convenient to use a 5½in (140mm) length of 2in × 2in (51mm × 51mm) timber for each. Mount between centres and turn to the dimensions shown in Fig 8.7, but only approximate the curve of the roof at this stage, leaving the top inch thicker to maintain support from the tailstock. The diameter of the body of the turret is 1½in (38mm), which fits the plain bore of a Multistar chuck

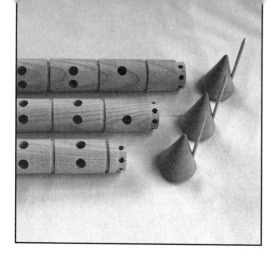

Fig 8.9
Three towers turned and grooved, with three roofs in iroko.

when fitted with 'B' jaws or larger; thus, after sanding the body, I parted off the turret and mounted it in the Multistar chuck to finish the pointed roof. An alternative would be to mount the blank on a screw chuck, with the tailstock giving support until the last part of the roof.

You will see that the base of each turret is 1¼in (32mm) in diameter, matching exactly the top of each buttress, to which it will be glued. First, however, you need to pierce five holes around the circumference of the turrets at 72° intervals, and with the centre heights ¾in (19mm) from the bottom of the piece. A marking guide is given in Fig 8.8: just place the turret base on the circle and mark it where the radiating lines cut the circle. I used a bench drill with a ½in (13mm) Forstner bit and with the turret resting in a 'V' cut made in a block of wood held in the drill table vice. The drill bit was taken down just beyond the halfway point of the thickness of the turret, so light was able to shine through all holes. Finish all turrets, but do not glue them into position yet, as the placing of the towers is much easier without turrets in the way.

51·43°

Fig 8.10
Marking guide for the seven piercings at the top of each tower: ⁹⁄₃₂in (7mm) diameter holes.

125 %

Fig 8.11
Positional guide for placing the towers. All towers are 1⅞in (48mm) in diameter at base. Dotted lines indicate drill centre positions at tower circumferences, and also bridge positions.

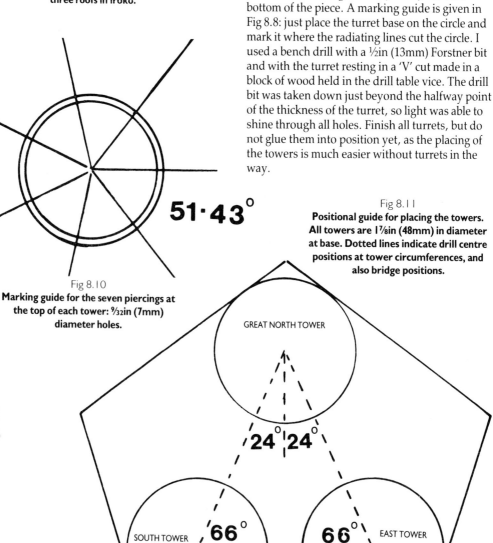

GREAT NORTH TOWER

24° 24°

SOUTH TOWER **66°**

66° EAST TOWER

GATE

Towers

There are three towers (odd numbers again!): the Great North Tower being 10⅝in (270mm) as a finished turning, and the others diminishing in 2in (51mm) increments anticlockwise. All have the same base diameter of 1⅞in (48mm), which reduces to 1¾in (44mm) at the top of two towers, and 1²¹⁄₃₂in (42mm) at the top of the smallest east tower. All this reduction is achieved in the first 2¾in (70mm), above which the tower walls are vertical and parallel. All three are turned from 2in × 2in (51mm × 51mm) timber.

For the Great North Tower, take a 12in (305mm) length of timber, mount between centres, and rough out. Mark the ends with a parting tool; the base of the tower should be ½in (13mm) away from the headstock end of the timber, and the top of the tower 10⅝in (270mm) from that base edge. Turn to a base diameter of 1⅞in (48mm) and top diameter of 1¾in (44mm). Finish the piece with a smooth curve from the base to a point 2¾in (70mm) up the tower, using a 1¼in (32mm) or 1½in (38mm) skew chisel or a heavy round-nosed scraper. Mark the ring positions at 2¾in, 5½in and 8¼in (70mm, 140mm and 210mm) and with a ⅛in (3mm) parting tool, cut grooves on the right-hand side of these marks ⅛in (3mm) deep. These will later accept iroko rings whose thickness will match the width of the grooves. Reduce the diameter of the top ½in (13mm) of the tower to 1⁷⁄₃₂in (39mm). Sand the surface and part off the piece, ensuring (for stability) that the base is very slightly concave.

Proceed to this point with the other two towers (*see* Fig 8.9).

The next job is to drill seven holes around the top of the tower at equal intervals (51.43° apart). I have given a marking guide (*see* Fig 8.10) to be used if you wish in the same way as that for the five turret piercings. The centres of the holes are halfway down the section with the reduced diameter, that is ¼in (6mm) down from the top. With the tower resting in the same 'V' grooved block as you used for the turrets, drill the seven holes with a ⁹⁄₃₂in (7mm) spurred wood drill, down to just beyond the centre of the timber.

Next, place all three towers into their final positions, but do not glue yet. It is worthwhile cutting out the pentagonal paper pattern (*see* Figs 8.11 and 8.12) and placing it in position under the towers so you can mark on the towers the drill positions of the apertures. Rotate each tower piece until you have it where the grain pattern is most pleasing. Mine, as you see from Fig 8.13, are arranged so that the grain on all three towers

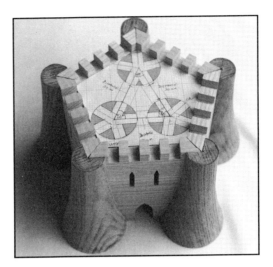

Fig 8.12
Assembled keep with pentagonal drawing to guide placing of towers.

Fig 8.13
Keep assembly, with the three towers in place.

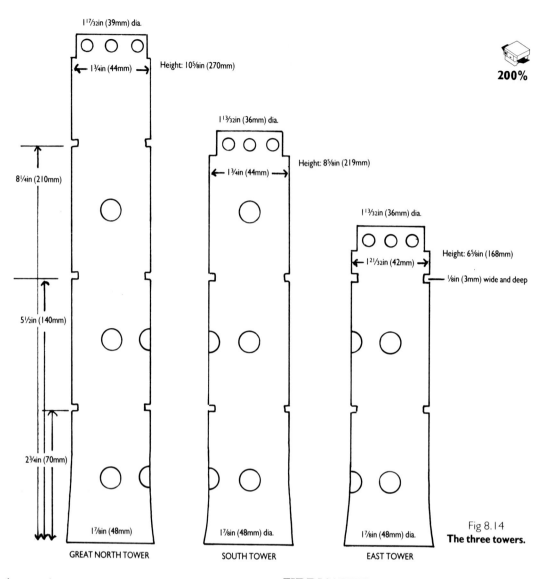

1¹⁷/₃₂in (39mm) dia.

← 1³/₄in (44mm) →

Height: 10⅝in (270mm)

200%

1¹³/₃₂in (36mm) dia.

← 1³/₄in (44mm) →

Height: 8⅝in (219mm)

1¹³/₃₂in (36mm) dia.

← 1²¹/₃₂in (42mm) →

Height: 6⅝in (168mm)

⅛in (3mm) wide and deep

8¼in (210mm)

5½in (140mm)

2¾in (70mm)

1⅞in (48mm)

GREAT NORTH TOWER

1⅞in (48mm) dia.

SOUTH TOWER

1⅞in (48mm) dia.

EAST TOWER

Fig 8.14
The three towers.

forms a sharp-rising inverted 'V' when viewed with the castle gate in front. Now, using the paper pattern, mark the position of the holes to be drilled. These are all ½in (13mm) holes drilled with the same Forstner bit as you used for the turrets, and with the tower resting in the same block of wood.

The holes are drilled equidistantly between the rings, so the actual centre heights are, as you will see from Fig 8.14, 13⁹/₁₆in, 4⁷/₃₂in and 6²⁹/₃₂in (345mm, 107mm and 176mm). There are three holes in the Great North Tower where it faces the South Tower, and two holes where it faces the East Tower. The South Tower is similar, and the smallest East Tower has only two sets of two holes. Don't drill too many!

You may now glue the three towers into their positions, after removing the paper pattern of course. The roofs and fiddly bits can all be added later.

FIDDLY BITS

Bridges
Before the roofs, parapets and rings can be added to the towers, it is necessary to cut and tailor-fit the seven bridges. They will be made to slide down snugly between adjacent towers, with a concave curve at each end to match the tower surfaces.

Cut from scraps of the same timber you used for the walls (¹¹/₁₆in (17.5mm) thick) five pieces 1⅛in × ⅝in (29mm × 16mm) and two pieces ¾in × ½in (19mm × 13mm), with a curve on the underside of ¾in (19mm) radius, all as shown in Fig 8.15. These sizes are slightly in excess of the actual length required, giving a little latitude for sanding to the exact size. I found that the easiest way to shape these little pieces was with a small drum sander on the lathe. I have a set of these, from ½in (13mm) to 2in (51mm) diameter, that fit on to rubber cylinders which expand to grip the

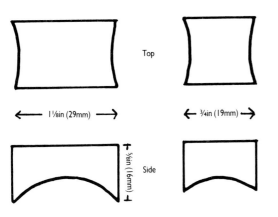

Fig 8.15
Bridges between towers.

North Tower to South Tower: three required at 1⅛in (29mm).

North Tower to East Tower: two required at 1⅛in (29mm).

South Tower to East Tower: two required at ¾in (19mm).

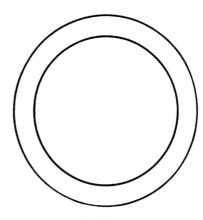

Fig 8.16
Bolection ring for towers (seven required). Internal diameter: 1½in (38mm); external diameter: 2in (51mm); thickness: ⅛in (3mm).

abrasive cylinders. I found the 1½in (38mm) diameter ideal. Mount the sanding drum on the lathe in a drill chuck fitted into the headstock morse taper. Bring the tool rest up close to the drum, and you should have no trouble shaping the ends of each piece. Watch the side as you go to check that the curve being sanded in is central and symmetrical, and check the piece frequently on the castle for fit. There will be variations from piece to piece, and when you achieve one which fits exactly, it helps to tape it to a piece of paper with the locations written on it. Note that the lowest bridges require sanding off the vertical, as the ends have to fit snugly up to the taper at the base of each tower. It doesn't take long; even if you waste a couple, you should have all seven ready for gluing in half an hour.

Tower Rings

Again, seven rings are required to fit into the grooves you have turned into the towers at 2¾in (70mm) intervals. This is achieved simply by breaking them in half along the grain and gluing them into the grooves. The process is called bolection (not quite true, as bolection is, strictly speaking, a moulding projecting beyond and covering the join between two pieces; in this case there is no join).

To make the rings, take a 2½in–3in (64mm–76mm) disc of iroko (or any other timber you may choose to contrast with your castle), mount it on a screw chuck and turn to the outer diameter of the ring required. True up the end of the piece, then turn

the tool rest at right angles so that it runs across the diameter of the timber. Mark the width of the ring required and push in your parting tool for at least ⅛in (3mm). Return the tool rest to its normal position, parallel with the lathe bed, mark off the thickness (⅛in (3mm)) you require, and push in the parting tool just to the left of that mark. If the thickness isn't exactly right, it is better to have it slightly too thick. It can easily be sanded to fit, whereas if it is too thin the gap would show.

Having parted off a ring and checked that it will fit into a groove, place it between two blocks of wood so that only half is showing. The grain must be parallel with the edges of the blocks. Then with the fingers, push down to snap the ring in two. You will find that iroko will break cleanly so that the joins will not show when glued up.

Parapets

There are three required, of course; one for the top of each tower. They can be fitted so that their top surface matches the point ½in (13mm) down from the top where there is a step, or as I have done, ⅟₁₆in–⅛in (2–3mm) above that point. The parapets are made in exactly the same way as you made the bolection rings; they are just a bit larger. Internal diameters vary, so check the diameters of your towers first. One small point is the depth of the parapet on the small East Tower. You can either have it nestling on the upper bolection ring, or you can increase its depth from ⁹⁄₁₆in (14mm) to ¹¹⁄₁₆in (18mm), to cover the turned groove with the one piece.

Roofs

Three pieces again here, all the same size and each turned on the screw chuck. It is not really important whether the grain is vertical or

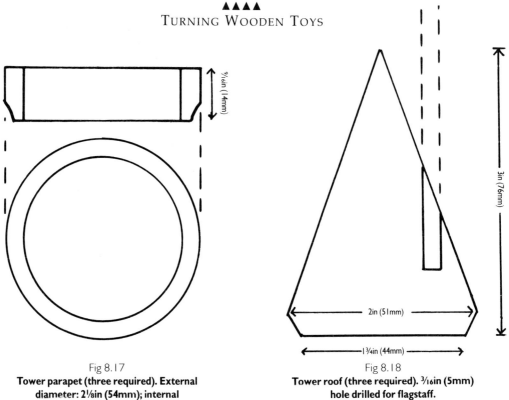

Fig 8.17
**Tower parapet (three required). External
diameter: 2⅛in (54mm); internal
diameter: two at 1¾in (44mm) and one
(East Tower) at 2¹/₃₂in (42mm).**

Fig 8.18
**Tower roof (three required). ³/₁₆in (5mm)
hole drilled for flagstaff.**

horizontal on the finished piece; it is up to you. I
chose to rough cut the blanks 3in (76mm) in
diameter from a 3in (76mm) thick plank of iroko,
and ensured that when they were glued to the
model, the side grain, which glows golden, faces
the front of the castle. Turn the three roofs to the
profile shown in Fig 8.18, remove from the chuck,
and sand the bottom surface. Drill a hole as shown
to take a ³/₁₆in (5mm) dowel flag pole sanded to a
point at the top. (However, if the model is

intended for a small child, then it is best to make
the flagpoles of some easily bendable material so it
will cause no damage if the child falls on it.) I
found that a ³/₁₆in (5mm) spur wood drill bit was
not satisfactory in the bench drill as it bent away
from the curve of the roof instead of biting in at
once. A high-speed metal drill bit was OK.
Alternatively you could drill from the bottom
upward.

Fig 8.19
**Great North Tower, grooved and drilled,
alongside roof, parapet and split bolection
rings.**

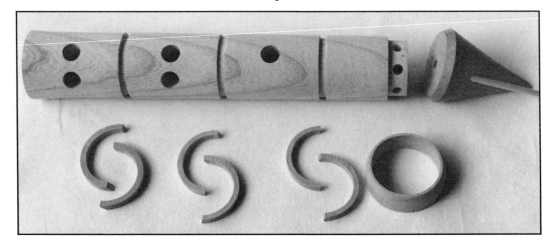

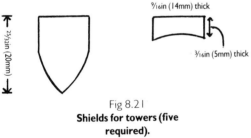

9/16in (14mm) thick

3/16in (5mm) thick

25/32in (20mm)

Fig 8.21
Shields for towers (five required).

FINAL ASSEMBLY

Glue the bridges into position first. As they are a snug fit, it is easiest to smear a little white PVA glue below each pair of holes, then slide the bridge down on to it, rather than gluing the ends of the bridge. You then avoid leaving a trail of glue all down the tower.

Next, fit the rings, checking each pair of half-rings first to see that they match. Next, add the parapets, and finally the roofs, checking that they are centrally placed on the towers. I added a ¼in (6mm) ring of cocobolo veneer beneath each parapet for contrast, but this of course is optional. Now at last you can glue the turrets into position.

FINISHING TOUCHES

I made little shields for the Baron's children. The shields are 9/16in (14mm) wide and 25/32in (20mm)

Fig 8.22
Castle Quint.

high, cut from 3/16in (5mm) thick scraps of ash (*see* Fig 8.21). The back of each shield is hollowed on the drum sander to match the curve of the turret surface, and this is done before the shield is cut out of its strip of wood. Each shield can then be painted in the designs shown in the colour section (between pages 92 and 93), using Humbrol enamel. Lest any of you accuse me of stealing your escutcheon, please note that these five relate to 1260. The blazons, however, are given in modern heraldic terminology. Finally, cut three pennants ½in × 1⅜in (13mm × 35mm) from 1/16in (2mm) thick ash, with the grain running lengthwise. Affix to the flagstaffs with instant glue and paint them red to indicate that the Baron is in residence.

CHAPTER 9

Noah's Ark

Although the chaps who wrote Chapter Six of Genesis said that Noah used gopher wood, I decided to use a timber which was a little less likely to split, and chose a dry blank of iroko. (Incidentally, gopher wood is a type of cypress.)

I thought that a ship's hull would be a nice modification to a simple bowl, and this one was turned from a piece of iroko which finished at 9¼in (235mm) in diameter and 3in (76mm) thick. A bow and stern post with rudder, again in iroko, were inset after turning.

The deckhouse, mast, main deck, companionway (ladder) and orlop (lower deck) are all removable, and the bilges are crammed with ship's stores, ranging from little water casks (turned in oak) and cases of food, to spare ropes and spars. There is even a rolled animal hide for tenting, for use after the flood.

Each of the two removable decks rests upon a ledge within the turned hull, and each is located with a small fixed dowel at the bow. The lower deck has animal stalls radiating from the centre. The original deckhouse (oblong in plan and made of iroko with walnut veneer shingles on its roof) may please you, but it occurred to me that at the time of the original, housing may well have been a little less sophisticated. I therefore designed and made an alternative deck, with a circular deckhouse turned in lime and thatched with straw. This latter is the one preferred by all the children who have seen it so far.

CUTTING LIST

Standard model
Hull: 1 blank 9¼in diameter × 3in thick
(235mm × 76mm)
Deck: ⁵⁄₃₂in (4mm) thick plywood for 2 discs each
8¾in diameter (222mm)
Rondavel deck and house
⁵⁄₃₂in (4mm) plywood:
1 disc 8¾in diameter (222mm)
1 blank 5⅜in (137mm) × 1³⁄₁₆in (30mm) thick
Roof from card and straw/dried grass
Linen thread

6 cocktail sticks
³⁄₁₆in (5mm) dowel: 12in (305mm)
walnut veneer 0.024in (0.6mm): 30in × 30in
(762mm × 762mm)

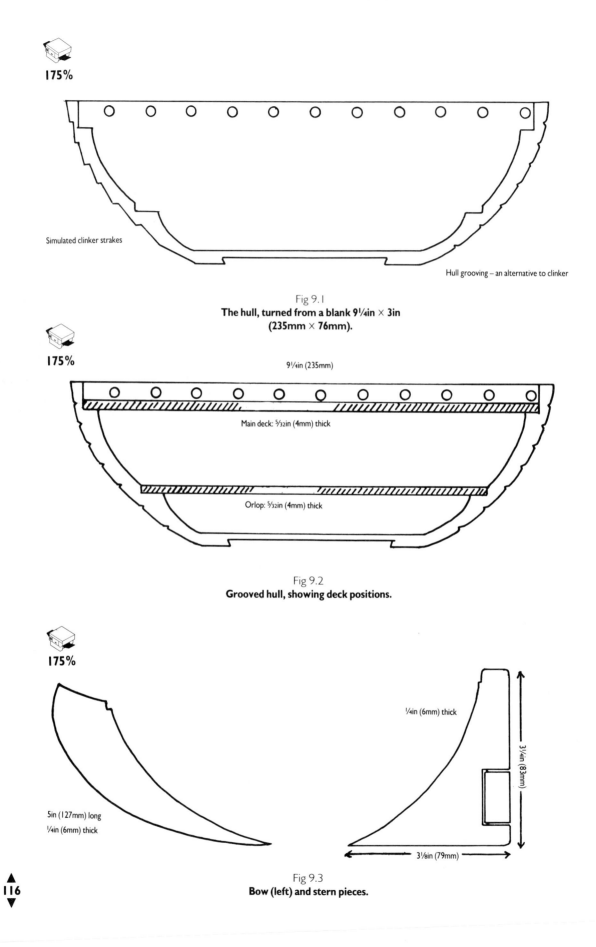

175%

Simulated clinker strakes

Hull grooving – an alternative to clinker

Fig 9.1
**The hull, turned from a blank 9¼in × 3in
(235mm × 76mm).**

175%

9¼in (235mm)

Main deck: ⁵⁄₃₂in (4mm) thick

Orlop: ⁵⁄₃₂in (4mm) thick

Fig 9.2
Grooved hull, showing deck positions.

175%

¼in (6mm) thick

3¼in (83mm)

5in (127mm) long
¼in (6mm) thick

3⅛in (79mm)

Fig 9.3
Bow (left) and stern pieces.

CONSTRUCTION

Hull

This is a straightforward piece of turning, similar to any bowl, but you will have to take special care to establish with accuracy the depths, below the rim (gunwale), of the two ledges upon which the two removable decks will rest. I used $\frac{5}{32}$in (4mm) plywood for the decks, as the edges will not show when the decks are in place, but if you vary the thickness, you will have to consider adjusting the ledge heights.

Take a dry turning blank of your chosen timber and mount it on a 6in (152mm) faceplate. Turn the curve of the hull, then decide how it is to be finished. You can leave it smooth of course, but if you decide to simulate clinker construction (overlapping horizontal planks), you can either cut the strakes with a flat scraper, or you can groove at regular intervals with the point of a skew chisel or similar point. Fig 9.1 shows clinker strakes at the bow and grooving at the stern. I used a 3in (76mm) expanding dovetail chuck to hold the piece when hollowing the hull, and the housing cut for this on the bottom surface was $\frac{1}{8}$in (3mm) deep. After sanding the exterior with your preferred progression of grits (I used 120, 180, 240 and 400), remove the workpiece from the faceplate and remount it on your dovetail chuck. True the rim and, with a parting tool, mark $\frac{1}{4}$in (6mm) in from the edge. This is the hull thickness at the gunwale: it will be thicker under the ledges which you will cut for the decks. Start to hollow out the hull, finishing the ledge for the main deck with your parting tool at $\frac{1}{2}$in (13mm) below the rim. This will give you a $\frac{1}{2}$in (8mm) high railing around the gunwale above the fitted deck into which you may later drill scupper holes.

Continue hollowing the hull, reducing the thickness below the top ledge if you wish, as shown in Fig 9.2. Establish the second ledge for the orlop deck at $1\frac{3}{8}$in (35mm) below the top ledge surface, $1\frac{27}{32}$in (47mm) below the rim of the hull. This will give you, when you allow for the thickness of the ply deck, $1\frac{7}{32}$in (31mm) between decks, in which space you will later fit your animal stalls. (For the benefit of the purists among you, and for fans of Horatio Hornblower, I do know that the word 'orlop' is the name of the lowest deck only in a ship with at least four decks, but I don't care; I like the name!)

Finish the hollowing, making very sure that the final depth in the bilges does not exceed $2\frac{11}{16}$in (68mm). This will ensure that there is $\frac{1}{8}$in (3mm) of wood left before you reach the recess you have already cut for the dovetail housing in the base.

You may, however, feel happier if you do not go so deep, but leave a slightly thicker base for safety.

Sand the inside of the turned hull. Mark in pencil fore and aft the positions for the bow and stern pieces. It looks best if these positions are on the end grain of the timber so that the side grain will show on the port and starboard sides of the hull.

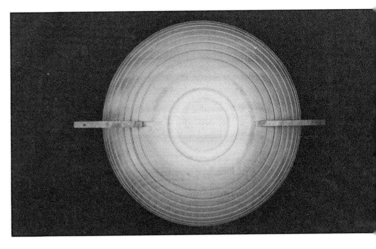

Fig 9.4
Underside of hull turning, with bow and sternposts in place.

With the piece still on the lathe but with the lathe switched off (or disconnected from the mains), you may now drill the scupper holes for water to drain off the deck. You may choose to limit these to the normal 24 stations of your indexing device (if you have one). However, I found it satisfactory to forget that and, without locking the headstock spindle, to drill the holes freehand with a $\frac{3}{16}$in (5mm) spurred bit in a hand-held electric drill. The holes are marked around the rim with centres $\frac{25}{32}$in (20mm) apart, and the centres set $\frac{3}{16}$in (5mm) down from the rim. This will mean that they are halfway between gunwale and deck surface – poor for drainage, but fine for aesthetics.

Remove the turned hull from the lathe. Cut the bow and stern pieces from scrap timber $\frac{1}{4}$in (6mm) thick. I cut $\frac{1}{4}$in (6mm) slices with the band saw from the timber left after cutting the hull circular blank from the original plank of iroko. Allow at least $\frac{1}{16}$in (2mm) extra on the curve which will be inset into the hull, as shown by the dotted lines on Fig 9.10. This amount is obviously dependent upon the depth of the finished housing cuts you make in the hull. The object is to avoid light shining through the bases of the clinker cuts or grooves.

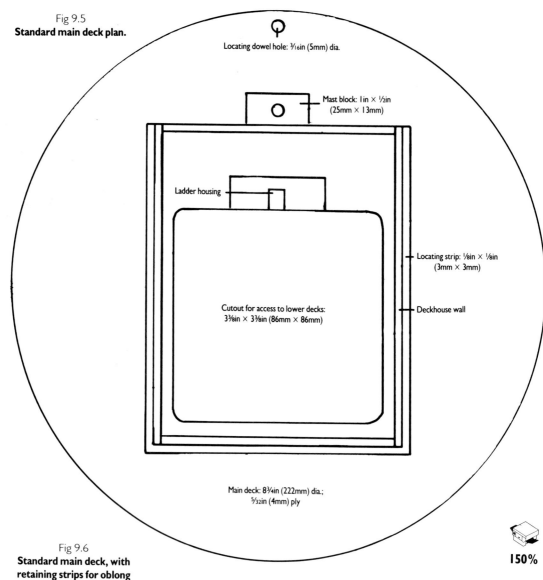

Fig 9.5
Standard main deck plan.

Locating dowel hole: ³⁄₁₆in (5mm) dia.

Mast block: 1in × ½in
(25mm × 13mm)

Ladder housing

Locating strip: ⅛in × ⅛in
(3mm × 3mm)

Deckhouse wall

Cutout for access to lower decks:
3⅜in × 3⅜in (86mm × 86mm)

Main deck: 8¾in (222mm) dia.;
⁵⁄₃₂in (4mm) ply

150%

Fig 9.6
**Standard main deck, with
retaining strips for oblong
deckhouse, mast block and
ladder housing.**

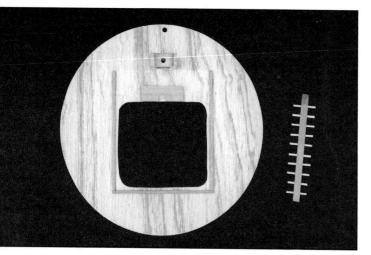

Place the hull upside down on the bench, and
accurately mark and re-check the ¼in (6mm) wide
grooves which must be cut in it: they must be
vertical and must not exceed the thickness of the
bow and stern pieces. Cut the grooves with a fine-
bladed coping saw or, as I did, with an X-acto fine
saw blade in a No. 3 handle, keeping the blade
within the drawn lines. Clean up the base of each
groove with a craft knife or a miniature X-acto
chisel held in the same handle.

Glue the bow piece into position. Take the stern
post and cut out the rudder with a fine blade in
the scroll saw. Drill holes for the rudder pintles
(axles) at the top and bottom of the rudder
aperture and set the rudder into position, using
thin nails with their heads snipped off (I used 1in

× ¹⁄₃₂in (25mm × 1mm) tacks. Glue the completed
stern piece, complete with its rudder, into
position (*see* Fig 9.4).

Main Deck

This is cut from a piece of ⁵⁄₃₂in (4mm) ply, and is
8¾in (222mm) in diameter. Choose a piece from
your stockist which is free from warp and, if
possible, with an interesting woodgrain on one
face. I was lucky to find some with a pronounced
grain pattern, but most are dull mahogany
substitutes. If you can only obtain the boring stuff,
don't worry; you can always veneer it with the
timber of your choice.

Check the deck disc for fit in the hull and, if
necessary, sand the periphery. With the grain
running fore and aft (i.e. from bow to stern), drill
a ³⁄₁₆in (5mm) hole through the deck at the bow
edge, just in from the edge of the disc and down
into the ledge. Glue a short length of ³⁄₁₆in (5mm)
dowel into the hole (in the ledge only, of course),
with the top of the dowel just flush with the deck
surface. This is the locating pin for the deck. Mark
in pencil the cut-out at the centre of the deck area
(*see* Fig 9.5), drill a pilot hole, and cut out on the
scroll saw.

Cut from ⅛in (3mm) scraps the four walls of the
deckhouse. I used scrap iroko rather than
plywood, as I did not want the laminations at the
edges of ply to be visible. Drill the portholes, three
in each of the bow and stern walls, and four in the
port and starboard walls (*see* Figs 9.7 and 9.8). I

Fig 9.9
**Standard deckhouse, with
shingle roof, and mast with
lashed spar.**

double drilled these for swank, first drilling at low
revolutions with a ⅝in (16mm) Forstner bit to a
depth of ¹⁄₃₂in (1mm), then with a ½in (13mm)
Forstner bit with its central spur point down into
the spur point hole left by the first drill bit. Drill
down now, right through the wall into a scrap
piece of timber below, to keep the edges crisp.

Assemble the deckhouse walls with white PVA
glue and cover the roof with strips of the same
timber in the same thickness, or less. Cut some
strips of veneer, preferably with variations of
colour across it; each strip should be ¹⁹⁄₃₂in (15mm)
wide with the grain running across the width.
Allowing a ³⁄₁₆in (5mm) overlap, mark the roof
surface in pencil with horizontal lines at ⅜in
(10mm) intervals. Cut the veneer strips into
random lengths to make shingle tiles and glue
them onto the roof surface with the grain running
vertically. Start, of course, with the lowest line, so
that the next will overlap (*see* Fig 9.9).

Cut three strips of timber ⅛in (3mm) square for
the locating pieces for the deckhouse. These may
be glued on to the deck, with the deckhouse in its
final position. The strips should be cut to fit left,
right and rear. The front of the deckhouse is held
in position by the mast housing block, which can
be cut from scrap 1in × 1¼in × ½in (25mm ×
32mm × 13mm). Drill this block vertically ³⁄₁₆in
(5mm) (to house the mast) and glue the block into
position. I drilled this block additionally ⅝in
(16mm) fore and aft to match the central porthole
in the front wall of the deckhouse.

All that is now required to complete the deck is a
small housing at the front of the central aperture,

Fig 9.7
Standard deckhouse (side elevation).

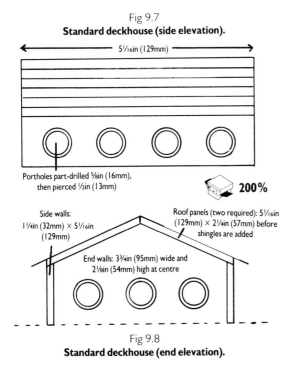

Portholes part-drilled ⅝in (16mm),
then pierced ½in (13mm)

200%

Side walls:
1¼in (32mm) × 5¹⁄₁₆in
(129mm)

Roof panels (two required): 5¹⁄₁₆in
(129mm) × 2¼in (57mm) before
shingles are added

End walls: 3¾in (95mm) wide and
2⅛in (54mm) high at centre

Fig 9.8
Standard deckhouse (end elevation).

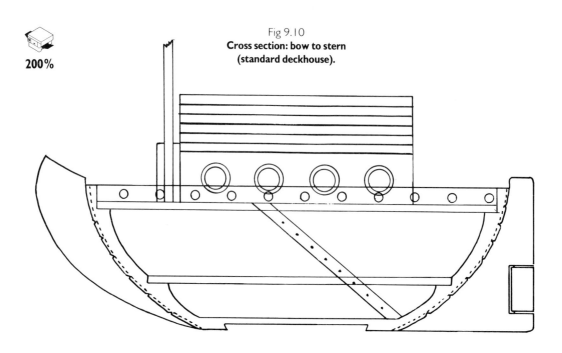

200%

Fig 9.10
**Cross section: bow to stern
(standard deckhouse).**

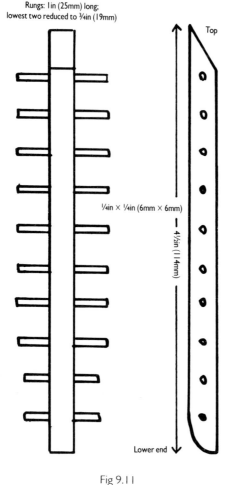

Rungs: 1in (25mm) long;
lowest two reduced to ¾in (19mm)

Top

¼in × ¼in (6mm × 6mm)

4½in (114mm)

Lower end

Fig 9.11
Ladder.

which will locate the top of the ladder. You may make this now or wait until you have completed construction. The ladder is made from a piece of iroko ¼in (6mm) square, drilled at ⅜in (10mm) intervals with holes 1/16in (2mm) in diameter (*see* Fig 9.11). The lower end is rounded to fit snugly into the curve at the rim of the bilge. The top is cut horizontally, flush with the deck housing piece which is ⅛in (3mm) thick, 19/32in (15mm) wide and 1¾in (44mm) long, with a central 45° indent which is cut and trimmed with a craft knife. The steps of the ladder are simply 1in (25mm) lengths of cocktail stick, glued into the 1/16in(2mm) holes.

Alternative Main Deck

For those who prefer something a little more ethnic, I offer a deckhouse which is similar to an African kraal or rondavel, thatched with straw. You need a different cutout in the deck for this, so I have made a second deck, as shown in Figs 9.13 and 9.14. The mast, mast block and ladder are the same as for the standard deck.

The size of the deck is unchanged, of course, as it will have to sit on the same top shelf, so cut out a disc of 5/32in (4mm) ply 8¾in (222mm) in diameter as before, and sand the edge if necessary to achieve a snug fit on its ledge within the hull. The locating pin is exactly as described above. Cut out a central hole as shown on Fig 9.13. It is not a complete circle as its front edge is placed to make an identically situated ladder housing. Instead of three strips of wood to locate the deckhouse, there is only one, this time of ply, curved to match the rear wall of the rondavel.

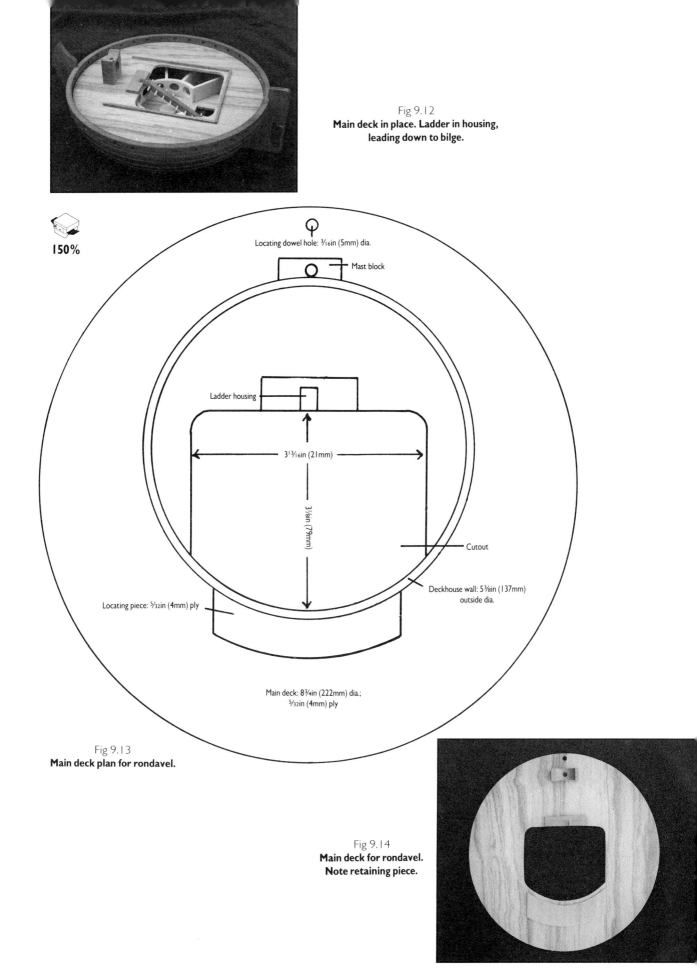

Fig 9.12
Main deck in place. Ladder in housing, leading down to bilge.

150%

Locating dowel hole: ³⁄₁₆in (5mm) dia.

Mast block

Ladder housing

3¹³⁄₁₆in (21mm)

3¹⁄₈in (79mm)

Cutout

Deckhouse wall: 5³⁄₈in (137mm) outside dia.

Locating piece: ⁵⁄₃₂in (4mm) ply

Main deck: 8¾in (222mm) dia.; ⁵⁄₃₂in (4mm) ply

Fig 9.13
Main deck plan for rondavel.

Fig 9.14
Main deck for rondavel. Note retaining piece.

Deckhouse No. 2

The wall of this house is a circle 5⅜in (137mm) in external diameter, 1³⁄₁₆in (30mm) high, and with a wall thickness of ⅛in (3mm). It was made by mounting on a screw chuck a disc of timber (in this case lime, because I happened to have it in stock) 1³⁄₁₆in (30mm) thick, and truing it on the lathe to a diameter of 5⅜in (137mm). Then, with the tool rest at right angles to the lathe bed, I pushed in a parting tool ⅛in (3mm) from the periphery, and continued the cut right through the timber, checking the constancy of the wall thickness as I proceeded. This left me with a ring of the correct size which needed only slight trimming with a craft knife at its

Glue the card roof cone on to the circular wall, which it will overlap by about ⅜in (10mm). You may now thatch it. I used real straw, taken from the fields around my village after the farmer had finished his baling, and I cut sound pieces into 2in (51mm) lengths, avoiding the natural joints. However, the real thing is out of scale by an enormous factor and, particularly on the second and top layers, I found that I had to cut the upper end of most of the pieces with a diagonal cut to make a point, in order to get them to fit.

You will do much better to use hay or other dried grasses, which have a much smaller diameter than straw.

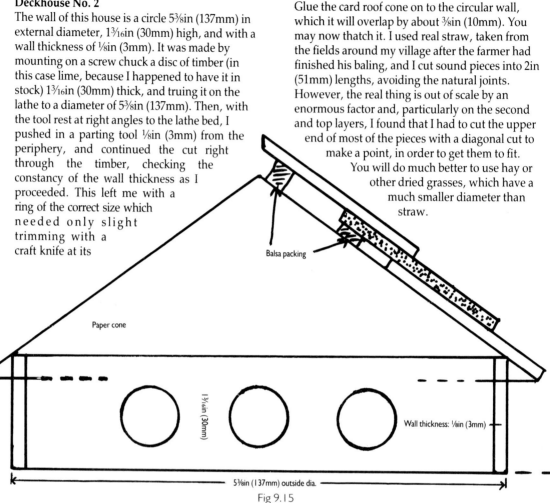

Balsa packing

Paper cone

1³⁄₁₆in (30mm)

Wall thickness: ⅛in (3mm)

5⅜in (137mm) outside dia.

Fig 9.15
Rondavel: thatched deckhouse.

base. The holes for the ports were cut in the same way as before, using ⅝in (16mm) and ¼in (8mm) Forstner bits, with the holes at 1³⁄₁₆in (30mm) centres. Check the true circumference of your turned ring of wood before you drill by placing a strip of paper around it; it should be 16¾in (425mm), which will allow 14 holes of the given diameter and spacing. If yours varies, then adjust the gaps between the holes accordingly. The ring was supported for the drilling operation by a semicircular piece of scrap, with its curve matching the curve of the inside of the workpiece, held in a vice on the drill table. The roof was made of thin card, cut from a circle 7⅜in (188mm) in diameter with a 50° segment cut out. The cut edges were brought together and overlapped to give a roof angle, from overhang to apex, of 35°. It is best not to make that angle any steeper; the thickness of the layers of thatch will in any case raise the height of the apex.

My straw pieces were affixed with white PVA

glue. The first layer was glued into place around the greatest (lowest) diameter of the roof cone, with the bottom end of each 2in (51mm) piece of straw flush with the rim. The next layer, with its ends at least ½in (13mm) in from the ends of the first layer, must be supported at the top ends if you wish to maintain the roof surface angle. The easiest way to do this is to glue a circle or small segments of balsa wood or expanded polystyrene on to the roof card, above the ends of the first layer (see Fig 9.15). However, if you use dried grass, you should have no trouble with the thickness of the thatching changing the roof line and you should need no packing.

The final piece to make, before going below deck, is the mast. This is simply a length of ³⁄₁₆in (5mm) ramin dowel. It is 7in (178mm) long, sanded to a blunt point at the top, and with a small semicircular indent filed ²⁵⁄₃₂in (55mm) below the point. This indent is the housing for the single spar, 5in (127mm) long, pointed at both ends, and

143%

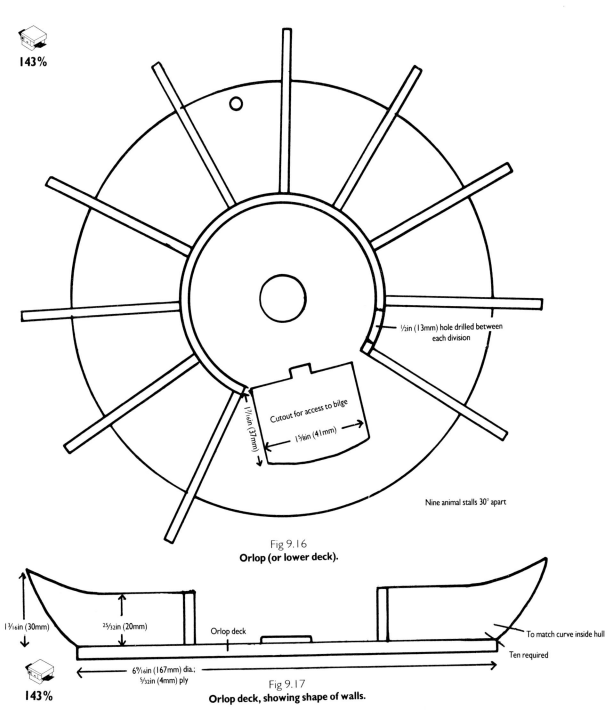

½in (13mm) hole drilled between
each division

Cutout for access to bilge

1⁷/₁₆in (37mm)

1⅝in (41mm)

Nine animal stalls 30° apart

Fig 9.16
Orlop (or lower deck).

1³/₁₆in (30mm)

²⁵/₃₂in (20mm)

Orlop deck

To match curve inside hull

Ten required

6⁹/₁₆in (167mm) dia.;
⁵/₃₂in (4mm) ply

143%

Fig 9.17
Orlop deck, showing shape of walls.

glued centrally on the mast. I finished it by lashing the joint with linen thread, the knot secured with a little dab of glue.

This completes the instructions for the hull and main deck.

Orlop or Lower Deck
Cut a circle 6⁹/₁₆in (167mm) diameter from ⁵/₃₂in (4mm) ply, then sand its edge if necessary to fit it into position on the lower ledge that you have

turned within the hull. Drill a ³/₁₆in (5mm) hole at the bow curve centrally and just within the rim, as before, down into the ledge, ensuring that the grain pattern of the deck ply runs fore and aft. Glue a small piece of ³/₁₆in (5mm) dowel into the hole in the ledge so that its top is just flush with the deck surface. Again, this is the locating pin for the deck. This deck has nine animal stalls grouped around a central circular area walled with a circle 3⅛in (80mm) in external diameter, and with a wall thickness of ⅛in (3mm) and height of ²⁵/₃₂in

Fig 9.18
**Side view of orlop, showing animal stalls
and access hatch.**

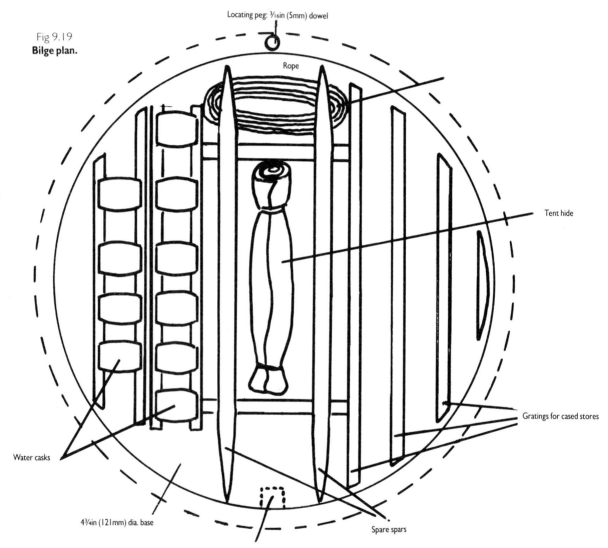

Locating peg: ³⁄₁₆in (5mm) dowel

Fig 9.19
Bilge plan.

Rope

Tent hide

Water casks

Gratings for cased stores

4³⁄₄in (121mm) dia. base

Spare spars

Position of ladder base

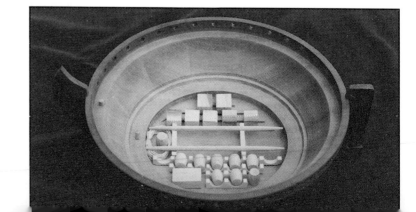

Fig 9.20
**Hull with bilge stores in
place, showing ledges for
main and orlop decks.**

(20mm). Cut out with the scroll saw the hole in the deck plywood which will give access to the stores in the bilge and which will allow the ladder to fit into its final position. Turn the central circular ring wall in exactly the same way as is described above for the rondavel deckhouse, by mounting a disc of timber on your screw chuck and cutting off a ring with your parting tool parallel with the lathe bed. Remove 90° of this ring as shown in Fig 9.16.

Mark lightly in pencil on the deck surface the position of the central ring, and also all 10 of the

The barrels for water were turned from a small piece of oak, turned between centres to a diameter of ⅜in (10mm), then mounted in a Jacobs chuck on the lathe headstock. It was then simple to shape and part off each barrel, using ½in (13mm) skew chisel. No finish was required for the surface of the barrels. The spare ropes were simply small coils of linen thread, wrapped around two fingers and then secured with a lashing of thread centrally. The tenting is a small piece of thin leather 2⅜in × 3⁵⁄₁₆in (60mm × 100mm), rolled with the suede side outward and tied with thread.

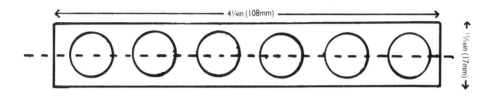

Fig 9.21
Cask rack: drill ⁷⁄₁₆in (12mm) holes, ³⁄₁₆in (5mm) apart, and saw along dotted line.

stall walls which radiate from it. Mark the wall positions on the ring, and the centre point of each division, and drill a ½in (13mm) hole at each centre point to give access to each stall. After sanding, glue the ring into position, with the 90° cutout facing aft. Cut a template to match the wall shape given in Fig 9.17, and check that its outer curve matches and fits neatly against the inner curve of the hull. Using that template, cut 10 wall sections from ⅛in (3mm) thick timber of the same type you used for the central ring wall. Glue all these into position as shown in Fig 9.18. If you have marked the centre of the orlop deck with the point of your compasses when drawing the deck rim and marking the position of the inner ring, you may glue a small disc of timber over the mark for neatness, if you wish.

Bilge and Stores
No deck to cut here, as it is in fact the flat bottom of your hull turning. However, since bilges usually have some water in them, I made racks and gratings for the casks and boxes of stores. Fig 9.19 is self-explanatory, though I expect that you will want to design your own layout. It is helpful to start with the two mountings which hold the spare spars, as these are central. Make sure there is enough space between the spars, when they are in position, to allow the ladder with its rungs to pass between them. If not, you can easily snip say ½₂in (1mm) off each side of the lower two rungs.

Fig 9.22
The ark sails off into the sunset.

The boxes of stores glued to the gratings were small cubes of oak, ¹⁹⁄₃₂in × ¹⁹⁄₃₂in × ⅜in (15mm × 15mm × 10mm), sanded on all sides. I show in Fig 9.21 my suggestion for quickly making the racks for the water casks. Well, that's it, except for the animals. You may either buy plastic or metal ones from your toy store, or make your own. One thought that occurs to me is that Noah didn't have a great deal of time between receiving his instructions from the Bearded Gent, and the onset of the flood. I doubt that he had time for a quick safari to collect the beasts from Ethiopia, Kenya and Tanzania. Think about it; what would you have had time to put aboard?

CHAPTER 10

Fantasy Bridge

This is a bridge over a river on an imaginary planet. I hope that it will stimulate the imagination of the child for whom it is built, as well as provide some happy hours of turning for you. Most of the turning is between centres, with some on the screw chuck. There is some miniature turning too, with the standard lamps on the bridge piers and the medallions over the arches. The basic bridge is a simple parabolic curve; the lamps also form a parabola, as do the leading edges of the piers. The centre pathway on the bridge decking, formed by the pierced railings, is for animals to cross, keeping them and their droppings away from the dwellings.

CUTTING LIST

Most of the timber for this project will be found in your scrap box. I have used a variety of timbers; Indian laurel, ash, iroko, chacahuante, beech, spalted hackberry and oak. However, the list below gives the quantities required if you choose to make all the towers of the same timber, and each one of a single piece.

Bridge:
¾in × 4¾in (19mm × 121mm ash:
56in (142cm) for sides and cross struts
2 sq ft (61 sq cm) of 1/16in (2mm) ply for decking
2 sq ft (61 sq cm) of 0.024in
(0.6mm) veneer for decking
4 sq ft (122 sq cm) of 0.024in (0.6mm) veneer
for arches 6in (152mm) wide, with the grain running
across the width

The surface veneer is your own choice, but I strongly recommend a very flexible veneer for filling the arches. (I used horsechestnut).

Towers:
1½in × 1½in × 1ft 6in (38mm × 38mm × 457mm)
2in × 2in × 9ft 3in (51mm × 51mm × 2819mm)
3in × 3in × 6in (76mm × 76mm × 762mm)
MDF, ¼in (6mm) thick: 2ft 0in × 6in
(610mm × 152mm) for rails
3/16in (5mm) dowel: 2ft 6in (762mm)
for lamp standards

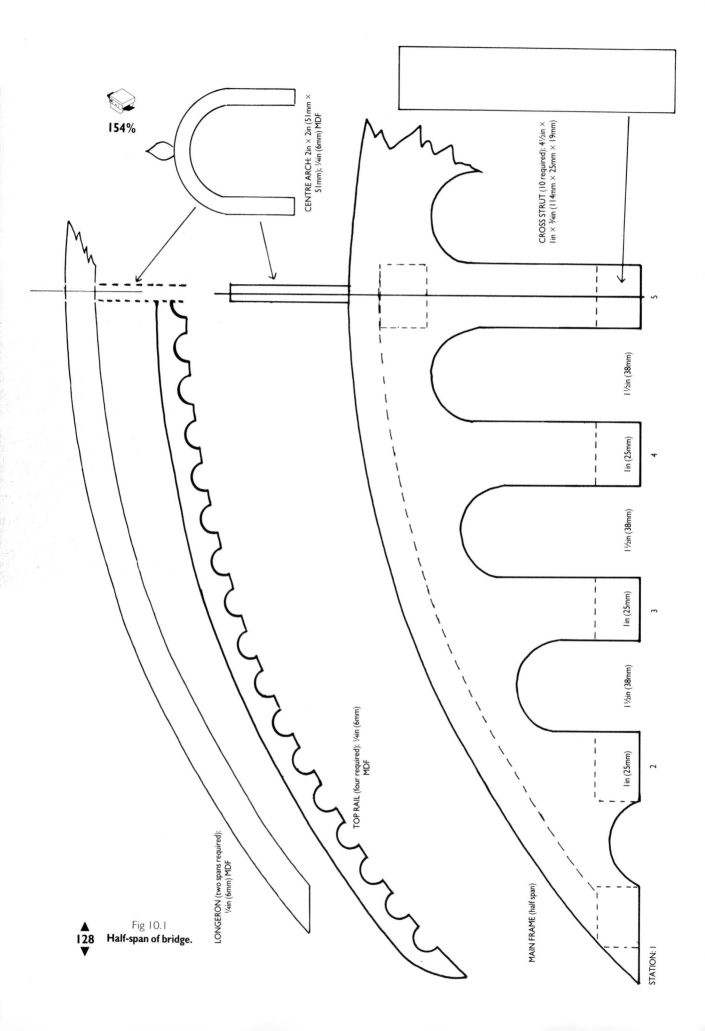

154%

CENTRE ARCH: 2in × 2in (51mm × 51mm); ¼in (6mm) MDF

CROSS STRUT (10 required): 4½in × 1in × ¾in (114mm × 25mm × 19mm)

1½in (38mm)

1in (25mm)

1½in (38mm)

1in (25mm)

1½in (38mm)

1in (25mm)

5

4

3

2

LONGERON (two spans required): ¼in (6mm) MDF

TOP RAIL (four required): ¼in (6mm) MDF

MAIN FRAME (half span)

STATION: 1

Fig 10.1

128 Half-span of bridge.

BRIDGE CONSTRUCTION

It is advisable to make the bridge before undertaking the turning of the towers. This will save making allowances for the thickness of the ply/veneer decking when cutting transversely on the tower units.

You will no doubt make your own modifications to the shapes I have designed if they do not please you, but I do suggest that you retain the curve which I have used for the bridge surface. I tried quite a number before settling on this one, which bears a resemblance to ancient hump-backed bridges on this planet. As for size, the original has a total span of 22in (559mm) and a width of 6in (152mm). You may choose to reduce this by 50% to economize on shelf space, in which case just halve all measurements.

Main Frame

First, cut the two spans from ¾in (19mm) timber. You will find that by reversing Fig 10.1 for marking the second curve, you can get both sides from a plank 38in (965mm) long and 4¾in (121mm) wide. You may use a band saw with a fine blade, or a scroll saw with a medium-to-coarse blade for the cutting. I found the scroll saw was easier to use for the bridge arches.

Cut the 10 cross struts from similar timber, 4½in (114mm) long. If the timber used for the main bridge sides differs from the ¾in (19mm) thickness which I used, then the length of the cross struts must be amended to achieve a final 6in (152mm) width of bridge. (I tried wider and narrower spans, but they just did not look right.)

From scrap timber, cut triangular fillets to strengthen the joints at each end of the cross struts. I cut a length of ½in × ½in (13mm × 13mm) timber and ripped it on the band saw with the table set at 45°. I then cut off lengths just under 1in (25mm), so that when glued into position, their ends did not foul the veneer to be applied under each arch.

Assemble the bridge frame as shown in Fig 10.2. There are nine base struts, one upper cross strut and 20 triangular fillets, all glued with white PVA glue. You may find it easiest first to glue one end of each cross strut to one side and then, when the glue has set, glue on the second side, holding it with rubber bands.

Decking

On the prototype, as you see from Figs 10.3 and 10.4, I decked the bridge with copaiba veneer,

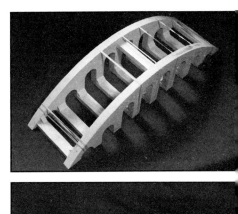

Fig 10.2
Bridge assembly with 10 cross struts. Note triangular fillets at joints.

Fig 10.3
Bridge frame with the two MDF longerons (deck supports) in position.

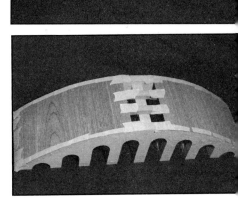

Fig 10.4
Partly affixed decking of copaiba veneer. N.B. For strength, use ¹⁄₁₆in (2mm) ply below the veneer.

which was supported by the bridge sides and also two curved longerons of ¼in (6mm) MDF (shown on Fig 10.1). However, it would yield a stronger surface if you were to plank the curved surface with ¹⁄₁₆in (2mm) ply first. If you do this, you do not really need the MDF longerons. Check the natural curve of your sheet of ¹⁄₁₆in (2mm) ply by bending between the fingers each way. Those I had in stock curved most easily across the 12in (305mm) width, rather than along the 24in (610mm) length, so it would have been necessary to cut four 6in (152mm) pieces, butting the 6in (152mm) sides together when planking the deck. You will find masking tape convenient to hold the planking in place whilst the glue dries. When set, cover with the veneer of your choice. Again, you will find that curvature is easiest when the veneer grain runs across the width of the bridge. Cut each piece slightly oversize, say ¹⁄₁₆in–⅛in (2–3mm), to allow for possible irregularities. Trim the edges after the glue is set. Don't worry about the edges of the ply-veneer showing, as you will cover these edges at the end of construction with ¼in (6mm) strips of veneer between towers.

was not flexible enough and split when following the curves, which are 1½in (38mm) in diameter. You could steam or soak the pieces of veneer, but it is easier to select a more flexible wood than ash. Sycamore might do, but I found that horsechestnut was ideal, and its colour almost matched the ash timbers. You can see in Fig 10.5 the planking being carried out. Note that each piece of veneer is cut a little oversize, and has the grain running across the width of the bridge. Glue with PVA and hold with masking tape until dry.

Fiddly Bits
The bridge piers (*see* Fig 10.6) can now be cut from the waste left after cutting the two bridge sides, but do not glue them in position until the very end of construction, as they would prevent the bridge assembly from being laid on its side. However, you can drill them for the standard lamps. Set your bench drill, with a ³⁄₁₆in (5mm) spurred drill bit in the chuck, for a depth stop of ½in (13mm). The holes are drilled in the pier pieces ¾in (19mm) back from the pointed nose of each piece. Cut the lamp uprights from ³⁄₁₆in (5mm) dowel,

Fig 10.5
Underside of arches, showing horse chestnut planking in the course of being applied.

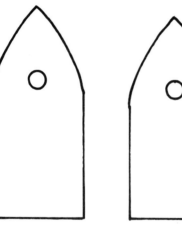

No. 5 (two required): 2¼in (57mm)   No. 4 (four required): 2⅛in (54mm)

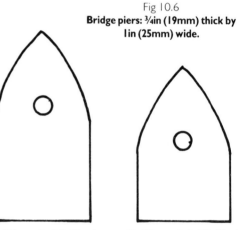

Fig 10.6
Bridge piers: ¾in (19mm) thick by 1in (25mm) wide.

No. 3 (four required): 2in (51mm)   No. 2 (four required): 1⅝in (41mm)

You may now cut (but do not glue yet) the bridge centre railings of ¼in (6mm) MDF (*see* Fig 10.1). These were cut on the scroll saw using a No. 3 blade; half-span lengths were cut as it proved impracticable to cut 22in (559mm) lengths on my scroll saw, which has a throat of only 14in (356mm). Also, moving the piece on the saw table to make the little semicircular cutouts was awkward, and my body got in the way too!

Planking
Finally, you must block in under the arches to hide the cross struts and to simulate solid construction. I first tried to do this with ash veneer to match the main timber, but I found that this

and drill a small hole (a ¹⁄₁₆in (2mm) bit is OK) ½in (13mm) from the top end of each piece to take a 1in (25mm) length of cocktail stick at right angles (*see* Fig 10.7). This is to lean a ladder against when servicing the lamps. It is convenient to rest each piece of dowel in a 'V' block of waste wood in the cross vice of your drill table. Mark the drilling spot with a sharp point so that the drill bit does not wander.

The lamps can be conveniently cut in multiples between centres. 14 are required altogether, and are easily shaped from ½in (13mm) dowel which you can turn yourself. The ½in (13mm) mini-jaws of the Multistar chuck are useful for this.

Each lamp is ½in (13mm) high and ½in (13mm) in diameter at the top, reducing to ⅜in (10mm) with your small skew chisel. Remove from the lathe, complete the parting off with a fine-bladed saw, sand the top and bottom, and glue the lamps onto their standards.

You may also now cut the medallions which are (eventually) glued between each tower. Turn a short length of contrasting timber (I used mahogany) between centres to a diameter which will fit your chuck. Reduce the outer end to ⅝in (16mm) diameter. With the rest at right angles to the lathe bed, push into the end of the workpiece a ⅛in (3mm) parting tool to a depth of 1/32in (1mm) or so. Replace the rest parallel to the lathe bed, and part off the disc with a thickness of ⅛in (3mm). Repeat until you have 18 of these, to be affixed after the assembly of the towers on the bridge.

cutouts needed to fit to the bridge structure. I made each of mine out of three pieces, but you can, if you wish, turn as one piece and cut out the section shown in Fig 10.9 in dotted lines.

To make up in three pieces, turn a piece of timber 1in (25mm) square and 3in (76mm) long, to a diameter of 1in (25mm). Part off two pieces of 1⅛in (29mm) and cut them in half lengthwise, to give four pieces with a semicircular cross section. Turn four discs of the same timber. In this case, I used Indian laurel. The discs are 1½in (38mm) in diameter and ¼in (6mm) thick. Finally, with a short length of 1in (25mm) diameter timber in the jaws of your spigot chuck (or in the plain bore of a Multistar chuck with 'A' jaws in contracting mode) turn four domes 1in (25mm) in diameter and ½in (13mm) thick. I used pine for these. Glue up as shown in Fig 10.9 and set aside for later.

Fig 10.7
Lamps (14 required): ½in (13mm) dia. top and ⅜in (10mm) dia. base. Plus lamp standards.

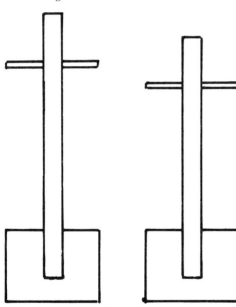

No. 5 (two required): 2¾in (70mm)   No. 4 (four required): 2½in (64mm)   No. 3 (four required): 1¾in (44mm)   No. 2 (four required): 1⅛in (29mm)

TOWER CONSTRUCTION

For convenience I have numbered the towers, No. 1 being the threshold pillar on the left of the upstream side of the bridge (*see* Fig 10.26). Numbering goes from 1 to 9 on this side, and 10 to 18 on the other (downstream) side. I will describe the making of each piece using this numbering system and mentioning the timber which I used, although you will use the timbers of your own choice.

Threshold Pillars (Stations 1, 9, 10 and 18)
These are the simplest pieces; the cross section of the lower ends are semicircles; there are no angled

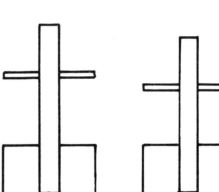

Fig 10.8
Arch medallions (16 required): ⅝in (16mm) dia. and ⅛in (3mm) thick.

Alternatively you may mount a length of 1½in (38mm) diameter timber in your chuck (or plain bore of Multistar size 'B'–'E' jaws) and turn the outer 1⅞in (48mm) to the finished shape. Part off and cut out the dotted line section, preferably

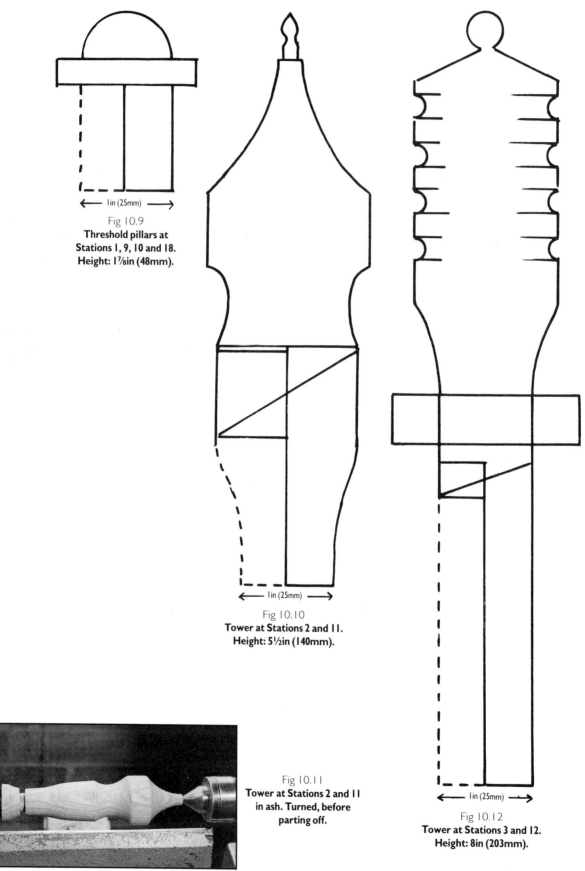

Fig 10.9
**Threshold pillars at
Stations 1, 9, 10 and 18.
Height: 1⅞in (48mm).**

←— 1in (25mm) —→

←— 1in (25mm) —→

Fig 10.10
**Tower at Stations 2 and 11.
Height: 5½in (140mm).**

Fig 10.11
**Tower at Stations 2 and 11
in ash. Turned, before
parting off.**

←— 1in (25mm) —→

Fig 10.12
**Tower at Stations 3 and 12.
Height: 8in (203mm).**

with a handsaw – much safer than trying to use a band or scroll saw. I used a slitting saw blade mounted in a No. 3 X-acto handle, with the workpiece held in the wood-lined jaws of a bench vice.

Stations 2 and 11

Take a piece of timber 2in × 2in × 6in (51mm × 51mm × 152mm), mount between centres and turn to the profile shown in Fig 10.10. As you see from Fig 10.11, I used a revolving centre in the tailstock, the point of which pierces the end of the timber. Don't worry about this, as you will later enlarge that hole with a ³⁄₁₆in (5mm) drill bit to take a small finial. Sand 120, 180, 240 and 400 grits, and part off the piece. Make a second piece to the same profile (I used white ash for one of these, and olive ash for the other).

Cut out the half section shown in Fig 10.10. The flat vertical surface left after the cut will butt onto the vertical surface of the bridge side at Station 2 and Station 11. Obviously, the diagonal cut made halfway through one piece will be the mirror image of the other, but it is easy to avoid cutting the wrong way. Place a bridge pier at the base of Station 2. Stand the tower on it (with no cut yet made) with the best grain pattern showing on the side of the tower away from the bridge. Using a pencil, mark on the tower the curve of the bridge deck surface. Remove the tower piece, mark the mean straight line which accommodates this curve and cut that straight line down to the centre of the cross section with an X-acto saw. You can do it on a band saw, but you run the risk of judder as it is such a short piece, and also you risk cutting off your digits. The same applies to the vertical cut from the base of the piece to meet the X-acto transverse cut, so for safety it is best to use a handsaw.

The little finial at the top of this piece is simply cut with a ½in (13mm) skew chisel from a short length of ³⁄₁₆in (5mm) dowel held in a Jacobs chuck, mounted in the morse taper of your headstock.

Stations 3 and 12

There are at least two ways of making this tower: (a) as a three-piece structure, or (b) as a one-piece turning with a ring slid onto it after finishing. The former was done because I took a short piece of timber from my offcut box, but it is much simpler to turn the latter, so I will give notes on that one only. Take a 9in (229mm) length of 1½in (38mm) of square timber. I used a piece of terminalia for these. Turn to the profile shown in Fig 10.13, checking that the lower 3½in (89mm) is a constant

Fig 10.13
Tower at Stations 3 and 12 in Indian laurel. Checking the 1in (25mm) base diameter.

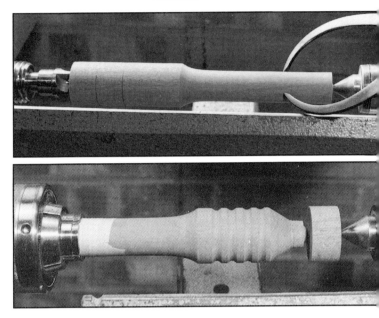

Fig 10.14
Tower at Stations 3 and 12, partly shaped now and reversed into the 'A' jaws of the Multistar chuck to finish finial.

1in (25mm) in diameter so that it will match the 1in (25mm) width of the bridge upright. With a ¼in (6mm) round scraper, or a ¼in (6mm) gouge, cut the five coves, which are ¼in (6mm) apart. Reduce the top of the piece, reverse into the 1in (25mm) bore of your chuck, and finish the ball finial with a ½in (13mm) skew (see Fig 10.14). It is best to protect the 1in (25mm) diameter end by wrapping it evenly with masking tape; this will prevent possible marking by the jaw segments. Part off outboard of the finial, which can be hand sanded if necessary to perfect its spherical shape.

Cut a 2in (51mm) diameter blank from a 3in (76mm) thick piece of timber (I used iroko here). Mount on a screw chuck on the headstock and bore out the centre to a depth of just over 1in (25mm) with a 1in (25mm) Forstner or sawtooth bit mounted in a Jacobs chuck in the tailstock. The lathe should be turning at low speed (I used 220rpm). True up the outboard end and the diameter and sand the surface with your usual progression of grits. Part off two rings, each ½in (13mm) thick, and check their fit on the stems of the two towers. Remove them temporarily so that you may cut out the half sections of the bases in exactly the same way as described above for the towers at Stations 2 and 11.

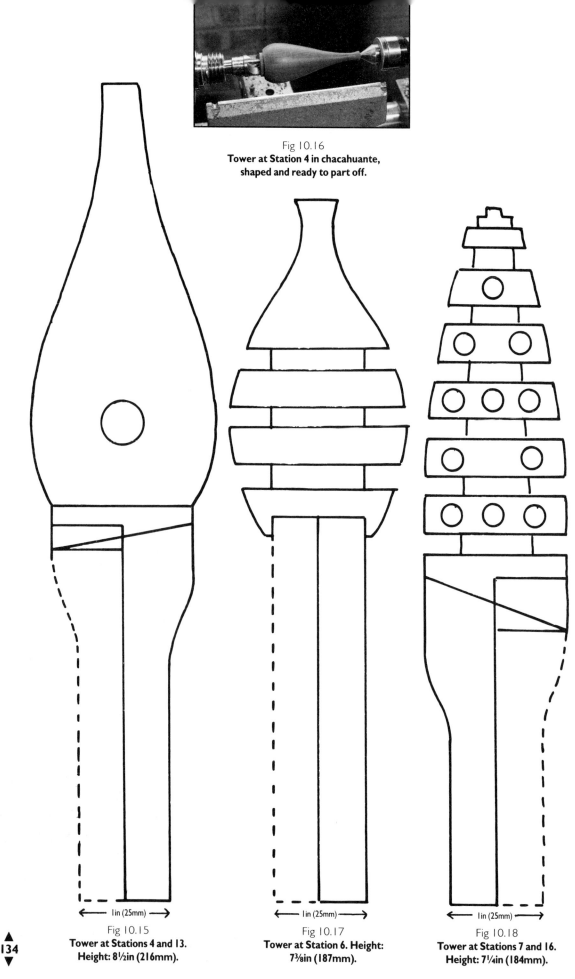

Fig 10.16
Tower at Station 4 in chacahuante, shaped and ready to part off.

← 1in (25mm) →

Fig 10.15
Tower at Stations 4 and 13. Height: 8½in (216mm).

← 1in (25mm) →

Fig 10.17
Tower at Station 6. Height: 7⅜in (187mm).

← 1in (25mm) →

Fig 10.18
Tower at Stations 7 and 16. Height: 7¼in (184mm).

Stations 4 and 13

These are each turned in two pieces; the bases in ash, one teardrop-shaped top in ash (countersunk at its base to accept its stem) and one in chacahuante with a flush base, to be glued on to its stem. Because it is simpler I recommend the latter, unless you wish to turn the whole tower in one piece of timber.

Mount a piece of ash 1½in × 1½in × 4½in (38mm × 38mm × 114mm) between centres and turn to the profile shown in Fig 10.15, with the top end finished at 1½in (38mm) and the lower end at 1in (25mm). Part off the piece to give a finished height of 4⅛in (105mm), and cut out the half section as before. You could simplify this if you wish by making a single turning, then cutting it in half lengthways to make two stems, each with a semicircular cross section. Your top piece can be glued to this quite satisfactorily, though a little part of the flat section of the stem will show when assembled.

Fig 10.16 shows the chacachuante blank mounted and turned to the profile given in Fig 10.15. This is sanded and parted off to give a length of 4⅜in (111mm). You will need to drill four holes at its greatest diameter. Mark with a pencil a line round the circumference of the piece 1in (25mm) up from its base. Mark four drilling stations with a sharp point at 90° intervals around the line. With a ½in (13mm) Forstner bit in the chuck of your bench drill and the workpiece held in the 'V' groove of a waste block on your drill table, bring the brad point of the drill down on to the marked locations and drill at low revolutions (I used 120rpm) into the timber to just beyond the centre. When all four holes have been drilled they will meet at the centre. Make another top section for Station 13, glue tops to stems and set aside for later assembly.

Station 6

Again, I made this as two separate turnings, the stem in ash and the top bulbous tower in knotty beech. The stem is a simple 1in (25mm) cylinder, finished, parted off at 4in (102mm) and sawn down the middle.

To make the top section, I mounted a beech blank 2in × 2in × 3½in (51mm × 51mm × 89mm) long on to a 1in (25mm) screw chuck. I had first counter-drilled the base of the piece as indicated in Fig 10.17, but this is not actually necessary. If you leave the base flat you may care to reduce the stem length slightly, so that the bulbous tower is closer to the bridge deck.

Turn the piece to the profile shown in Fig 10.17,

using a parting tool to achieve the grooves whilst leaving 1in (25mm) at the centre within those grooves to match the diameter of the stem. Finish, part off and glue to the stem.

Stations 7 and 16

These are another pair I made from terminalia. Again, take care when cutting transversely so that you get the slope of the cut correct for the station you use. The shape is turned from a blank 1½in × 1½in × 8in (38mm × 38mm × 203mm) mounted between centres. Incidentally, the lathe speed for all these pieces was 1150–1200rpm, except for the first roughing out of the larger diameters when I reduced it to 900rpm. I am lucky in having variable speeds on my machine, but if you have the usual pulleys and drive belt, then select the nearest speeds.

For the towers at Station 7 and 16, as you see from Fig 10.19, first turn the base section to 1in (25mm) diameter, sloping up to 1½in (38mm) by the time you are 2½in up from the base. Cut the six grooves with a parting tool. Those you see in Fig 10.19 were made with a ⅛in (3mm) parting tool with the end ground askew. With a straight push into the wood at 90° to the lathe bed the tool cut a groove, the base of which sloped in towards the top of the piece. Now, with a gouge or scraper, shape the outside of the piece to give a curve matching the profile in Fig 10.18. With the lathe switched off and using a 24 station index wheel, ³⁄₁₆in (5mm) holes were drilled in the rings of this piece. The bottom and third rings have eight holes (at Stations 3, 6, 9, 12, 15, 18, 21 and 24), the second and fourth rings have four holes (at Stations 6, 12, 18 and 24) and the fifth ring has four holes (at Stations 3, 9, 15 and 21).

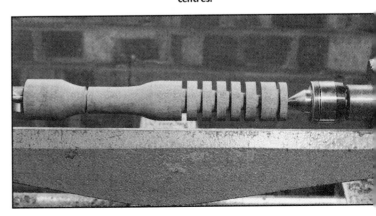

Fig 10.19
Tower at Stations 7 and 16, partly turned between centres.

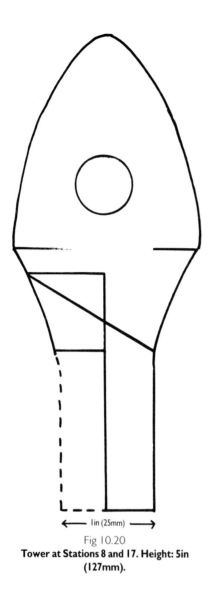

← 1in (25mm) →

Fig 10.20
Tower at Stations 8 and 17. Height: 5in (127mm).

Fig 10.21
Tower at Stations 8 and 17, rough turned between centres.

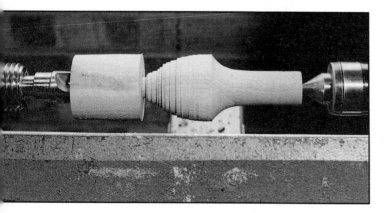

Now part off the tower, cut out half the stem in the usual way, having marked the transverse cut whilst it was up against the bridge, and set aside.

Stations 8 and 17
These bullet-shaped small towers, each with three holes around the circumference, are turned from timber blanks 2in × 2in × 5½in (51mm × 51mm × 140mm). I used beech for one piece and spalted hackberry for the other. The beech piece is shown on the lathe in Fig 10.21, and the blank was 2in (51mm) longer than was necessary. This was because the shape was, like all the others, decided upon whilst the wood was actually spinning. It is quite good fun to make it up as you go along.

So, turn your blank between centres, and reduce the stem to a 1in (25mm) diameter for at least a length of 1¾in (44mm), preferably 2in (51mm). This is so that the profile does not extend laterally to obscure the curve of the bridge arches, to which it is adjacent. Rough turn the head of the bullet, part off, and remount in the bore of your chuck in order to finish the head. As before, protect the stem by wrapping it with masking tape.

Remove from the lathe, hold the piece next to its final location, mark the line of the bridge and cut out as before. Using a 'V' block as support, drill three holes, each ⅝in (16mm) in diameter, at 120° intervals around the head. One of the holes should face either the bridge, or directly away from it. Drill with a Forstner bit slowly to just beyond the centre of the wood so that all three holes meet in the middle and light shines through.

Station 5
This is one of the two largest, central towers and it was made in three sections: the stem in ash, the main body in olive ash, and the roof in oak. You can make it all from one blank 2½in × 2½in × 10in (64mm × 64mm × 254mm), or in two sections, the main one 2¼in × 2¼in × 8in (57mm × 57mm × 203mm) plus a separate disc for the roof piece. I suggest a three-part construction.

Take a blank of ash 1½in × 1½in × 6in (38mm × 38mm × 152mm), turn to a cylinder and reduce the base 2in (51mm) to a diameter of 1in (25mm) like all the others, to match the bridge upright. You may, if you wish, cut four decorative grooves as shown in Fig 10.22, just for variety. Sand the surface, part off to give a 5in (127mm) length, and cut out as usual (see dotted line on Fig 10.22). Note that this piece and the one at Station 14 are the only ones whose transverse cuts are horizontal (90° to the vertical axis of the tower) because they are, of course, located at the crown of the bridge.

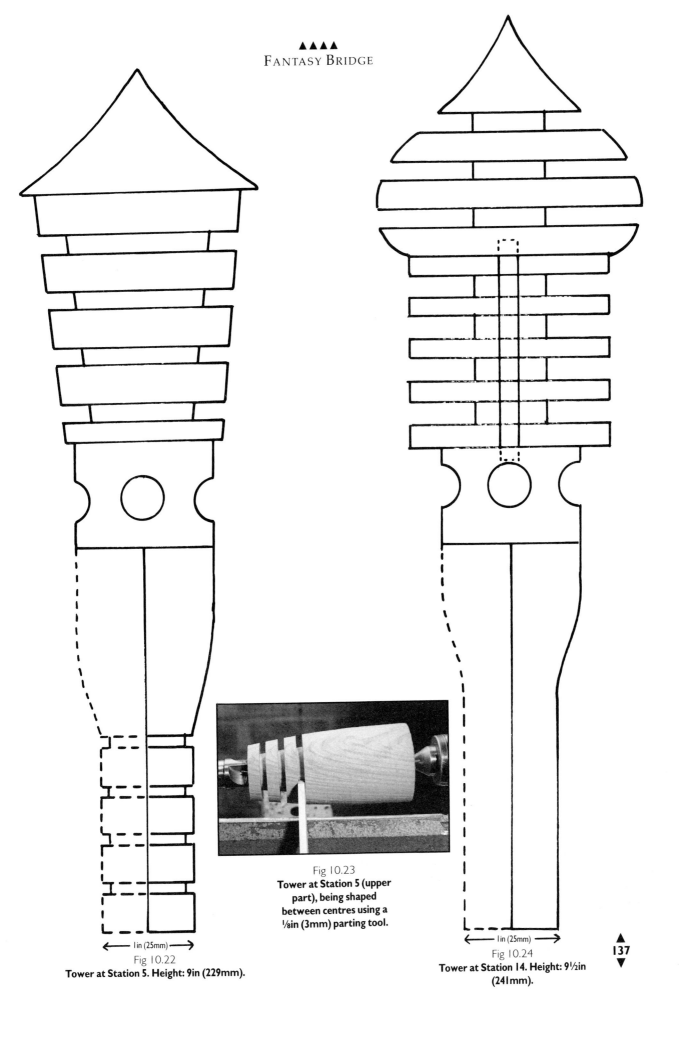

Fig 10.23
Tower at Station 5 (upper part), being shaped between centres using a ⅛in (3mm) parting tool.

← 1in (25mm) →
Fig 10.22
Tower at Station 5. Height: 9in (229mm).

← 1in (25mm) →
Fig 10.24
Tower at Station 14. Height: 9½in (241mm).

Drill four holes at 90° intervals around the 1½in (38mm) diameter of the top of this stem, with centres ⅝in (16mm) below the top surface. The body of the tower is turned from a piece of olive ash 2¼in × 2¼in × 2⅝in (57mm × 57mm × 67mm). In this case the length is exact, unlike all the others given above where allowance has been made for parting off. For this piece, the marks of the four-prong drive centre and the tailstock centre point do not matter, as they will be hidden when all the parts are glued up.

Turn to the profile shown in Fig 10.22 and cut the grooves with a ⅛in (3mm) parting tool with its point ground askew, as was done for the towers at Stations 7 and 16 (*see* Fig 10.23). Finally, put a 2⅝in (67mm) diameter disc of oak 1½in (38mm) thick (or more) on to your screw chuck, and turn the roof piece. A large round-nose scraper is a convenient tool to use to refine the flattish curve of this piece. Glue all three sections together, checking concentricity before the glue sets.

Station 14

You can repeat here if you wish the tower opposite (No. 5 as described above) either in the same or different timbers. I chose to vary the design, and made a piece which finished a little taller, has an onion dome, and revolving floors.

The stem is exactly the same in timber and dimensions as No. 5, so I need not repeat those notes. Just drill a vertical hole ³⁄₁₆in (5mm) in diameter and, say, ⅛in to ⁵⁄₃₂in (3mm to 4mm) deep at the centre of the top of the stem, to take a length of ³⁄₁₆in (5mm) dowel. Turn a piece of ash to 2⅛in (54mm) diameter, mount on your screw chuck, drill ¼in (6mm) centrally, and part off five discs, each ¼in (6mm), thick.

Do the same with a cylinder 1in (25mm) in diameter, parting off four washers of the same thickness. You can, as I did, cut little ¼in × ¼in (6mm × 6mm) notches in alternate discs, but that is optional. Glue a 2⅜in (60mm) length of ³⁄₁₆in (5mm) dowel vertically into the ash stem and, when the glue is dry, thread the 2⁵⁄₃₂in (55mm) and 1in (25mm) discs onto it alternately.

Mount on your screwchuck a disc 2⅛in (54mm) in diameter and 2¼in (57mm) thick, and turn the onion dome (I used iroko for this), grooving it to match the floors below. Finish the surface, remove from the chuck and, using the screw hole, glue the piece on to the top of the dowel which bears the discs. You can first push on a large washer of newspaper to stop glue from joining the roof to the top disc, and tear the paper away later.

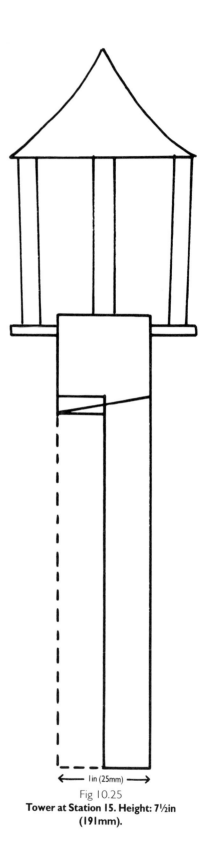

← 1in (25mm) →

Fig 10.25

Tower at Station 15. Height: 7½in (191mm).

Station 15

This is the last of the 18 stations. As you see, this tower is similar to a lantern on a pole. The stem is quite simple: 1in (25mm) in diameter, and finished to a length of 4¾in (121mm). Part off from the lathe, mark on it the position of the bridge deck as usual, and cut out as per the dotted lines on Fig 10.25.

The tower head is basically a short turning 1⅜in (35mm) in diameter at the base, 1½in (38mm) in diameter at the top, and 1¾in (44mm) high. Turn this on the lathe after drilling a ¼in (6mm) deep hole of 1in (25mm) diameter in its base. You should find that your four-prong drive centre will fit this hole if you turn between centres, or you can use the screw chuck as the screw hole will be hidden on assembly.

Cut eight lengths of ³⁄₁₆in (5mm) dowel to the exact height of the head piece (1¾in (44mm)) and glue them vertically around it at 45° intervals. Turn the roof from a disc of oak 2in (51mm) in diameter and 1⅛in (29mm) thick. Also turn a thin ¹⁄₁₆in (2mm) disc 2in (51mm) in diameter, with a 1in (25mm) central hole (I used a scrap of chacahuante for this). Glue together the stem, disc, head and roof.

FINAL ASSEMBLY

You now have a smooth surfaced bridge, a box of completed towers, and assorted fiddly bits (piers, medallions and lamps). It is time to put the whole lot together.

Lay the bridge on its side and glue on the threshold pillars and towers, covering Stations 1 to 9. Check before gluing that when the respective pier is in place (that is, flush with the bottom of the bridge upright), the base of the tower touches the pier surface. If there is a gap, you have two

options: make the transverse cut on the stem a little higher or, after final assembly, fit a little veneer strip around the base of the tower stem. You can see in Fig 10.26 that I did this on the centre tower (No. 5), using a ¼in (6mm) strip of Rio rosewood veneer with the grain running across the strip, so it would bend easily.

When the glue has set, turn the assembly over and add the pillars and towers for Stations 10 to 18. You will find it convenient to hold the assemblies in position with masking tape.

Cut some lengths of veneer into strips ¼in (6mm) wide, matching or approximating the colour of the bridge deck (I use copaiba for the deck and mahogany for the strips). Cut them to fit between the towers and glue them into position with the centre of the strips' top edge flush with the bridge surface. After the glue has dried, you can trim to match the bridge curve with a scalpel. Glue on the medallions above each bridge arch. As you see, mine are glued with their bottom edges at the apex of the arch curves, but you may prefer them equidistant between the veneer strips and the arches.

Glue all the piers into position with their lamp standards. Finally, glue the central MDF arch with its finial into position centrally on the bridge crown and, when the glue has set, fit the four curved MDF rails to butt on to the arch.

Construction is now complete, and you can leave it plain or apply some finish. A glossy surface can be achieved with plastic coating (but be careful it doesn't glue the rotating discs of Tower 14). Alternatively, you can do as I did and apply a single generous coat of Danish oil, with the excess wiped off after five minutes. This darkened all the timbers and showed their grain patterns to advantage.

CHAPTER 11

Starship Moth

This is the starship *Moth*. It is strange to think that only a century ago men questioned the existence of 'flying saucers'; now we have a whole series of them built on, or near, earth. This vessel is one of a series designed by von Lorenz, and built between 2063 and 2083. They are all trading vessels, and none has ever been armed. As we all know, distant commercial trips can be lucrative; the diamonds brought back by *Moth* from Rigel IV actually covered the cost of her building, just in the one voyage.

The designer took advantage, from the start, of the then recent advances in piezzo power extraction. The di-lithium process, developed in the U.S.A. by Roddenberry, has largely been superceded by Rorschach, whose work on crystals triggered the development of quick growth in a vacuum. When this process came on stream commercially in the No. 2 Lunar factory, it was timely for this class of ship, which is powered by a giant quartz monolith with power take-up through crystal rods. The main drive is by ion motor, with five outlet venturis, and altitude control is by means of 16 plasma jets around the rim of the ship.

The Mark I design in this class had rotational controls, using vectored thrust outlets on the sides of four of the five ion venturis. However, it became a matter of pride for the pilots to carry out all manoeuvres using plasma jets only, and vectored thrust was therefore deleted in the later models.

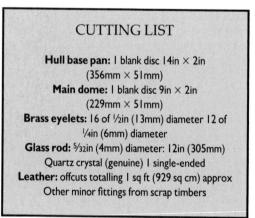

CUTTING LIST

Hull base pan: 1 blank disc 14in × 2in
(356mm × 51mm)
Main dome: 1 blank disc 9in × 2in
(229mm × 51mm)
Brass eyelets: 16 of ½in (13mm) diameter 12 of
¼in (6mm) diameter
Glass rod: ⁵⁄₃₂in (4mm) diameter: 12in (305mm)
Quartz crystal (genuine) 1 single-ended
Leather: offcuts totalling 1 sq ft (929 sq cm) approx
Other minor fittings from scrap timbers

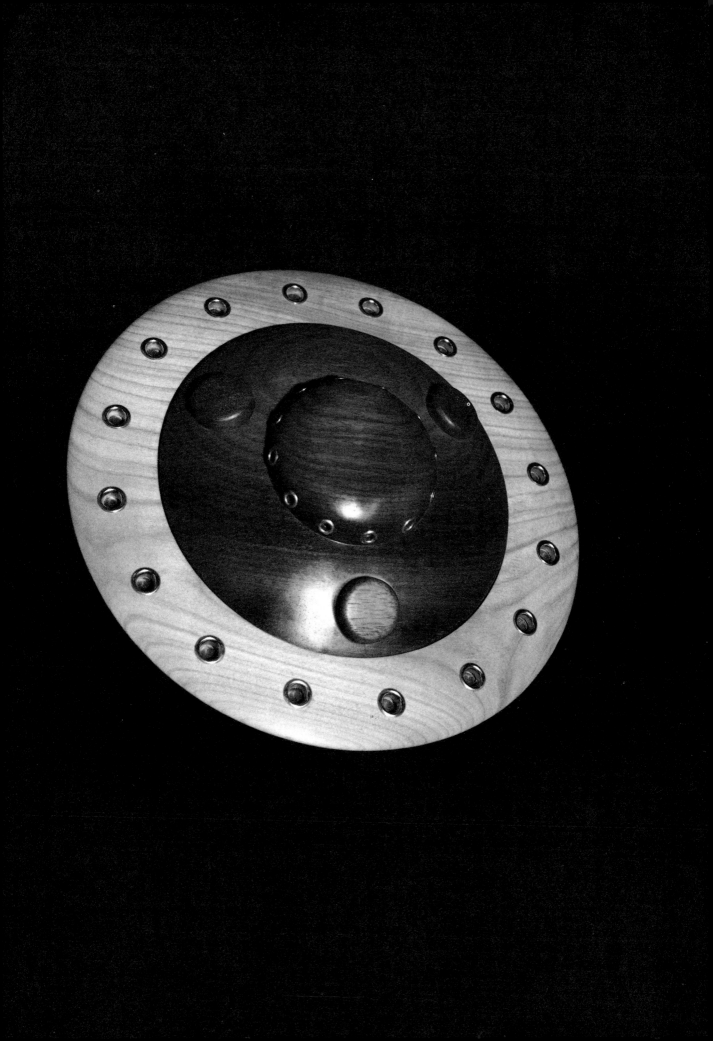

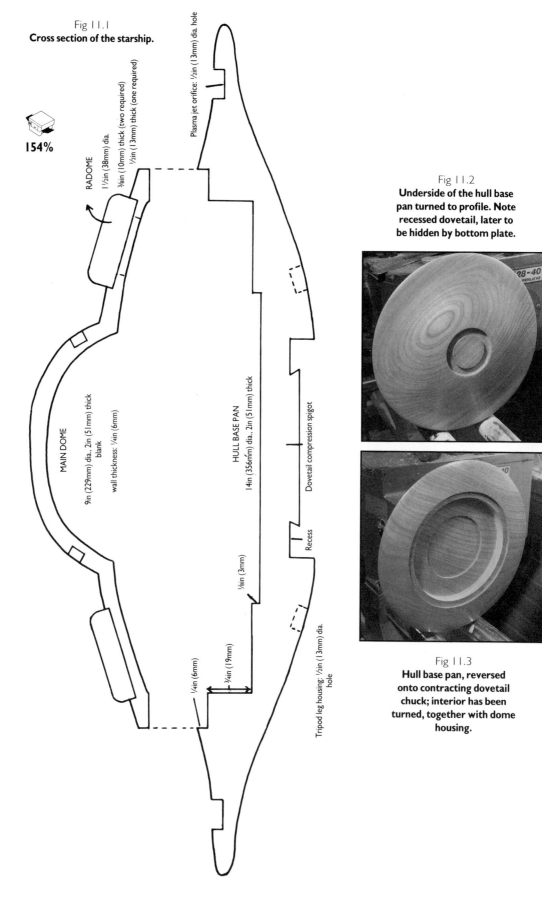

Fig 11.1
Cross section of the starship.

154%

RADOME
1½in (38mm) dia.
⅜in (10mm) thick (two required)
½in (13mm) thick (one required)

Plasma jet orifice: ½in (13mm) dia. hole

MAIN DOME
9in (229mm) dia., 2in (51mm) thick blank
wall thickness: ¼in (6mm)

HULL BASE PAN
14in (356mm) dia., 2in (51mm) thick

Dovetail compression spigot

Recess

⅛in (3mm)

¼in (6mm)
¾in (19mm)

Tripod leg housing: ½in (13mm) dia. hole

Fig 11.2
Underside of the hull base pan turned to profile. Note recessed dovetail, later to be hidden by bottom plate.

Fig 11.3
Hull base pan, reversed onto contracting dovetail chuck; interior has been turned, together with dome housing.

CONSTRUCTION

Hull-base Pan

If you can turn a bowl and a platter, you will have little difficulty in the turning of this project. I used a blank of cherry 14in (356mm) in diameter for the base of the starship. If you do use this size, you need a facility of a 14in (356mm) swing, inboard or outboard, or have a swinging headstock on your lathe to enable this size blank to turn outside the lathe bed. If you do not have one of these on your machine, reduce the scale of the drawings a little.

First mount the blank on your large faceplate. (I use a cast-iron 10in (254mm) diameter faceplate.) Ensure that the retaining screws are within a radius of 4in (102mm) from the centre of the timber (8in (203mm) diameter circle), so that the holes will be turned away when you hollow out the centre of the upper face.

Next, true up the circumference of the disc at low revolutions (I used 250rpm to start with). The weight of the blank may be 20 pounds (9 kilos) or so, depending on the timber you use, and there is quite a bit of vibration when the piece is eccentric. To guide you when you start to shape the underside, hold a pencil to the side of the blank and describe a line ½in (13mm) from the headstock face (and 1½in (38mm) from the face nearest the tailstock, of course). This line is the centre of the thin edge of the saucer, which is ½in (13mm) thick near the rim.

Now, skim the face of the blank to help true it up and reduce vibration, then cut a housing for your large compression dovetail chuck jaws (I used a Multistar with 'D' jaws, which accept a 2½in (64mm) spigot). Note that the dovetail is recessed rather than flush with the surface of the blank, and has a 3½in (89mm) circle cut around it to allow the jaws to enter the timber (see Figs 11.1 and 11.2). The reason for this is that the whole housing is later plugged with a 3½in (89mm) disc, which is the bottom plate, bearing five ion drive venturis.

Before you go any further, it is a good idea to make card or thin ply templates for the hull curves. Photocopy Fig 11.1 at 154% to bring it up to full size, then trace the templates from this, using carbon paper over the card. You will need two for the base (internal and external curves) and two for the dome. They will guide you when shaping the upper and lower radii of each piece. Shape the underside of the base, bringing the curve up to within ¼in (6mm) of the peripheral pencil line. When you are satisfied that the curve

matches the template, sand and finish the surface. You will find that vibration decreases as you remove material, and you may gradually increase speed up to about 600rpm, or whatever lower speed is comfortable for you. Don't forget that at these revolutions, the rim of the disc is moving quite quickly past the tool. I worked out that 14in (356mm) diameter at 600rpm means that a point on the rim is moving at 50 miles per hour (assuming that the figures I dredged up from my schoolboy memory are correct; i.e. 88 feet per second = 60mph).

I found that I achieved a better finish by sanding by hand, rather than using velcro discs on an electric drill. I used 120, 180 and 240 grit papers, with a piece of plastic foam between paper and fingers. My finish was a coat of melamine applied with the blank stationary (sanding sealer is good, too), followed by a final touch with fine sandpaper and a coat of wax polish (a 50/50 mix of beeswax and carnauba).

Remove the workpiece from the faceplate and remount it on your contracting dovetail chuck. True up the face now toward you and mark a 4½in (114mm) radius, 9in (229mm) diameter circle, which is the outer limit of the recessed shelf which will hold the dome of the starship. The depth of this shelf is ¼in (6mm), and its width is ½in (13mm). Next, draw another circle 4in (102mm) radius, 8in (203mm) diameter, which is the inner edge of the dome shelf. Inside the smaller circle, cut away to a depth of ¾in (19mm), using the tool of your choice – gouge or scraper. It is convenient to use a parting tool, pushed straight into the wood, to cut the vertical edge of this recess. Now with the same tool, cut the dome shelf to a depth of ¼in (6mm). Finally, draw a 2½in (64mm) radius, 5in (127mm) diameter circle, and recess this a further ⅛in (3mm) using a square-ended scraper to get the floor of it flat.

Finish the top side of the hull pan with sandpaper and sealer, but wax only the outer rim; that is, outside the 8in (203mm) deep recess. Later you will be fitting and lining the interior, and wax does not accept glues.

Now mark out the locations of the holes which will carry the ½in (13mm) brass eyelets. There are 16 holes at 22½° intervals and with centres 1in (25mm) in from the rim (see Fig 11.4). Produce with ruler and pencil the lines from the centre of the piece out through the centre of each marked 1in (13mm) circle. Stick a piece of masking tape at each location and mark the centres accurately on the tape. You can now drill out to a depth of ¼in

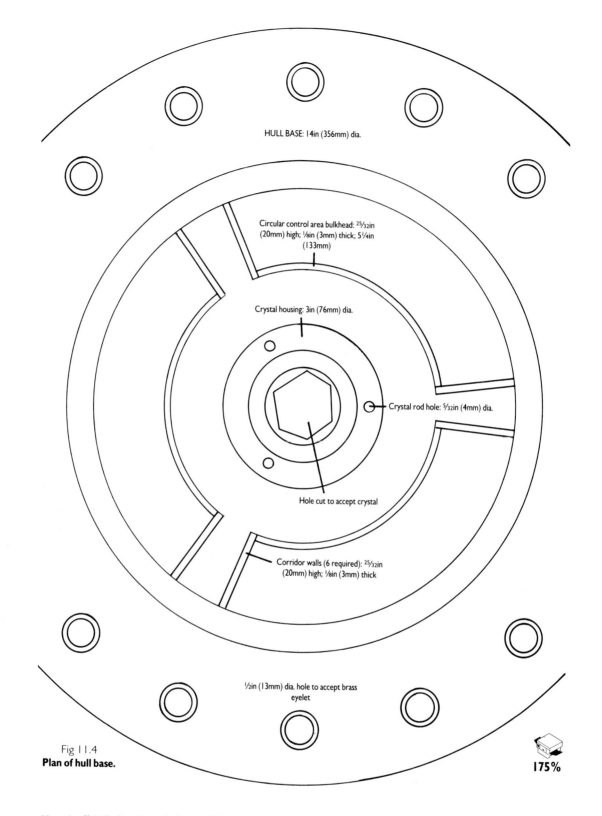

HULL BASE: 14in (356mm) dia.

Circular control area bulkhead: $^{25}/_{32}$in (20mm) high; $^1/_8$in (3mm) thick; $5^1/_4$in (133mm)

Crystal housing: 3in (76mm) dia.

Crystal rod hole: $^5/_{32}$in (4mm) dia.

Hole cut to accept crystal

Corridor walls (6 required): $^{25}/_{32}$in (20mm) high; $^1/_8$in (3mm) thick

$^1/_2$in (13mm) dia. hole to accept brass eyelet

Fig 11.4
Plan of hull base.

175%

(6mm), all 16 holes. Rest the base of the piece on the horizontal table of your bench drill, and use a ½in (13mm) Forstner bit at low revolutions and light pressure.

Now is the point to leave the turned piece alone for a while, preferably in the location where it will live in future. Dependent upon how dry the timber was to start with, there could well be some movement, i.e. distortion of the saucer. It will be

due partly to the drying of the newly exposed timber, and partly to the release of tensions which existed in the wood in its original form.

I used air-dried cherry wood. The blank was not split when I bought it and it has not split subsequently, but its surfaces were less than flat and the diameter across the grain differed from that along the grain by some ¼in (6mm). After the turning described above, I found soon afterwards that the edge wobbled when it turned on the lathe, and two days later the recess of the dome was less than circular (oval by about $\frac{1}{16}$in (2mm)). So leave the piece, if you can, to stabilize, and then remount on the lathe and skim it again to true, especially the dome recess. Incidentally, I found that the padauk, which I used for the dome, was dimensionally much more stable, so you might consider that for the base too.

When you have checked, and if necessary re-skimmed the base, you can remove it from the chuck and complete the 16 plasma jet orifices. Having used a Forstner bit, you will have unsightly depressions at the base of each hole, where the spur of the bit has dug in. Cut from the scrap leather 16 discs $\frac{1}{2}$in (13mm) in diameter, or use a punch, which is quicker. I used a short length of steel tube $\frac{1}{2}$in (13mm) in internal diameter with the rim at one end ground at 45° to give a sharp circular cutter. With a piece of scrap leather on a piece of softwood, a smart tap with a hammer will cut a disc in no time.

Glue the discs into the bases of the holes, suede side down (the smooth finished side of the leather will retain less dust). I used Evostick glue for this. Now set in the brass eyelets with a couple of tiny dabs of epoxy (Araldite Rapid) under the rim of each. Set aside the piece at this stage. Fitting out can proceed after you have made the main dome to fit the recessed shelf you have cut in the base.

Main Dome

I used a 2in (51mm) blank disc of African padauk for this. To fit the recess which you have cut in the base, you need a blank slightly larger than 9in (229mm), as you will lose a little in the truing. If you can get only an exact 9in (229mm) diameter blank in your chosen timber, then it is best to reverse the order of manufacture. Make the dome first, then cut the base to fit it afterwards.

In fact I could only obtain a disc of the required thickness with a larger diameter 11in (279mm), so my first job was then to remove (cut off with a parting tool) a 1in (25mm) wide ring from the blank. I will have a use for that ring one day. ('Ho-ho', says my wife, who knows that my workshop has been stuffed for 30 years with things which might come in handy one day!)

Mount the disc on your faceplate, making sure that the screws are outside the middle 4in (102mm) diameter that will form the raised centre of the dome. I drilled for my screws on a circle of 7in (178mm) diameter (1in (25mm) in from the rim) and the holes were turned away later.

Make sure you have your two templates. For the underside I actually used a single template the full 9in (229mm) width, as you see from Fig 11.5. It is slightly easier to use than one which covers the radius only, unless you mark the centre point of the depression which you will cut in the underside.

True the rim and face of the blank at fairly low revolutions (although this blank is not as heavy as the 14in (356mm) cherry blank, despite the greater specific gravity of the padauk (cherry is SG 0.58; African padauk is 0.72).

Mark a 4in (102mm) radius, 8in (203mm) diameter circle, which is the inner limit of the flat under-rim of the dome, and start hollowing within that circle. Use gouge and/or scraper as you prefer (I did most of this section with a heavy duty 1½in (38mm) round-nosed scraper). Check the curvature as you go, using the template. Finish the underside by sanding and wax polishing. I found that the padauk did not need a sanding sealer.

Fig 11.5
Underside of dome finished, with card template to check curves.

Remove the workpiece from the faceplate in order to turn and finish the upper surface of the dome. You need to hold the piece, with its hollow underside, on the lathe with the unworked face toward the tailstock. You can use a glue chuck, which is a plain disc of timber or plywood, with the piece held on by the underside of the rim with hot-melt glue. You may use paper, a ring of thick brown wrapping paper. If you use paper, you will need to clean up the rim after you have separated the disc and dome with a knife. I was not happy about using either of those methods as there was a lot of mass in the piece. My answer was to make a wood chuck. This was simply a 12in (305mm) disc of ¾in (19mm) thick ply, as shown in Fig 11.6. Cut

Fig 11.6
12in (305mm) chuck plate turned from ¾in (19mm) ply, recessed on its reverse to accept expansion dovetail chuck jaws, and recessed on its face to accept rim of dome.

Fig 11.7
Dome mounted on plywood chuck plate; at this stage it is held by tailstock bearing on a scrap disc of timber.

a disc from sheet ply and mount it on your screw chuck. It does not matter if the screw goes right through the ply. True up the rim, and cut a housing for your expanding dovetail chuck jaws (I used a Multistar with 'D' jaws again). Then reverse the piece onto the dovetail chuck and cut a housing of 9in (229mm) external diameter, with a width of, say, 1in (25mm), and a depth of ¼in (6mm).

Make the diameter a little under 9in (229mm) to start with, then enlarge it exactly to fit the already

turned rim of the dome piece. (You may have turned it in such a way as to yield a rim a little less than 9in (229mm), and you need a reasonably good fit.) Now drill a couple of holes in the disc so that you can, with stick or finger, push off the finished turning from the ply chuck if it is tightly held.

Now mount the partly worked dome on to the disc, base toward headstock. Bring up your tailstock, but don't let its point pierce the timber. Place a piece of scrap wood between, to avoid marking the top of the dome. (If you do make an indentation, don't worry; you can always stick a navigation light on it later!) If the workpiece rotates in the plywood chuck, you can increase the pressure of the tailstock ram just a little. If you are worried about marking the dome with the scrap wood, put some masking tape over the dome centre (*see* Fig 11.7).

You can now proceed to shape almost the whole of the dome's top surface, except for the little bit covered by the scrap timber. Use your card template to check curvature; if you do this accurately, you will end up with a dome thickness of ¼in (6mm). If you get worried, then stop, retract the tailstock ram to release the piece, and check its thickness with callipers or fingers. If the depth of the retaining groove in the plywood chuck is greater than the required thickness of the dome rim, don't hesitate to shove your narrow round-nosed scraper into the ply in order to achieve what you want – but make sure that you leave enough to locate the workpiece!

Sand and polish the outer part of the dome now, before you go on to the centre. Shape the exterior of the raised centre as much as possible, then stop the lathe and fix the workpiece on to the plywood chuck with bits of masking tape all round. Now withdraw the tailstock completely and bring the tool rest across the lathe bed to finish the shaping at the top of the dome. I used a heavy duty square-ended scraper for this, only a small part of which was in contact with the curve at any one moment. Sand, polish and then, as shown in Fig 11.8, drill the portholes in the central dome wall. There are 12 holes, at 30° intervals, and they do not need to go right through the wood. Use your index device to mark and drill. If you do not have one, then cut a paper circle with a 4in (102mm) hole at its centre. Mark the paper with 12 equal divisions and slip it over the dome, then mark off in line with the divisions on the paper. Brass eyelets of nominal ¼in (6mm) size actually need a 0.256in (6.5mm) hole, so it is best to use a 0.275in (7mm) drill. The underside of the eyelet rims can

Fig 11.8
Drilling dome portholes ¼in (6mm) to accept brass eyelets.

then seat themselves quite well on the curve of the dome. Glue with epoxy, as you did with the plasma jet orifices.

Radomes

The final part of the dome assembly is to make and fit the three radomes, which each serve a 120° arc. You will find that, on its own, the dome is rather difficult to lift off the starship base. This is solved by making one of the radomes removable, and drilling a finger hole below it. The removable one is a little thicker than the other two, for better grip. The other two are glued permanently in place. Mount a scrap piece of padauk (or whichever timber matches the one you have used for your dome) 2in × 2in × 3in (51mm × 51mm × 76mm) approximately, with the grain across the piece. True the face, and turn the piece to a diameter of 1½in (38mm). Sand and polish the face and sides, and part off to give a thickness of ⅜in (10mm). Then make another one exactly the same, and finally the removable one, finishing its thickness at ½in (13mm) (see Fig 11.1).

Fig 11.9
Bottom plate assembly.

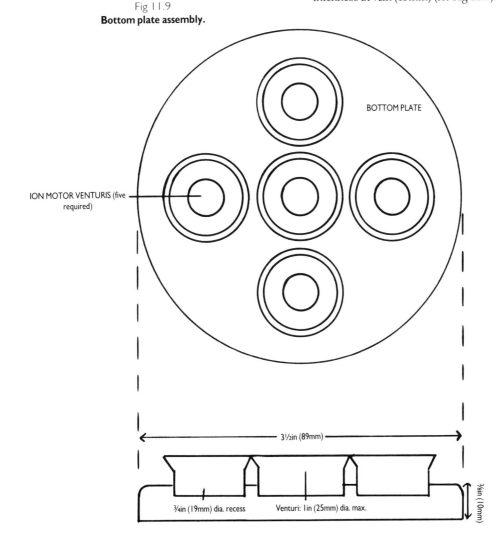

BOTTOM PLATE

ION MOTOR VENTURIS (five required)

3½in (89mm)

⅜in (10mm)

¾in (19mm) dia. recess   Venturi: 1in (25mm) dia. max.

Fig 11.10
Bottom plate, turned to fit base hole and to cover the recessed dovetail. Four of the five ion motor venturis in position.

The recesses in the dome, to accept these radomes, were made with a 1½in (38mm) Forstner bit, with the workpiece on the flat table of the bench drill, inclined to the left at an angle of 20° from the horizontal. I was a bit worried about holding the dome still on the steel table, and I was right, as it slips very easily. The solution was a scrap piece of carpeting, rubberized on the underside, placed between steel table and wooden dome. You could use a clamp, but I was afraid of cracking the dome, and so held it in position with my hand whilst bringing down the drill bit, turning at low revolutions (160rpm) to a depth stopped at ⅛in (3mm).

In two of these depressions glue the thinner radomes. For the third, use a 1in (25mm) Forstner bit, and drill within the 1½in (38mm) depression, right through. Use a *very* gentle pressure on the drill, as you run the risk of splitting the timber as the drill breaks through to the underside. Leave the drill table at 20° ready for the holes to accept the tripod legs.

Bottom Plate

This is a disc of timber ⅜in (10mm) thick, with a diameter of 3½in (89mm), to fit inside the recess at the base of the starship, covering the dovetail spigot (*see* Fig 11.9). The plate itself was turned on the screwchuck from a scrap piece of timber just over the required diameter. It was then trued on face and edge, and its rim was rounded off. Use callipers to measure the diameter as you turn. For safety, you might care to stop the lathe, move the tool rest, and bring up the starship's base to the plate to check the fit. It does not need to be a tight fit, as the plate will be glued into position (unless you are worried about further distortion of the base, in which case, a push fit only will allow

access for later re-skimming of the housing shelf for the dome). Part off the disc and mark and drill the five depressions, each ¾in (19mm) in diameter and ⅛in (3mm) deep, to accept the five ion motor venturis. These can be turned either in the plain bore of your chuck in compression mode, or between centres. I used a small skew chisel point to recess the face a little. Glue the venturis into position and, whilst the glue is drying, you can turn the three tripod legs.

Tripod Legs and Pads

As you see from Fig 11.11, these are quite simple turnings between centres. Each is 2⅜in (60mm) long with three sections of ²⁵⁄₃₂in (20mm), each with a different diameter: ½in (13mm) at the top ¹¹⁄₃₂in (9mm) at the centre, and ⁹⁄₃₂in (7mm) at the bottom. The ends may be parted off square. I used oak for the legs, with the grain running lengthwise, but you will use the timber of your choice.

The three pads are hemispheres, with a diameter of 1⅛in (29mm), and were made of padauk. Turn a piece of your chosen timber 1¼in (32mm) square and about 5in (127mm) long, between centres, to a

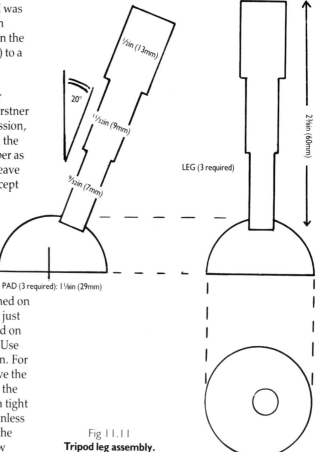

Fig 11.11
Tripod leg assembly.

cylinder. Reduce 2in (51mm) of one end to a diameter to fit inside the bore of your contracting chuck. (I turned this spigot end to ¾in (19mm), to be held in the ¾in (19mm) mini jaws of the Multistar.)

As shown in Fig 11.12, with the timber in the jaws of the chuck, withdraw the tailstock and round off, then sand and polish the end of the timber to give a hemisphere of the required diameter. Part off, and make two more identical pieces. These three pads must now be drilled with a ⁹⁄₃₂in (7mm) bit to accept the legs. The holes are drilled at 20° off the vertical, and your drill table should still be set at this angle. To make the holes uniform, I made a little jig for this operation – just a strip of

scrap timber with a 'V' cut out of one side (to locate the pad), and nailed onto a small sheet of ply which was held on the drill table with a clamp. It was located so that the spur of the drill entered ¼in (6mm) from the centre top of the pad. Drill the holes to a depth of about ⅛in (3mm) or so – it is not critical, as long as they are all the same depth. Glue the legs into position on the pads. As you see from Fig. 11.13, I drew the angle on a scrap piece of timber, and chocked the leg at the correct angle, whilst the glue set (10 minutes with epoxy).

Again using the piece of rubberized carpet – or something similar – as a pad, drill the three holes in the base of the starship pan to accept the tops of

Fig 11.12
Parting off one of three tripod leg pads.

Fig 11.13
Tripod legs with pads.
Note: one is being supported by scrap block at correct angle whilst glue dries.

Fig 11.14
Underside of hull, with hydraulic retracting legs in position.

the tripod legs, using a ½in (13mm) drill bit. Leave the drill table at 20° and mark the three positions for drilling at 120° intervals, 2¾in (70mm) from the centre of the workpiece. Set the drill stop to give a depth of ¼in (6mm). With the starship base upside down, glue in the tripod leg/pad assemblies and the bottom plate assembly (*see* Fig 11.14).

You have now finished the hull and all its external fittings.

FITTING OUT

Piezzo Crystal and Housing

The crystal is a real one – a single-ended natural quartz crystal with one end cut flat with a diamond saw. You can buy them with the end already cut and polished, from most lapidary or rockhound shops, or else craft fair exhibitors who deal in stones. These single-ended crystals are much cheaper than the double-ended ones (i.e. facets coming to a point at both ends), as the latter are in demand for crystal healing purposes. At the time of writing, a suitable crystal costs about half what you would have to pay for the timber blank of the starship dome.

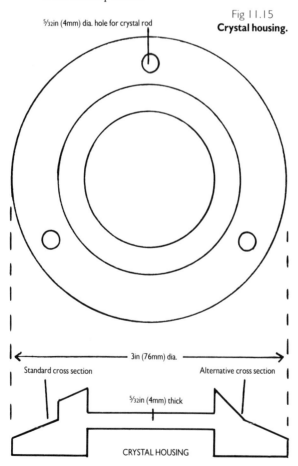

⁵⁄₃₂in (4mm) dia. hole for crystal rod

Fig 11.15
Crystal housing.

3in (76mm) dia.

Standard cross section

Alternative cross section

⁵⁄₃₂in (4mm) thick

CRYSTAL HOUSING

Measure across the flats and widest points of your crystal, to determine the minimum diameter of the centre of the housing you will now need to turn for it. The centre (thin) section of the housing shown in Fig 11.15 is 1½in (38mm) in diameter, and the piece can be turned quite easily on a screw chuck, reversing the piece halfway to hollow the underside. Note that Fig 11.15 shows two alternative cross sections for the wall. Make the thin centre about ⁵⁄₃₂in (4mm) thick (it is an advantage to use a soft timber; I used a piece of lime, which can be cut easily in any direction).

Place the base of the crystal in the centre of the housing and draw round it with a pencil. You can now cut out the waste. You may find it easiest to cut away most of it with a fine blade on the scroll saw, and just trim the six-sided hole with a scalpel (*see* Fig 11.4). Drill three holes (*see* Fig 11.15) at 120° intervals around the rim of the housing to accept the crystal rods.

The rods are of glass: ⁵⁄₃₂in (4mm) diameter glass rod. You can use borosilicate laboratory glass (pyrex type) or plain lead glass, which has a lower melting point and can be bent over the flame of a domestic gas cooker hob. I used borosilicate rod, which bends in the flame of a butane gas torch such as is used for stripping paint.

Hold the rod with its end in the hottest part of the flame (just beyond the point of the centre core of the flame) until it glows and becomes rounded. Then apply the flame 1in (25mm) along the rod. In a few seconds it will glow, and bend under its own weight. You can help it along with steel tweezers. You need 1in (25mm) at right angles to a 2⅛in (54mm) stalk. When you have achieved a right angle, remove the rod from the flame and lean it against a block of wood so that it cools for a minute or so in the air (not with the hottest part on

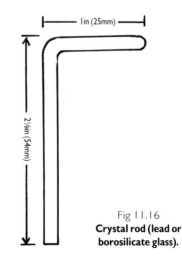

1in (25mm)

2⅛in (54mm)

Fig 11.16
Crystal rod (lead or borosilicate glass).

Fig 11.17
**Main deck: control centre complete with
crystal and receptor rods, plus three
compartments, all lined in plum suede
(including a furnished crew's dormitory).**

the wood). Do not roll the end on wood to round
it as the hot glass will pick up scorched black ash.
Measure 2⅛in (54mm) from the bend, score that
point with a fine triangular file, and you can snap
off the piece with your fingers. There is no need to
round off the snapped end, as it will be within the
mount. Make two more rods in the same way.

To represent the control knobs around the
housing, I used a 0.02in (0.5mm) drill in a pin
chuck to drill seven holes between each of the
rods, and inserted glass-headed dressmaking pins
in different colours. The pattern and sequence is
up to you, but you will need to snip off with pliers
about half the steel shank of each pin so that the
glass head is flush with the timber. Glue the
housing into position centrally in the hull base,
and push a disc of leather inside it to cushion the
crystal.

Main Bulkheads
These walls are arranged around the central
control area, and comprise a ring, pierced at 120°
intervals to give three corridors, each with
doorways into the three living areas. The ring and
six short walls are all ²⁵⁄₃₂in (20mm) high and ⅛in
(3mm) thick.

To turn the circular bulkhead, mount a disc of
timber ²⁵⁄₃₂in (20mm) thick or more and 5¼in
(133mm) or more in diameter, on your large screw
chuck. True the periphery and the face, and mark
with a parting tool the internal diameter of the
ring which you will part off. This diameter should
match that of the depression 5in (127mm) in
diameter, which you cut earlier in the floor of the
starship. Skim the rim of the disc until you have
reached the required wall thickness of ⅛in (3mm);
then, with the tool rest back at right angles to the
lathe bed, push in your parting tool to create the
ring. Open up the groove a little on the side
nearest the centre to give room for the tool so that
it will not bind, and go in until you have parted off
the ring completely. If the blank disc is thicker
than ²⁵⁄₃₂in (20mm), you can go in, say, just ⅞in
(22mm), then move the rest to a position parallel
to the lathe bed, and part off the required ²⁵⁄₃₂in
(20mm) width.

Prepare some strips of timber of the same type as
your circular wall, ²⁵⁄₃₂in × ⅛in (20mm × 30mm)
in cross section. Cut six lengths 1½in (38mm) for
the corridor walls, and cut out doorways centrally
in each, ⅜in (10mm) wide and ½in (13mm) high.

Mark the positions of the walls on the base of the living quarters, and cut segments of the ring wall to fit. Without the corridor walls in position, there is a gap ¾in (19mm) between the ends of the curved segments. The walls align with the radii lines, so the gap between a pair of short walls is slightly larger at the rim than at the joins with the circular wall. Glue all bulkheads into position.

You can now line all compartments. I used leather for this, cut from offcuts. All floor sections and the outer walls are in plum-coloured leather with the suede side showing (i.e. smooth finished side glued to the wood). The inside vertical face of the circular wall is lined in black suede.

The leather is cut easily using a scalpel (Swann-Morton No. 3 handle, No. 10A blade) and a steel ruler for the straight edges. I made a thin card template to fit each section first (rather than tracing the shapes from the drawings, from which I may have deviated slightly). I then cut out the leather by taping the correctly shaped template over it and cutting around it. This may seem tedious, but it avoids any wastage of leather. Minor errors in length can usually be overcome by the natural stretch of the leather, but don't bank on it. Check your leather for stretch first. My plum suede was very pliable, but the black had no more stretch than cardboard, and had to be cut accurately.

Fig 11.18
Cargo deck (removable).

125%

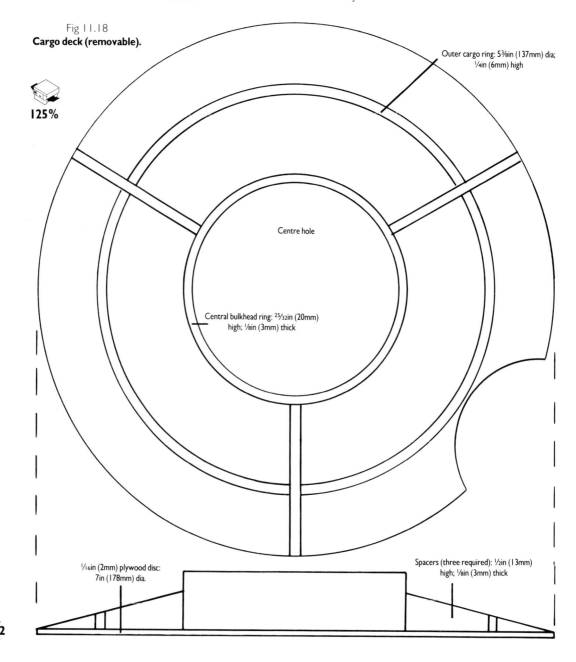

Outer cargo ring: 5⅜in (137mm) dia; ¼in (6mm) high

Centre hole

Central bulkhead ring: ²⁵⁄₃₂in (20mm) high; ⅛in (3mm) thick

¹⁄₁₆in (2mm) plywood disc: 7in (178mm) dia.

Spacers (three required): ½in (13mm) high; ⅛in (3mm) thick

Glue the pieces of leather in separately, using Evostik on the underside (its smooth surface) only. None is needed on the wood. Once again in this series of projects, I have given only the minimum of furnishings so as to give you plenty of scope for your own personalized interiors. I have just made bunks and cupboards from small scraps of wood for the crew's dormitory, which is in Green Sector. Each of the three sectors of accommodation is identified by a different coloured light: red, white and green. These are indicated by glass cabochons glued to the relative black wall of the control area. These cabochons are marketed by Fimo modelling clay, and are accessories for their costume jewellery sets. You can get them from craft supply shops.

Cargo Deck

This is an optional extra, and you may care to dispense with it in order to give free view of the more interesting-looking living quarters. However, every craft of this class has a cargo area; it is what the vessel is for. These ships were not built as bulk carriers, but haul only high-value cargoes: rare earths, gold, platinum, precious gems and organic medicines, all of which take up relatively little space.

The deck is basically a disc 7in (178mm) in diamter, cut from a sheet of $\frac{1}{16}$in (2mm) plywood. There is a 2$\frac{3}{4}$in (70mm) diameter central hole, so the disc fits around the quartz crystal with its rod and housing. Note that there is another cut-out; a curved bite from the rim, which can be aligned with the finger hole under no. 3 radome.

In the same way as you turned the circular bulkhead for the living quarters, turn and part off another ring for the cargo deck central bulkhead, from a disc with minimum dimensions of 3$\frac{1}{8}$in (79mm) diameter and $\frac{25}{32}$in (20mm) thick. The interior diameter of the ring should match the 2$\frac{3}{4}$in (70mm) diameter of the hole at the deck's centre.

There are three triangular hold dividers, but note that their highest point is $\frac{1}{2}$in (13mm) maximum. If you exceed this, the dome will not seat on its rim. The ring bulkhead is okay, as it fits inside the raised centre of the dome.

I have cut another ring 5$\frac{3}{8}$in (137mm) in diameter, which further divides the area. The purpose of this is to retain cargo should it be moved by centrifugal force. The ring is only $\frac{1}{4}$in (6mm) high and could, if you wished, be made from bent strip wood.

The whole surface and the outside of the ring bulkhead was then lined with black suede. Again, each piece was cut according to a card template which was cut to fit first. You will find that most – if not all – black leathers are chrome tanned, and the cut edge shows as light grey. When you have lined the cargo area, it is neater if you paint these edges (and the inner side of the circular bulkhead) with black dye.

Make up cargo boxes and crates from small scraps of wood, and put the larger ones near the centre so the dome seats well.

I leave you now, to complete your fitting out.

Fig 11.19
Completed vessel with dome removed to show cargo deck in place.

Fig 11.20
Completed vessel with dome removed.

CHAPTER 12

Nautilus

I have read Jules Verne's *20,000 Leagues under the Sea* several times, and when the idea of turning a model submarine came to my mind, the *Nautilus* seemed to be the natural prototype. Right from the start of the design, I wanted to avoid the usual cylindrical shape, and decided to make a hull which was flattened to a horizontal oval in its cross section. My ideas were to hint at the shape of a skate (or rather a halibut, which is truly deep-sea pelagic), to hint at Victorian engineering, and to provide more comfort for the crew than I found when I went aboard a real submersible.

I would class this project as the most difficult of all those in this book, so far as actual turning is concerned. The hull is formed from two slices of a hollow cigar which is made up from 10 sections (of which eight are hollow rings) glued together. If you prefer to simplify the idea, you could leave the whole thing solid, in which case you might reduce the scale, as the hull would be quite heavy. Alternatively, you could go as far as the hollowing out, but fit out the exterior only, or just halve the turned hull longitudinally, in which case you would not need a centre horizontal frame.

The hull is not the only piece of turning; there are various other parts to be made on the lathe, including the engine and external propulsion unit.

The fitting out of the hull is quite good fun, and there is ample scope for your own ideas, as I have assigned only the minimum of furnishings for each compartment. All compartments, except for the engine room at the stern, are lined in leather with the suede side up, to make it comfortable.

I could not omit one particular feature which stuck in my mind – a large pipe organ on which Captain Nemo played Bach. As you see from Fig 12.17, this is amidships, so the sound will reverberate in the conning tower.

CUTTING LIST

Hull: 1¹³⁄₁₆in (46mm) thick ash:
6in × 36in (152mm × 914mm)
for hull sections B C D E F G
4in × 18in (102mm × 457mm)
for hull sections A H I J and the conning tower
Frame: ³⁄₈in × 6³⁄₈in × 24in long
(10mm × 162mm × 610mm) oak
(this is enough for the cradle too)
Other fittings: wooden fittings from scrap
10 brass eyelets ½in (13mm) in diameter
8 brass eyelets ¼in (6mm) in diameter
1 roll motor vehicle trim strip ⅛in (3mm) wide
Leather offcuts to 1 sq ft (929 sq cm) approx

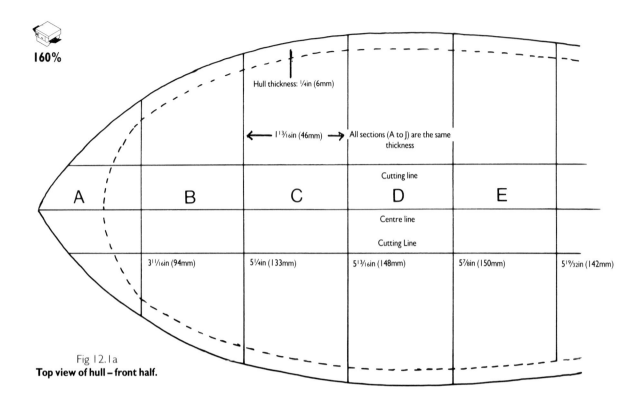

160%

Hull thickness: ¼in (6mm)

← 1¹³⁄₁₆in (46mm) → All sections (A to J) are the same thickness

Cutting line

| A | B | C | D | E |

Centre line

Cutting Line

3¹¹⁄₁₆in (94mm)   5¼in (133mm)   5¹³⁄₁₆in (148mm)   5⅞in (150mm)   5¹⁹⁄₃₂in (142mm)

Fig 12.1a
Top view of hull – front half.

CONSTRUCTION

Hull

There are 10 sections, marked A to J, all of discs or rings of the same thickness. I purchased ash which, when planed, finished at 1¹³⁄₁₆in (46mm) thick. Don't worry if you cannot match this. Get the nearest you can to that thickness, and mark new lines on your hull drawing to correspond to the joints you will achieve with your particular timber thickness. Then carefully measure the actual diameter of the joint (port to starboard). I have marked Fig 12.1 with the diameter at each joint, as you will later need to finish the rings on the lathe to those measurements. There is another point to watch, before you start. It is important to achieve the same grain direction in each of the 10 pieces. As you can see in Fig 12.4, the grain gives the appearance of the shell having been carved from a solid piece of timber. Indeed, as an alternative to ring construction, you can hollow out the hull from one piece of wood, if you can get a 6in × 6in (152mm × 152mm) cross section which is dry and stable. Cut out the 10 blanks from the plank timber, marking them on their flat faces as you go with their sequential letter, preferably with a bold felt-tip for ease of identification.

Disc A (the nose or bow piece) should have, at its junction with piece B, a diameter of 3¹¹⁄₁₆in

(94mm). Add a little for safety (I allowed ⁵⁄₃₂in (4mm) on all diameters), so cut a disc of 3²⁷⁄₃₂in (98mm) and mark the centre clearly with the point of your compasses when you draw the circle on the wood.

Disc B must be larger and, as you see from Fig 12.1 (a), will finish with a diameter of 5¼in (133mm) at its junction with disc C, so cut the blank disc B at a 5⅜in (137mm) diameter. Continue in this way until you have 10 discs, A to J, with the following diameters:

A – 3²⁷⁄₃₂in (98mm); B – 5⅜in (137mm); C – 6in (152mm); D – 6¹⁄₁₆in (154mm); E – 5¾in (146mm); F – 5¾in (146mm); G – 5³⁄₁₆in (132mm); H – 4⁵⁄₁₆in (109mm); I – 3⅛in (79mm); J – 1¹³⁄₁₆in (46mm).

All discs will have their centres marked, and have an identifying letter.

If you use a 6in (152mm) plank for the largest discs, and a 4in (102mm) plank for the smaller discs, check when you cut the first disc from the smaller plank that the grain will match. For example, blank G, cut from the 6in (152mm) plank, will match F, but blank H, cut from the 4in (102mm) plank, may not match, because it may be the wrong way round. If this is the case, just reverse it and mark its identifying letter on the

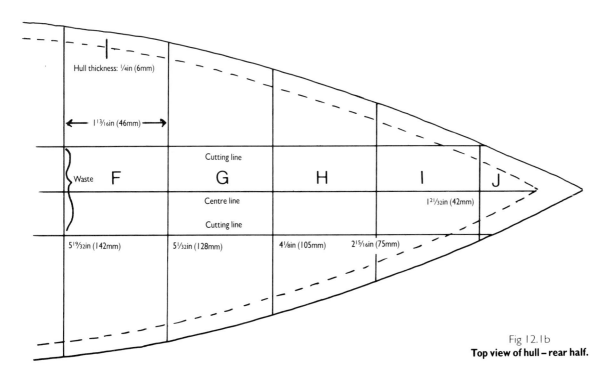

Fig 12.1b
Top view of hull – rear half.

other side; if you have to reverse this one, then do the same with blanks A, I and J.

Now that you have 10 discs (or a number commensurate with your timber thickness), mount disc A the wrong way round (i.e. with the marked side toward the tailstock) onto a screw chuck. True up the disc and cut a dovetail for a compression chuck (I used a Multistar with 'C' jaws). Reverse the piece onto the dovetail chuck and partially hollow out to a depth of about 1in (25mm). Ensure that the diameter nearest the tailstock finishes at 3¹¹⁄₁₆in (94mm). I suggest that you leave a wall thickness of ⁵⁄₁₆in (8mm). Do not narrow this piece down to a point, but leave it as shown in Fig 12.2, a little larger than the chuck jaws, as it will later have to carry another five rings of timber.

Now remove chuck and hull section A (still mounted) from the lathe, and mount disc B on a screw chuck with the marked face toward the headstock. Using callipers to check the diameters of both faces, and a cardboard template for the edge shape, finish the periphery of the piece to a diameter of 3¹¹⁄₁₆in (94mm) on the headstock face, and 5¼in (133mm) on the face nearest the tailstock.

Now, with the tool rest at right angles to the lathe

bed, part off a ring, looking along the parting tool to direct it at the same angle as the side of the disc. Try for a wall thickness of ⁵⁄₁₆in (8mm), but err on the thicker side as you will true the interior later.

Proceed in the same way with discs C, D and E. The next step is to glue discs A to E together in sequence, but first check the reach of the tool you will use to skim the interior to achieve a constant wall thickness of ¼in (6mm). I do not have a

Fig 12.2
First section of hull (bows), turned on compression chuck.

Stewart Hooker, and used a side-cutting scraper with a short handle. Having turned a new, long and strong handle for it, I still felt comfortable only when the scraper over-reached the supporting tool rest by 6in (152mm); that is, just enough to cope with pieces A to D. If you feel the same, just glue A, B, C and D together with white PVA glue, ensuring that the grain patterns all match, and doing your best to achieve concentricity to avoid wobble when you turn the composite piece later. Apply a weight on top and leave overnight if possible.

Meanwhile, you can proceed with the second half of the hull shell, involving discs F to J. If you do not have, or do not wish to use, a revolving headstock, it is easier to part off a ring from a disc when the direction of cut is slightly left to right, rather than reaching across to cut outward. Consequently, the discs for the stern half should be mounted with the marked side reversed, i.e. facing the tailstock. This will preserve continuity of grain pattern.

Reverse disc J onto a compression chuck (after you have removed that chuck from your glued up bow shell) and, leaving plenty of thickness, finish the diameter furthest from the chuck to $1^{21}/_{32}$in (42mm), to match ring I. Glue up G, H, I and J, whilst the glue is drying (again under a weight), you can go back to the front half of the shell.

Mount the composite shell, comprising pieces A, B, C and D, on your contracting dovetail chuck and, at low revolutions (300–500rpm) and taking *light* cuts, true up the interior of the piece with your side-cutting scraper. You do not need to sand and finish the interior at this stage; it is easier to sand after the two shells have been cut from the whole turning. Indeed, if you intend to fit out the interior, you must not use any wax on the interior at all. You may now remove the piece from the lathe, and glue on ring E. When the glue is dry, finish shaping the interior again, when your tool will not have to enter more than 2in (51mm) (*see* Fig 12.3).

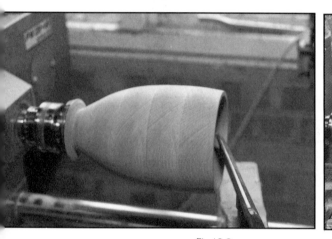

Fig 12.3

Front five sections of hull glued up, with interior being skimmed.

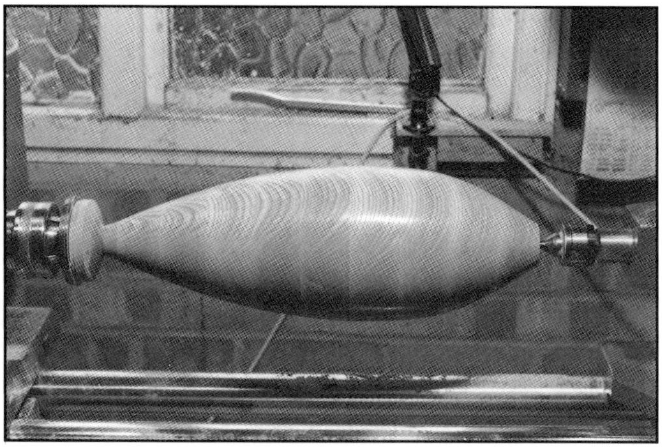

Mount disc F on your screw chuck in this way, and finish to a diameter of $5^{19}/_{32}$in (142mm) on the tailstock side, and $5^{1}/_{32}$in (128mm) on the headstock side. Then part off a ring, again with a wall thickness of $5/_{16}$in (8mm). When reversed, the $5^{19}/_{32}$in (142mm) diameter will match ring E. Similarly, cut rings from discs G, H and I to the dimensions shown in Fig 12.1 (b).

Treat disc J in the same way as disc A. Mount it on a screw chuck first, to cut a compression dovetail. Your drilled hole for the chuck screw can go right through the piece, as the hole may be used later for centring onto your revolving tailstock centre, once you have finished the exterior of the completely assembled shell.

Fig 12.4

Hull, with curves refined at bows and stern; sanded and sealed.

Mount the rear half shell pieces G. H, I and J on your compression chuck and true the interior in the same way as the front half, described above. Then add ring F and, after the glue is dry, refinish as before.

Check that the rims of the two half shells are true and flat. They may now be glued together, ensuring again that the grain patterns match. You may use the lathe itself as a cramp to hold the two pieces together, achieving gentle pressure with the tailstock wheel.

When the glue is dry, you may true up the exterior of the piece, which now resembles an airship in shape. Use low revolutions to start with, and take

Fig 12.5
**Using tool rest to mark longitudinal
centre point.**

light cuts with a small-nosed tool. Reduce the bow and stern pieces (A and J) in diameter, as shown in Fig 12.4, sand with your usual series of grits (I use 120, 180, 240 and 400 grit velcro discs) and apply a coat of sanding sealer or melamine.

Before removing the piece from the lathe, mark the longitudinal centre line and the two parallel lines which mark the cuts you will make to create the hull halves. It is difficult to draw a straight line on a complex curve, and I found it easiest to use the tool rest as a guide.

Disconnect your lathe from the mains for safety, and lock your headstock spindle with the most prominent and attractive side grain of the wood uppermost. Set the height of your tool rest to the centre of the workpiece (i.e. the height of the tailstock point which carries one end of the turned piece). Now move the tool rest and its mounting along the lathe bed, keeping the rest abutting the timber and marking the centre line with a pencil as

you go (*see* Fig 12.5). Do the same with the cutting lines, parallel to the centre line, and 1in (25mm) above and below it. If the post of the tool rest is not long enough to rise to the height of the top line, then clamp a piece of strip timber to it.

When plotting the hull curves, I tried several variations of the final hull cross section and found that the most pleasing was the one achieved by a central longitudinal cutout of 2in (51mm), that is 1in (25mm) either side of the centre line. This gives a maximum external height of the hull (including the frame) of $3^{15}/_{16}$in (100mm), which allows plenty of room for fitting out the lower hull shell.

Next comes the bit that made me a little nervous – cutting the shells using the band saw. The upper part of the cut may be kept accurate because you can see the blade cutting along the line; unseen, however, is the bottom cut, which could be slicing away more shell than you require to be removed!

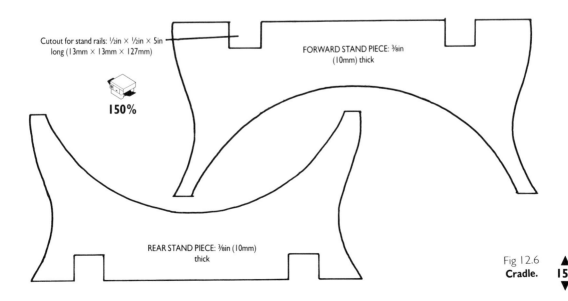

Cutout for stand rails: $^{1}/_{2}$in × $^{1}/_{2}$in × 5in
long (13mm × 13mm × 127mm)

150%

FORWARD STAND PIECE: $^{3}/_{8}$in
(10mm) thick

REAR STAND PIECE: $^{3}/_{8}$in (10mm)
thick

Fig 12.6
Cradle.

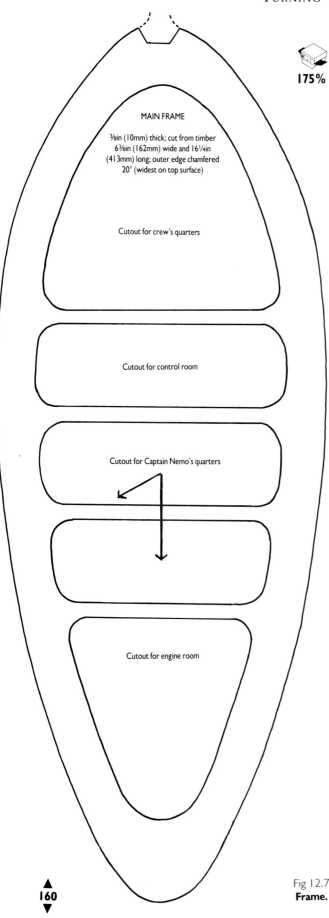

175%

MAIN FRAME

⅜in (10mm) thick; cut from timber
6⅜in (162mm) wide and 16¼in
(413mm) long; outer edge chamfered
20° (widest on top surface)

Cutout for crew's quarters

Cutout for control room

Cutout for Captain Nemo's quarters

Cutout for engine room

There are several ways round this (or you may have your own preferred method). You can cut by hand with a tenon saw, doing each side separately. You can glue a cradle onto the centre section, which is 2in (51mm) wide, keeping the base of the cradle flat to slide smoothly over the band saw table. You can first band saw along the centre line, then trim each half shell separately, following just outside the final cut line at the top of the shell, whilst keeping the bottom edge of the shell clear of the blade.

I used the last alternative and, of course, found that the cut edges were not flat in either direction. This is not a problem: glue two sheets of coarse alox abrasive paper onto a sheet of ¾in (19mm) or thicker MDF board. Place the half shell, cut side down, on the paper and, wearing rubber kitchen gloves for good grip, slide the shell back and forth. You will soon achieve a flat edge ready for final assembly. Of course, you may be lucky enough to have a belt sander, in which case you can avoid this primitive washerwoman approach.

After you have sanded the interior of the two shells, you can start making the exterior fittings. This is a good time to make the cradle, which will hold the completed model and which is useful for holding the lower shell whilst you add its interior features. The cradle is a simple affair, and its parts are shown in Fig 12.6. It can be cut from the same timber as the horizontal hull frame, and its curved cutouts match the curves of rings D and F.

Frame

This is a horizontally mounted pierced piece to which the lower shell is eventually glued, and upon which, with locating pins, the upper shell will rest.

Nautilus has a pointed ram at the bows, for attacking and piercing enemy vessels. To save timber, it is best to cut the ram separately, and set it into the front of the frame afterwards.

The frame is shown in Fig 12.7, and was cut from a plank of oak ⅜in (10mm) thick. You could use plywood, but I did not, as I do not like to see the laminations. You could use MDF in, say, ¼in (6mm) thickness, in which case it would look better treated with wood dye, which it accepts very evenly. The plank of oak I used looked thicker than I cared for, and I reduced the apparent thickness by chamfering the edge at a 20° angle. In this way, the wider top surface reflects light, and the lower, narrower edge is in shadow and less noticeable.

Fig 12.7
Frame.

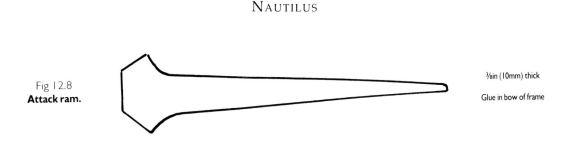

Fig 12.8
Attack ram.

⅜in (10mm) thick

Glue in bow of frame

The frame is cut on the scroll saw (or with a fret saw) to finish ⅜in (10mm) larger all round than the hull shells. Cut the bow ram from the same timber as the frame so that its stub fits neatly into the cutout in the frame nose. It improves the appearance if the bottom surface of the ram is cut to angle up 10° to 15°. Glue the ram into position.

From now on, most of the glue used was epoxy two-part resin (Araldite Rapid), so that I did not have to wait more than 10 minutes before handling each fixed part. (The exception was the glue used for the suede lining, of which more later.)

Upper Hull

Conning Tower
This was cut from a piece of ash 2in × 2in × 4⅝in (51mm × 51mm × 117mm) on the band saw. When the vertical sides and rounded ends are

sanded smooth, mark a line ¼in (6mm) below the top, all around the piece, and remove this slice on the band saw. Use a fence so the cut is kept smooth. Mark a line around the slice ¼in (6mm) in from its edge, and remove the centre on the scroll saw. This will give a rim piece ¼in × ¼in (6mm × 6mm) in cross section, which may be glued to the top of the conning tower after the cut surfaces have been sanded smooth.

The conning tower block must now be made to fit the top of the hull. You can if you wish mark all around the conning tower whilst it is held in its final position, and cut out that section of the hull shell on the scroll saw before setting the conning tower into the hole. I preferred to leave the hull intact, and shaped the bottom of the tower to fit.

The curve at each side of the conning tower is shown in Fig 12.9, and you will have cut that curve on the band saw. There are also the curves

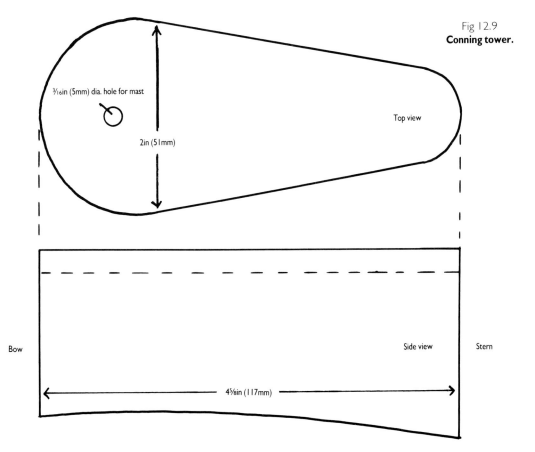

Fig 12.9
Conning tower.

³⁄₁₆in (5mm) dia. hole for mast

2in (51mm)

Top view

Bow

Side view

Stern

4⅝in (117mm)

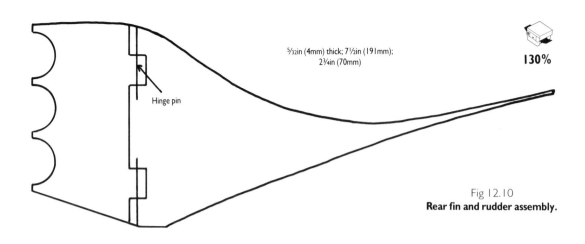

5/32in (4mm) thick; 7½in (191mm);
2¾in (70mm)

130%

Fig 12.10
Rear fin and rudder assembly.

Hinge pin

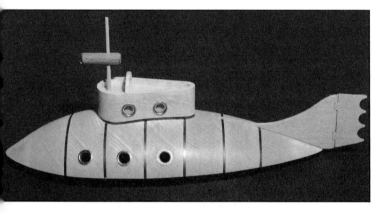

Fig 12.11
**Upper shell of hull, complete with conning
tower, fin and rudder, mast and
searchlight.**

from port to starboard, and the curve fore and aft
at the centre line. I found the easiest way to
encompass all these was to hollow the underside
of the tower, partly with a woodcarving gouge
with the block held in the wood-lined jaws of a
vise, and partly with a 2in (51mm) diameter flap
wheel mounted in a Jacobs chuck on the lathe. A
little bit of time and trouble will give you a good
fit. Don't worry if you hollow too deeply; the
epoxy around the rim will hold it well.

Drill two portholes each side with a ½in (13mm)
Forstner bit, and glue into each a ½in (13mm)
brass eyelet. As I could see the marks left by the
brad point of the bit, I first lined the bottom of
each hole with a ½in (13mm) disc of leather.

Add the mast, which is a length of ³⁄₁₆in (5mm)
dowel on which is threaded the underwater
searchlight which Captain Nemo used. This is
simply a turned rod of hardwood (I used bodo,
but any timber will do) finished to a ½in (13mm)
diameter, and drilled ³⁄₁₆in (5mm) vertically for the
mast. The searchlight lens is a glass cabochon,
mirror backed. These are obtainable from craft
shops and are put out by Fimo as accessories for

their costume jewellery. A packet includes two
clear, plus one green and one red. You might care
to use the coloured ones as lenses for port (red)
and starboard (green) navigation lights. If you do,
the lamps would look good mounted on the hull
next to, but not on, the conning tower.

Rudder
The fin and rudder assembly is a simple cutting,
made on the scroll saw with a fine blade (I used a
No. 3 – 0.013in (0.34mm) thick, 20tpi). Cut out the
profile shown in Fig 12.10. The semicircular
cutouts at the trailing edge of the rudder are ⅝in
(16mm) in diameter. You will find that the fine
blade will cope with the right-angled changes of
direction when cutting the hinge line. When the
rudder is cut away from the fin, sand (or trim with
a craft knife) all the vertical parts of the junction
between the two, so that they are rounded. This
will permit the rudder to turn on its pintles (or
hinge pins). Sand the rudder so that its thickness
is reduced toward the trailing edge. Do not try for
a feather edge, which would be too fragile; just
reduce the thickness to about half.

The pintles are made from two ordinary

130%

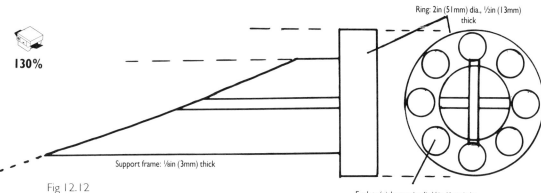

Ring: 2in (51mm) dia., ½in (13mm) thick

Support frame: ⅛in (3mm) thick

Fig 12.12
Nemo propulsion unit.

Eyelets (eight required): ¼in (6mm) dia.

Drill ⁹⁄₃₂in (7mm) dia. holes

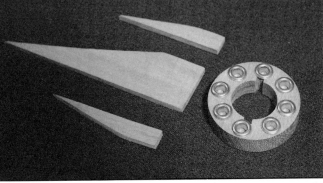

Fig 12.13
Nemo propulsion unit parts.

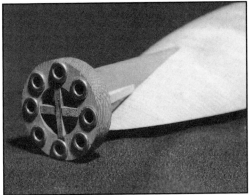

dressmaking pins. Hold fin and rudder together with masking tape. Mount between wood-lined jaws on the cross vise of your drill table, then drill accurately and vertically downwards with a 0.0196in (0.5mm) drill bit held in a pin chuck within your normal drill chuck. Turn the piece upside down and repeat for the pin hole at the base. Tap in the two pins (snip off any excess length if necessary) and the assembly is complete. It may now be glued onto the rear of the upper hull shell.

Top Hull Trim

Little is now required to complete the top shell of the hull. There are three portholes on either side of the hull, as you see from Fig 12.11. Because of the complex curvature of the hull exterior, the brass eyelets used to frame the portholes will not sit neatly if you drill too near the bows. Mine are drilled in sections C, D and E only, centrally in each section, and 1in (25mm) up from the edge which sits on the frame. Drill (as on the conning tower) using a ½in (13mm) Forstner bit at slow speed and with very light pressure, so that fine shavings are taken by the bit. The inside of the shell rests on a scrap block of timber, and light pressure ensures that little strain is put upon the glue joints between the hull sections.

Fig 12.14
Nemo propulsion unit, assembled onto underside of hull stern.

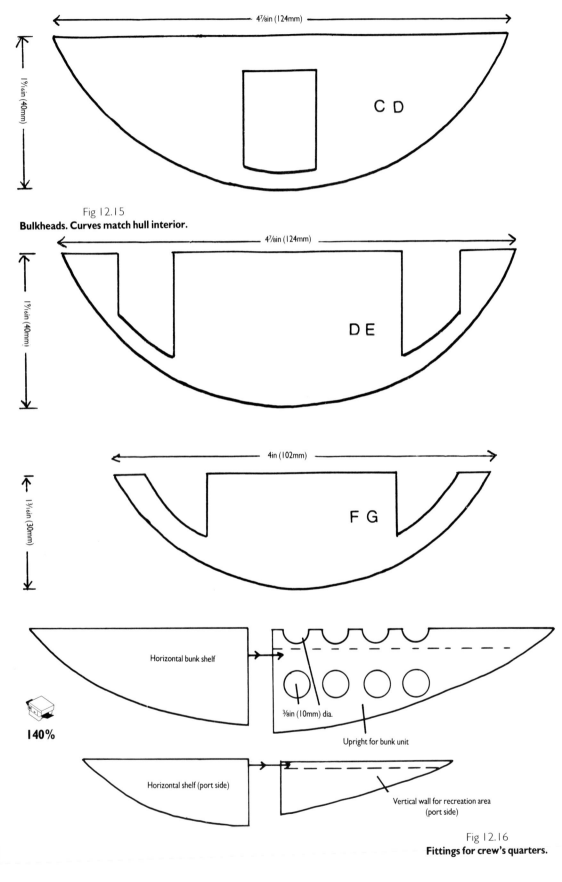

4⁷⁄₈in (124mm)

1⁹⁄₁₆in (40mm)

C D

Fig 12.15
Bulkheads. Curves match hull interior.

4⁷⁄₈in (124mm)

1⁹⁄₁₆in (40mm)

D E

4in (102mm)

1³⁄₁₆in (30mm)

F G

Horizontal bunk shelf

140%

⅜in (10mm) dia.

Upright for bunk unit

Horizontal shelf (port side)

Vertical wall for recreation area
(port side)

Fig 12.16
Fittings for crew's quarters.

In the case of the hull portholes, drill right through the shell, then set the ½in (13mm) brass eyelets in with epoxy. You can buy these eyelets from any good dressmaking shop or haberdasher.

You can now add the trim, if you wish. I found that, by covering the actual joins between the hull sections, the monolithic effect of the grain pattern is greatly enhanced. That is a fancy way of saying that it looks like one lump, not ten! Of course, you risk being accused of hiding poor joints.

The trim I settled on was a ⅛in (3mm) wide, self-adhesive trim strip used for motor cars. The colour I used was charcoal, but brown would be better if you can get it. The advantage of this strip is that it can be applied to follow the complex curves, which wood veneer will not do unless you cut the curves accurately first in the veneer; trim strip is easier.

Finally, place the top shell accurately on the frame, hold it in place with masking tape and/or rubber bands, and drill two holes, one at the bow and one at the stern, down through the shell into the frame. Use a ³⁄₁₆in (5mm) drill bit, then glue two stubs of ³⁄₁₆in (5mm) dowel into the hull holes, trimming and sanding their tops flush when the glue has set. The lower ends of the stubs will fit into the locating holes in the frame. The upper hull is now complete.

Lower Hull

First sand the interior of the lower hull shell, if you have not already done so. There is no need to seal or wax, as most of the interior surface will later be covered.

Nemo Propulsion Unit

This is the only external fitting for the lower shell and comprises only four pieces: a fin, two cross struts, and the propulsion ring. Figs 12.13 and 12.14 shows the parts and the finished assembly.

Cut the fin and struts on the scroll saw from ⅛in (3mm) stock (I used a slice of Indian laurel, to match the upper fin and rudder). Check the upper edge of the fin to ensure that it matches the curve of the hull at the stern. If not, sand as necessary.

Mount a piece of timber 2in × 2in × 2in (51mm × 51mm × 51mm) on the screw chuck, turn to a cylinder, and hollow out the centre to a diameter of 1in (25mm) and a depth of just over ½in (13mm). Then part off a ring ½in (13mm) thick, which is the body of the propulsion unit. Cut two notches in the interior surface to accept the fin. Mark and drill eight holes at 45° intervals, centred

¼in (6mm) in from the outer circumference. The holes should be deep enough to accept ¼in (6mm) brass eyelets to form the water jet outlets, and these may be glued in with a small dab of epoxy under the rim of each.

Glue the rim to the fin, then fit the two cross struts at right angles to the fin. Their trailing edges should fit inside the ring, flush with the rear surface. Finally, glue the assembly to the hull.

Bulkheads

Before fitting out, you should cut the interior bulkheads, and if necessary, tailor them to fit. These are the semicircular crosspieces which divide the compartments. There are only three: one with a central doorway, lies between the crew's quarters and the control room; the second is between the control room and Captain Nemo's quarters; and the third is between Nemo and the engine room. Numbers Two and Three have access cut out to port and starboard, so the crew can get round past the pipe organ and reach either side of the engine.

Cut the three bulkheads to the profiles given (*see* Fig 12.15), and chamfer the lower curved edges to fit the hull. The edge of the first slopes slightly up toward the bow, the centre one is virtually flat, and the rear bulkhead slopes up toward the stern. A few moments with knife and sandpaper will achieve a good fit.

You will see that the placement of the bulkheads is at the joints between sections of the hull; the first at C/D, the second at D/E, and the final one at F/G. Check the final position before gluing in by placing the frame onto the shell after temporarily setting the bulkheads into place. It is neater if you align the top of each bulkhead with the corresponding crossbeam of the frame. As you see, the engine will abut the last crossbeam (and bulkhead), and the organ is supported by the centre beam.

Crew's Quarters

The bow section, comprising the volume forward of the first bulkhead, includes the hull sections A, B and C. There are only a few pieces of timber (or MDF if you wish) to cut for this: the upright and top shelf of the bunk unit on the starboard side, with three little dividers athwartships (left to right, me hearties), and the upright and horizontal surface of the flat area on the port side, which represents a table, or a recreation area.

Cut these pieces (the two uprights, at least) from ⅛in (3mm) timber. (I used a slice of Cameroun

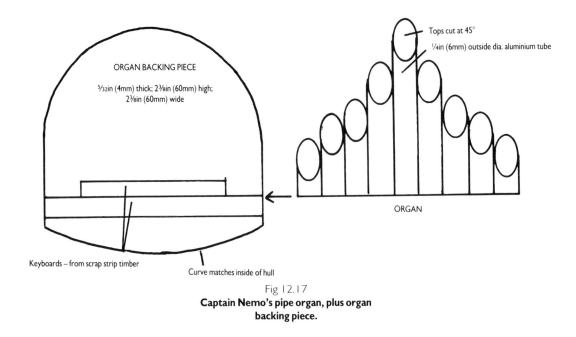

ORGAN BACKING PIECE

5/32in (4mm) thick; 2⅜in (60mm) high;
2⅜in (60mm) wide

Tops cut at 45°

¼in (6mm) outside dia. aluminium tube

ORGAN

Keyboards – from scrap strip timber

Curve matches inside of hull

Fig 12.17
**Captain Nemo's pipe organ, plus organ
backing piece.**

padauk which is red and tones well with the
suede leather representing the carpeting.) Again,
you will have to chamfer the curved edges to fit
the hull. The bunk unit has holes drilled in a
horizontal line near the base to represent
apertures for lower bunks, but you don't need to
put in a shelf, as it would not be seen.

When these units have been fitted and glued in,
you can line the compartment. The upper bunk
dividers were added after the leather lining.

Fig 12.18
Close-up of bow section, fitted out.

You don't have to use leather, but it does have
advantages: it is soft and pliable, and it can be
stretched or pushed along a little without
corrugating, to cover minor cutting errors. Also, it
smells good. Incidentally, the glue used for all the
leather pieces was Evostik, applied to one face
only (the smooth 'right' side of the leather), and
not the base timber. If you apply glue to both
surfaces you get instant adhesion, whereas a little
slip is often useful. There is a further advantage to
using suede. In the case of the crew's quarters you
have to butt several pieces together. With suede, a
light brushing with an old but clean toothbrush
hides the joins and smooths the nap into one
direction.

Alternatives to leather, should you choose to use
them, are: plain wood, cloth, sprayed flock (you
would need to mask certain areas), or paint (matte
is preferable to gloss).

I obtained my leather from Croggons, who supply
by weight (*see* page 170). If you decide to use
leather, proceed as follows: for the crew's
quarters, cut and fit a central strip between the
two uprights, with one end of the strip abutting
the bulkhead and the other end overlapping the
bows a little. This excess can be trimmed with a
scalpel later. Cut, fit and glue in two quadrants of
leather to fit the port and starboard horizontal
areas. Finally, cut two strips to line the sides, the
lower long edge of each butting up to the curved
edge of the horizontal piece. Again, if the strips
are higher than the edge of the hull, trim later.
The actual join between wood and leather, at the
edge of the shell, will be hidden by the frame,

which is not glued into place until the whole hull has been fitted out.

Any extras you wish to add to the rather spartan crew's quarters, I leave to your own taste and imagination.

Control Room

Once again, I have left this quite simple, with space for you to add extras if you wish. The rear of the front bulkhead is fitted with instruments and gauges. These are simply ¹⁄₁₆in (2mm) sections cut from a ¼in (6mm) OD aluminium tube, plus flat steel washers, and rings cut from a ½in (13mm) OD plastic tube, all affixed with epoxy.

The steering wheel is ¾in (19mm) and ³⁄₁₆in (5mm) thick, cut from a dowel of iroko mounted on a small screw chuck. Eight holes of ¹⁄₁₆in (2mm) diameter are drilled around the circumference at 45° intervals to accept ¼in (6mm) lengths of cocktail stick. The wheel is fixed to its supporting pillar by another short length of cocktail stick acting as an axle. If you require the wheel to rotate, do not glue it to the axle, but glue a small ³⁄₁₆in (5mm) disc onto the end of the axle as a stop, after pushing the wheel onto the axle.

Cut a strip of leather with a width equal to the distance between first and second bulkheads, and of a length to take it from port to starboard of the hull. Cut a ½in (13mm) hole at its centre (to allow the wheel assembly to be glued to the hull), and fix the leather into position. Trim port and starboard edges, and glue the wheel assembly into position.

Nemo's Quarters

Apart from the Captain'a musical indulgence, this section again is finished in severe style, so add any bits you fancy.

Organ

This is a simple representation, comprising four pieces of timber and nine organ tubes, all cut from ¼in (6mm) OD aluminium tubing. As you can see from Fig 12.17, the pipes are of ascending lengths, with the tallest at the centre. All are cut at 45° at the top, and all have little air slots near the base. Every timber and alloy part was cut on the scroll saw, using the same blade for both metal and wooden parts.

As you will detect from Fig 12.18, the prototype model had No. 2 bulkhead of oak, twice the thickness of the others, so I butted the organ tubes up to the bulkhead, and added a semicircular backing piece to the pipes with the base of the backing glued to the excess thickness of the bulkhead. It is slightly easier for you to make the bulkhead the same thickness as the others, and cut one backing piece (as shown in Fig 12.17) to cover the whole organ, which is glued up with epoxy.

Cut the chair for the organist from a scrap of oak ³⁄₈in (10mm) thick (left over from the frame) and use the same scrap timber for the captain's bed. You will see from Fig 12.20 that the underside of the bed is curved to fit the hull (i.e. thicker timber nearest the centre of the vessel). Cutting this curve, with the bed base on its side on the scroll saw's table, leaves you with a piece of waste ideal for the bedhead.

So, first install the organ. Next, line the compartment with leather. To accommodate the

Fig 12.20
Close-up of stern section, fitted out.

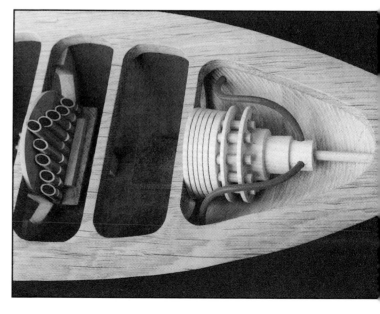

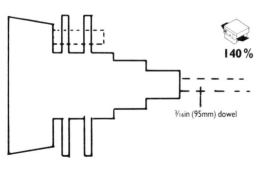

140 %

³⁄₁₆in (95mm) dowel

Engine turning: 2in (51mm) dia; 2⅝in (67mm) long

Fig 12.19
Engine.

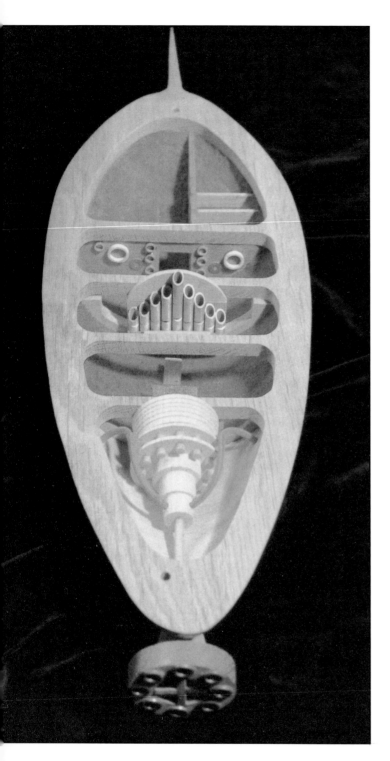

Fig 12.21
Lower hull shell, fitted out: bow section is crew quarters, followed by control room, then Nemo's quarters with his pipe organ, finally the engine compartment.

hull curvature, cut the leather fore and aft, from rear edge into the centre point, and mark and cut out the overlap. You now have a long 'V' shaped gusset and the leather will snug down; brushing the suede will obscure the join. Glue the bed and bedhead into position, covering the bed with a small piece of suede.

Engine Compartment

This won't take you too long, as there is no suede lining and no fittings – just an engine block with a shaft and two hydraulic tubes.

The whole engine block is turned from a piece of ash 2in × 2in × 3½in (51mm × 51mm × 89mm), with grain running lengthwise, rounded between centres and then held in a compression chuck for shaping. The first $\frac{11}{16}$in (17mm) of the block reduces slightly in diameter from bow end to the stern end, then follows a deep groove ⅛in (3mm) wide, and two flanges of 2in (5mm) diameter separated by a ¼in (6mm) groove. Two more reductions of diameter complete the block. Cut five lines in the forward section of the block with a pointed tool.

Sand and part off from the lathe. Drill a $\frac{3}{16}$in (5mm) hole into the narrow end for the shaft (of $\frac{3}{16}$in (5mm) dowel) the rear end of which is chamfered to fit the curve of the hull at the extreme stern. Trim with a knife the underside of the two flanges so that the whole unit will sit on the hull, butting up to the rear bulkhead and crossbeam.

Now, with the front end of the engine block sitting on the drill table, drill $\frac{3}{16}$in (5mm) holes gently through both flanges at ⅜in (10mm) centres, and cut, insert and glue ¾in (19mm) lengths of $\frac{3}{16}$in (5mm) dowel (as shown in Fig 12.20) into the holes. Drill $\frac{1}{16}$in × ⅛in (2mm × 3mm) holes, 45° from horizontal and 45° from the centre line of the hull. These holes are left and right on the rear of the engine casing. Now drill a ⅛in (3mm) hole on each side of the inside of the hull just abaft the rear bulkhead (these holes should not be deeper than $\frac{3}{16}$in (5mm) or you will pierce the hull). These four holes accept the hydraulic flexible pipes which were made from two neoprene 'O' rings, cut once so that they could be set in an 'S' bend between hull and engine block (no glued was needed).

With the engine glued into place, your hull is fitted out. Glue the oak centre frame to the lower hull shell, holding the assembly with rubber bands until the glue is set.

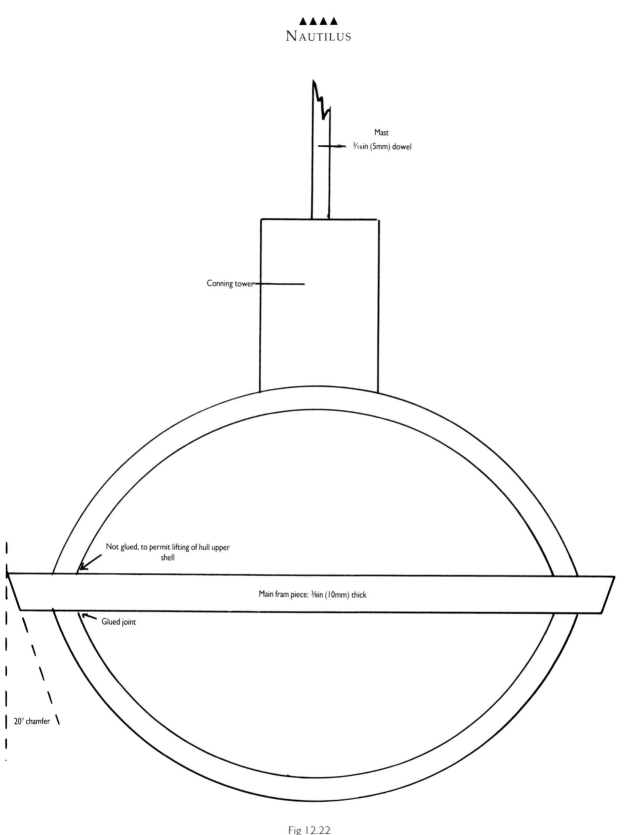

Mast
³⁄₁₆in (5mm) dowel

Conning tower

Not glued, to permit lifting of hull upper shell

Main fram piece: ³⁄₈in (10mm) thick

Glued joint

20° chamfer

Fig 12.22
Cross section of finished hull (across section D).

Suppliers

Yandle & Sons Ltd
Hurst Works
Martock
Somerset
TA12 6JU

Tel: (0935) 822207

Native and exotic timbers and blanks.

Craft Supplies Ltd
170 The Mill
Millers Dale
Nr Buxton
Derbyshire
SK17 8SN

Tel: (0298) 871636
Fax: (0298) 872263

Native and exotic timbers and blanks.
Machinery, tools and turning equipment.

The Working Tree
Milland
Nr Liphook
Hampshire
GU30 7NA

Tel: (042) 876505
Fax: (042) 876679

Native and ecologically sustainable timbers.

Art Veneers Co. Ltd
Chiswick Avenue
Industrial Estate
Mildenhall
Suffolk
IP28 7AY

Tel: (0638) 712550
Fax: (0638) 712330

Native and exotic veneers.

J. Croggon & Son Ltd
Manor Tannery
Grampound
Cornwall
TR2 4QW

Tel: (0726) 882413

Leathers of all kinds.

W. Hobby Ltd
Knights Hill Square
London SE27 0HH

Tel: (081) 761 4244

Hobbyist and modelling sundries and
materials.

Metric Conversion Table

Inches to Millimetres and Centimetres						
mm = millimetres cm = centimetres						
inches	mm	cm	inches	cm	inches	cm
⅛	3	0.3	9	22.9	30	76.2
¼	6	0.6	10	25.4	31	78.7
⅜	10	1.0	11	27.9	32	81.3
½	13	1.3	12	30.5	33	83.8
⅝	16	1.6	13	33.0	34	86.4
¾	19	1.9	14	35.6	35	88.9
⅞	22	2.2	15	38.1	36	91.4
1	25	2.5	16	40.6	37	94.0
1¼	32	3.2	17	43.2	38	96.5
1½	38	3.8	18	45.7	39	99.1
1¾	44	4.4	19	48.3	40	101.6
2	51	5.1	20	50.8	41	104.1
2½	64	6.4	21	53.3	42	106.7
3	76	7.6	22	55.9	43	109.2
3½	89	8.9	23	58.4	44	111.8
4	102	10.2	24	61.0	45	114.3
4½	114	11.4	25	63.5	46	116.8
5	127	12.7	26	66.0	47	119.4
6	152	15.2	27	68.6	48	121.9
7	178	17.8	28	71.1	49	124.5
8	203	20.3	29	73.7	50	127.0

About the Author

Terry Lawrence has been making things in wood for fifty years, and designing them for most of that time. He has been an amateur artist for 25 years, working in all media, though now preferring watercolour.

In his working life Terry was employed for 27 years by the Crown Agents in London, and then escaped the 'rat race' spending 10 years running a self-sufficiency smallholding in Cornwall.

Terry is now retired, which gives him much more time than before to express himself in the workshop. As the neighbours are quite close, he expresses himself rather quietly, and has learned to use the most mild of epithets.

He has concentrated on making toys because they are fun and because he has four children who, when young, appreciated things made especially for them. In those days, the toys had to pass the 'Lawrence test', where Dad had to stand on the object. If it did not break, then it would be strong enough for the kids.

The acquisition of a lathe has expanded his ideas greatly, and although the items in this book would not necessarily stand the twelve (and a little bit more now) stone test, they are designed rather more imaginatively.